Microprocessor 1

Series Editor
Jean-Charles Pomerol

Microprocessor 1

Prolegomena – Calculation and Storage Functions – Models of Computation and Computer Architecture

Philippe Darche

iSTE

WILEY

First published 2020 in Great Britain and the United States by ISTE Ltd and John Wiley & Sons, Inc.

ISTE Ltd
27-37 St George's Road
London SW19 4EU
UK

www.iste.co.uk

John Wiley & Sons, Inc.
111 River Street
Hoboken, NJ 07030
USA

www.wiley.com

Library of Congress Control Number: 2020938715

British Library Cataloguing-in-Publication Data
A CIP record for this book is available from the British Library
ISBN 978-1-78630-563-3

MIX
Paper from responsible sources
FSC www.fsc.org FSC® C013604

Contents

Quotation

Every advantage has its disadvantages and vice versa.

Shadokian philosophy[1]

1 The Shadoks are the main characters from an experimental cartoon produced by the Research Office of the Office de Radiodiffusion-Télévision Française (ORTF). The two-minute-long episodes of this daily cult series were broadcast on ORTF's first channel (the only one at the time!) beginning in 1968. The birds were drawn simply and quickly using an experimental device called an *animograph*.

The Shadoks are ridiculous, stupid and mean. Their intellectual capacities are completely unusual. For example, they are known for bouncing up and down, but it is not clear why! Their vocabulary consists of four words: GA, BU, ZO and MEU, which are also the four digits in their number system (base 4) and the musical notes in their four-tone scale. Their philosophy is comprised of famous mottos such as the one cited in this book.

Preface

Computer systems (hardware and software) are becoming increasingly complex, embedded and transparent. It therefore is becoming difficult to delve into basic concepts in order to fully understand how they work. In order to accomplish this, one approach is to take an interest in the history of the domain. A second way is to soak up technology by reading datasheets for electronic components and patents. Last but not least is reading research articles. I have tried to follow all three paths throughout the writing of this series of books, with the aim of explaining the hardware and software operations of the microprocessor, the modern and integrated form of the central unit.

About the book

This first work in a five-volume series deals with the general operating principles of the microprocessor. It focuses in particular on the first two generations of this programmable component, that is, those that handle integers in 4- and 8-bit formats. In adopting a historical angle of study, this deliberate decision allows us to return to its basic operation without the conceptual overload of current models. The more advanced concepts, such as the mechanisms of virtual memories and cache memory or the different forms of parallelism, will be detailed in the following volumes with the presentation of subsequent generations, that is, 16-, 32- and 64-bit systems.

The first volume addresses the field's introductory concepts. As in music theory, we cannot understand the advent of the microprocessor without talking about the history of computers and technologies, which is presented in the first chapter. The second chapter deals with storage, the second function of the computer present in the microprocessor. The concepts of computational models and computer architecture will be the subject of the final chapter.

The second volume is devoted to aspects of communication in digital systems from the point of view of buses. Their main characteristics are presented, as well as their communication, access arbitration, and transaction protocols, their interfaces and their electrical characteristics. A classification is proposed and the main buses are described.

The third volume deals with the hardware aspects of the microprocessor. It first details the component's external interface and then its internal organization. It then presents the various commercial generations and certain specific families such as the Digital Signal Processor (DSP) and the microcontroller. The volume ends with a presentation of the datasheet.

The fourth volume deals with the software aspects of this component. The main characteristics of the Instruction Set Architecture (ISA) of a generic component are detailed. We then study the two ways to alter the execution flow with both classic and interrupt function call mechanisms.

The final volume presents the hardware and software aspects of the development chain for a digital system as well as the architectures of the first microcomputers in the historical perspective.

Multi-level organization

This book gradually transitions from conceptual to physical implementation. Pedagogy was my main concern, without neglecting formal aspects. Reading can take place on several levels. Each reader will be presented with introductory information before being asked to understand more difficult topics. Knowledge, with a few exceptions, has been presented linearly and as comprehensively as possible. Concrete examples drawn from former and current technologies illustrate the theoretical concepts.

When necessary, exercises complete the learning process by examining certain mechanisms in more depth. Each volume ends with bibliographic references including research articles, works and patents at the origin of the concepts and more recent ones reflecting the state of the art. These references allow the reader to find additional and more theoretical information. There is also a list of acronyms used and an index covering the entire work.

This series of books on computer architecture is the fruit of over 30 years of travels in the electronic, microelectronic and computer worlds. I hope that it will provide you with sufficient knowledge, both practical and theoretical, to then specialize in one of these fields. I wish you a pleasant stroll through these different worlds.

IMPORTANT NOTES.– As this book presents an introduction to the field of microprocessors, references to components from all periods are cited, as well as references to computers from generations before this component appeared.

Original company names have been used, although some have merged. This will allow readers to find specification sheets and original documentation for the mentioned integrated circuits on the Internet and to study them in relation to this work.

The concepts presented are based on the concepts studied in selected earlier works (Darche 2000, 2002, 2003, 2004, 2012), which I recommend reading beforehand.

Philippe DARCHE
June 2020

Introduction

In this book, we will focus on the microprocessor, the integrated form of the central unit. It introduces basic concepts from the perspective of sequential execution. This first volume, presenting the field's introductory concepts, is organized into three chapters. The first two present the calculation and memory functions which, along with communication, are the computer's three primary functions. The last chapter defines concepts concerning computational models and computer architectures.

1

The Function of Computation

As in music theory, we cannot discuss the microprocessor without positioning it in the context of the history of the computer, since this component is the integrated version of the central unit. Its internal mechanisms are the same as those of supercomputers, mainframe computers and minicomputers. Thanks to advances in microelectronics, additional functionality has been integrated with each generation in order to speed up internal operations. A computer[1] is a hardware and software system responsible for the automatic processing of information, managed by a stored program. To accomplish this task, the computer's essential function is the transformation of data using computation, but two other functions are also essential. Namely, these are storing and transferring information (i.e. communication). In some industrial fields, control is a fourth function. This chapter focuses on the requirements that led to the invention of tools and calculating machines to arrive at the modern version of the computer that we know today. The technological aspect is then addressed. Some chronological references are given. Then several classification criteria are proposed. The analog computer, which is then described, was an alternative to the digital version. Finally, the relationship between hardware and software and the evolution of integration and its limits are addressed.

NOTE.– This chapter does not attempt to replace a historical study. It gives only a few key dates and technical benchmarks to understand the technological evolution of the field.

1 The French word *ordinateur* (computer) was suggested by Jacques Perret, professor at the Faculté des Lettres de Paris, in his letter dated April 16, 1955, in response to a question from IBM to name these machines; the English name was the Electronic Data Processing Machine.

1.1. Beginnings

Humans have needed to count since our earliest days (Ifrah 1994; Goldstein 1999). Fingers were undoubtedly used as the first natural counting tool, which later led to the use of the decimal number base. During archeological excavations, we have also found notched counting sticks, bones and pieces of wood. The incised bones of Ishango, dated between 23,000 and 25,000 years BC, provide an example (Figure 1.1).

Figure 1.1. *Ishango's incised bones (source: unknown). For a color version of this figure, see www.iste.co.uk/darche/microprocessor1.zip*

Counting sticks were used during antiquity, as well as pebbles, hence the word calculus, from the Latin *calculus* which means "small pebble". Knotted ropes were also used for counting, an example being the Incan *quipu* (Figure 1.2). This Incan technique (dating ≈ 1200–1570) used a positional numbering system (*cf.* § 1.2 of Darche (2000)) in base-10 (Ascher 1983).

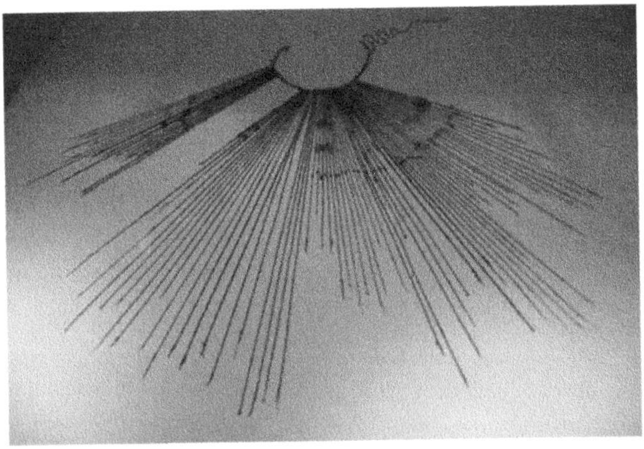

Figure 1.2. *A quipu (source: unknown). For a color version of this figure, see www.iste.co.uk/darche/microprocessor1.zip*

The need for fast and precise computation necessitated the use of computing instruments. Two exemplars are the abacus and the slide rule. The abacus is a planar calculating instrument, with examples including the Roman (Figure 1.3(a)) and the Chinese (Figure 1.3(b)) abacus. The latter makes it possible to calculate the four basic arithmetic operations by the movements of beads (or balls) strung on rods, which represent numbers.

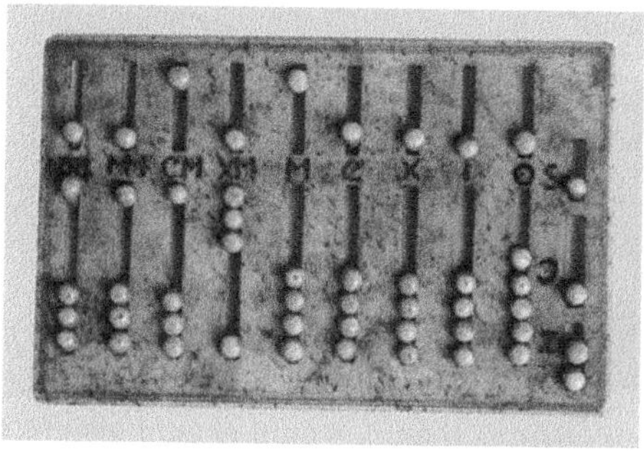

a)

b)

Figure 1.3. *Roman abacus (a) between the 2nd and 5th Centuries (© Inria/AMISA/Photo J.-M. Ramès); Chinese abacus (b). For a color version of this figure, see www.iste.co.uk/darche/microprocessor1.zip*

The 17th Century saw the introduction of mechanical computing machines, and the beginning of the history of computers is generally dated from their appearance. They met the need to systematically calculate tables of numbers reliably and quickly. These machines naturally used the decimal base. The most famous is undoubtedly the adding machine called the Pascaline (1642), named after its inventor, the philosopher and scientist Blaise Pascal (1623–1662). Numbers were entered using numbered wheels (Figure 1.4). The result was visible through the upper slits. Complementation made it possible to carry out subtraction (*cf.* exercise E1.1). But the first description of a four-operation machine was Wilhelm Chickard's machine (1592–1635), which appeared in a letter from the inventor to Johannes Kepler in 1623 (Aspray 1990). The end of the 17th Century and the following one were fruitful in terms of adding machines. Consider, for example, machines by Morland (1666), Perrault (1675), Grillet (1678), Poleni (1709), de Lépine (1725), Leupold (1727), Pereire (1750), Hahn (1770), Mahon (1777) and Müller (1784). A logical continuation of this trend was the multiplying machine by Gottfried Wilhelm Leibniz (1646–1716), which was designed in 1673 but whose implementation was delayed because of the lack of mechanical manufacturing precision in the 17th Century. For more information on this technology, we can cite the richly illustrated book by Marguin (1994) introducing the first mechanical calculating machines.

Figure 1.4. *An example of a Pascaline at the Musée des Arts et Métiers (source: David Monniaux/Wikipedia[2]). For a color version of this figure, see www.iste.co.uk/darche/microprocessor1.zip*

The mathematician Charles Babbage (1791–1871) marked the 19th Century *a posteriori* with two machines: the Difference Engine and the Analytical Engine.

The first machine was intended for the automatic computation of polynomial functions with printed results in order to build trigonometric and logarithm tables for the preparation of astronomical tables useful for navigation. At the time, logarithm tables were expensive, cumbersome and often out of print (Campbell-Kelly 1987, 1988, Swade 2001). They were calculated by hand, a tedious method that was the source of many errors. We can cite as an example those of De Prony (1825) for assessment, which was studied among others by Grattan-Guinness (1990), of which Babbage was aware. This machine reportedly allowed the successive values of a polynomial function to be calculated by Newton's finite difference method (see, for example, Bromley (1987) and Swade (1993)). Figure 1.5 presents a prototype, with all the details of this construction given in Swade (2005). It was never produced during his lifetime because of the enormous cost of manufacturing the mechanics. It was not until May 1991 that the second model, called the "difference machine no. 2", was implemented at the London Science Museum where it was also exhibited (Swade 1993).

2 URL: http://upload.wikimedia.org/wikipedia/commons/8/80/Arts_et_Metiers_Pascaline_dsc03869.jpg.

Figure 1.5. *Replica of the first Babbage difference machine*[3]*. For a color version of this figure, see www.iste.co.uk/darche/microprocessor1.zip*

The second machine (Figure 1.6) could compute the four basic arithmetic operations.

3 URL: http://iamyouasheisme.files.wordpress.com/2011/11/babbagedifferenceengine.jpg.

Figure 1.6. *Babbage's analytical machine (© Science Museum/Science & Society Picture Library). For a color version of this figure, see www.iste.co.uk/darche/microprocessor1.zip*

It introduces the basic architecture of a computer and its programming (Hartree 1948). Indeed, as illustrated in Figure 1.7, it was composed of a mill, which played the role of the modern Central Processing Unit (CPU), and a store, which played the role of main storage. It also implemented the notion of registers (major axes) and data buses (transfer paths). Integers were internally represented in base-10 using Sign-Magnitude or Sign and Magnitude Representation (SMR, *cf.* § 5.2 in Darche (2000)) in base 10. Extensive details of its operation are given in Bromley (1982). For the same technological and financial reasons previously mentioned, its construction has never been completed.

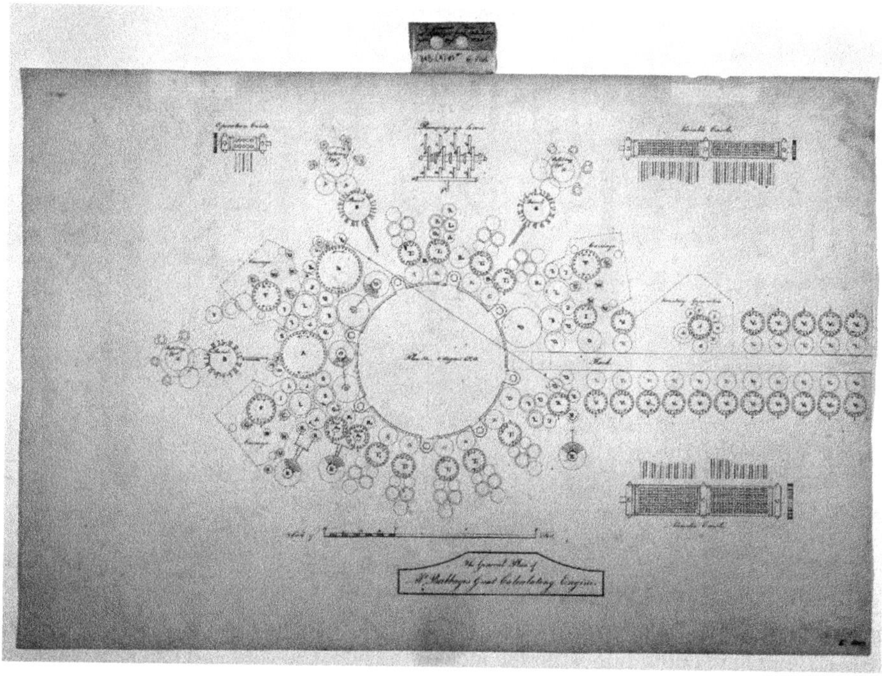

Figure 1.7. *One of the plans for Babbage's analytical machine (© Science Museum/Science & Society Picture Library). For a color version of this figure, see www.iste.co.uk/darche/microprocessor1.zip*

To program the machine, Babbage proposed the punched card. The latter had been invented by Basile Bouchon in 1725 for the weaving industry in the form of a strip of perforated paper. Jean-Baptiste Falcon improved it by transforming this strip into a string of punched cards linked together by cords. These cards made it possible to store a weaving pattern (Figure 1.8). This principle was further improved and made truly usable by Joseph Marie Jacquard with his famous loom (*cf.* Cass (2005) for a notice by J. M. Jacquard from 1809). Essinger (2004) tells the history of this machine. The latter was not the only programmable machine of the time. The music box with pegged cylinder was another form. In Babbage's machine, program instructions and data were entered separately using two decks of cards. Babbage had a collaborator, Ada Lovelace, who is considered the first programmer in history to have written a Bernoulli number algorithm for this machine (reproduced in Kim and Toole (1999)). However, we should not conclude that Charles Babbage is the source of the modern computer because of the influence of his ideas on the design of modern computers (Metropolis and Worlton 1980).

Figure 1.8. *Falcon's loom. For a color version of this figure, see www.iste.co.uk/darche/microprocessor1.zip*

The history of the modern computer can also be traced back to the 1880s with the invention of mechanography for the United States Census Bureau (Ceruzzi 2013). Hermann Hollerith took up the idea of the punched card and mechanized data processing to calculate statistics (Hollerith 1884a,b 1887). Figure 1.9 shows his statistics machine, composed of a hole punch called a press, with a tabulator that read and counted using electromechanical counters, and a sorter called a sorting box.

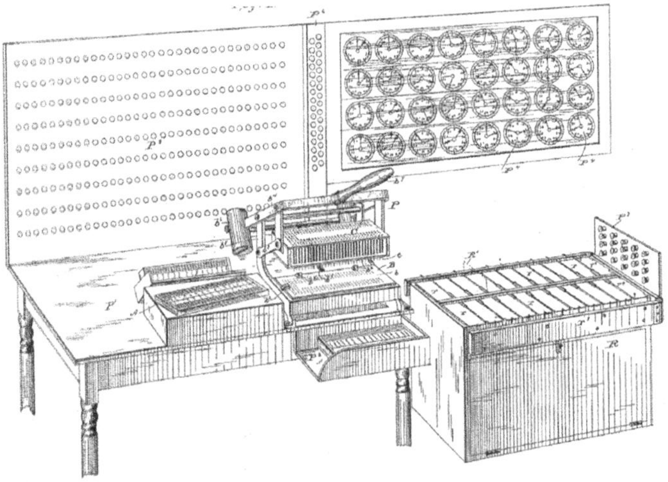

Figure 1.9. *Statistical machine (Hollerith 1887)*

As previously described and illustrated in Figure 1.10, the computer in its current form is the result of technological progress and advances in the mathematical fields, particularly in logic and arithmetic. Boole's algebra offered a theoretical framework for the study of logic circuits (*cf.* § 1.3 of Darche (2002)). For example, the American researcher Claude Elwood Shannon illustrated the relationship between Boolean logic and switch and relay circuits in his famous article (Shannon 1938). Thus, a link was established between mathematical theory and manufacturing technology. A study by Shannon (1953) described the operation of 16 Boolean functions in two variables using 18 contacts, and was able to show that this number of contacts was minimal. The mathematical aspect of switching has been studied in particular by Hohn (1955). Technology played a major role because it had a direct impact on the feasibility of the implementation, the speed of computation, and the cost of the machine.

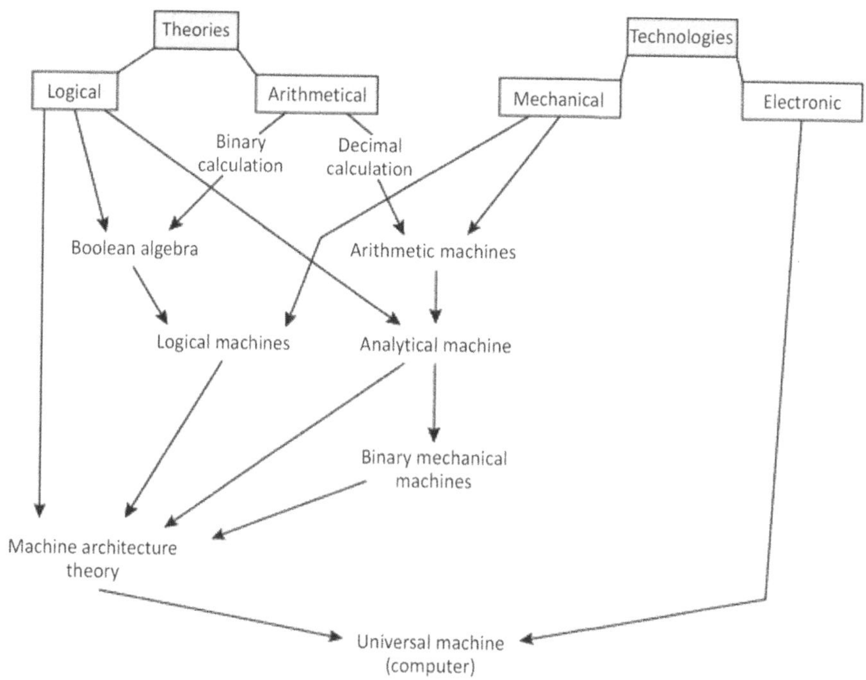

Figure 1.10. *Evolution of concepts and technologies in the development of calculating machines (from Marguin (1994))*

1.2. Classes of computers

There are several possible ways to classify computers. One is primarily related to the hardware technology available at the time, as presented in Tanenbaum (2005). For this reason, we will speak of technological generations. The transition from one generation to the next is achieved by a change in technology or by a major advance. Table 1.1 presents these generations in a simplified manner.[4]

Technological generations	Dates
0 – mechanical	1642–1936
1 – electromechanical	1937–1945
2 – tube	1946–1955
3 – transistor	1956–1965
4 – integrated circuits SSI – MSI – LSI	1966–1980
5 – integrated circuit VLSI	1981–1999
6 – integrated circuit GSI – SoC – MEMS	2000 to present

Table 1.1. *Generations of calculating machines and computers based on component technologies*

Generation 0 (1642–1936) consisted of mechanical computers, as presented in the previous section. Mechanography appeared at the end of the 19th Century to respond in particular to the need for automatic processing of statistical data, initially for the census of the American population. Its technology naturally evolved towards electromechanics. A historical examination of mechanography in relation to "modern" computing was conducted by Rochain (2016).

Generation 1 was that of the electromechanical computer (1937–1945). The basic component was the electromechanical relay (Figure 1.11(a)) comprised of a coil that moves one or more electrical contacts on command (i.e. if it is electrically powered). Figure 1.11(b) presents its equivalent electric diagram. Keller (1962) describes the technology of the time. The implementation of a logical operator in this technology was described in § 2.1.2 of Darche (2004). In 1937, George Stibitz, a mathematician from Bell Labs, built the first binary circuit, an adding machine, the Model K (K for Kitchen) in electromechanical technology (Figure 1.11(c)). One of the pioneers of this generation in Europe was the German Konrad Zuse. His first

4 The dates provided are for illustrative purposes only because the transition from one generation to the next is obviously gradual.

machine, the Z1, begun in 1936 and completed two years later, was a mechanical computer powered by an electric motor. The first electromechanical relay computer, the Z2, was completed in 1939. It was built using surplus telephone relays. The Z3 (storage of 1,800[5] relays, 600 for the computing unit and 200 for the control unit, according to Ceruzzi (2003)), whose construction began 1938 and ended in 1941, used base-2 floating-point number representation. The Z4, started in 1942, was completed in 1945. Rojas (1997) describes the architecture of the Z1 and the Z3, and Speiser (1980), that of the Z4. In the United States, Harvard's Mark I, also called Automatic Sequence Controlled Calculator (ASCC) by IBM, was built by Howard Aiken between 1939 and 1944. Bell Laboratories built six models of computers using this technology between 1939 and 1950 for military and scientific use (Andrews 1982). Andrews and Bode (1950) describe the use of the Model V from Bell Laboratories. The calculation speed of these computers is estimated at 10 operations/s.

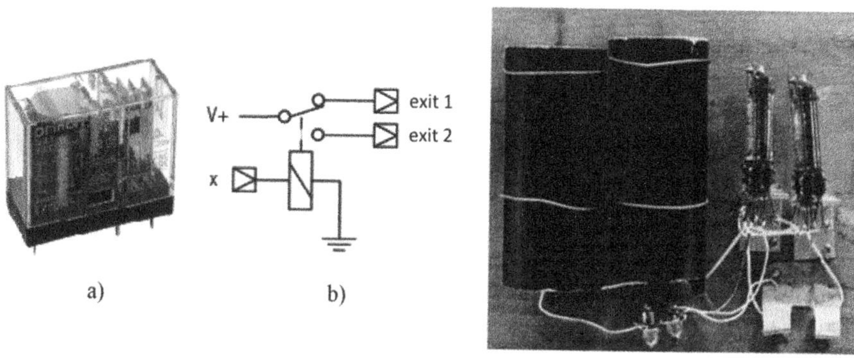

a) b) c)

Figure 1.11. *A modern electromechanical relay, its equivalent electrical diagram, and the Model K adder. For a color version of this figure, see www.iste.co.uk/darche/microprocessor1.zip*

The subsequent generations used electronic components, beginning in the 1946–1955 period with the electronic tube, also known as the vacuum tube (thermionic valve). This component has rectification, amplification, and switching functions. It was the latter that was exploited in this case. As shown in Figure 1.12(a), a tube is a bulb, made of glass in this implementation, that is sealed under vacuum or filled with an inert gas. Inside are electrodes: the cathode, the grid(s) and the anode. Electrons migrate from the cathode to the anode via thermionic effect, subsequently passing through one (triode) or more grids (tetrode, pentode and higher), which

5 1400 in Zuse (1993) and Weiss (1996).

modulates the flow. Figure 1.12(b) illustrates the resulting dimensions of a circuit board in this technology.

a) b)

Figure 1.12. *An RCA 5965 type electronic tube and an IBM 701 electronic board (source: IBM). For a color version of this figure, see www.iste.co.uk/darche/microprocessor1.zip*

Table 1.2 shows the main computers of generations 1 and 2.

(Beginning of the project –) operational computer	**Name**	**Designers**	**Country**	**Key features**
1936–1938	Z1	Zuse	Germany	Mechanical computer driven by electric motor
1939–1942	ABC	Atanasoff/Berry	United States	First electronic calculator (non-programmable)
1943	Colossus	Thomas Harold Flowers	Great Britain	First electronic computer to use a stored program
1939–1944	Harvard Mark I	Howard Aiken	United States	Electromagnetic computer based on Harvard architecture (*cf.* § 3.4.2)
1942–1945	Z4	Zuse	Germany	Electromechanical computer

1943–1946	ENIAC	Eckert/Mauchly (Moore School of Electrical Engineering University of Pennsylvania)	United States	Second electronic computer (reprogrammable via wiring)
1946–1952	EDVAC	Eckert/Mauchly/von Neumann	United States	Electronic computer based on von Neumann architecture
1948	Manchester Baby[6]	Williams/Kilburn	Great Britain	First electronic computer to use a stored program
1949	Manchester Mark I[7]	Williams/Kilburn	GB	Second electronic computer to use a stored program
1947–1949	BINAC	Eckert/Mauchly	USA	First commercially available electronic computer
1946–1949	EDSAC	Wilkes	GB	Electronic computer implementation of von Neumann architecture
1951	Whirlwind I	MIT	USA	Electronic computer
1951	UNIVAC I	Eckert/Mauchly	USA	Commercially available computer
1945–1952	IAS machine	John von Neumann (Princeton)	USA	Implementation of von Neumann architecture
1952	701	IBM	USA	First commercially available scientific computer from this company
1954	704	IBM	USA	Scientific computer with floating-point operations
1957	709	IBM	USA	Improved version of 704

Table 1.2. *Reference computers for generations 1 and 2*

Generation 3 (1956–1965) saw the emergence of electronic computers with diodes and discrete transistors.[8] These two components have the same function –

6 The Manchester Baby was the nickname given to the *Manchester Small Scale Experimental Computer*.

7 The official name of the Manchester Mark I was the *Manchester Automatic Digital Computer or Machine* (MADC or MADM). According to Reilly (2003), the correct date should be June 21, 1948, the date on which the computer became operational.

8 As opposed to "integrated".

rectification and amplification respectively – as the electronic tube, but at a much lower size, supply voltage, consumption of current and cost by a factor 10, 20 and 30 (orders of magnitude) respectively for the first three criteria. In addition, reliability and switching speed both increased. The transistor (Figure 1.13(a)), a contraction of the words "transfer resistor", was invented in 1948 (Bardeen and Brattain 1950). Its history is retraced in Brinkman (1997), and *Scientific American* (1997); IEEE (1998). A Bipolar Junction Transistor (BJT) (Figure 1.13(a)) is a sandwich of three layers of doped semiconductor materials (germanium or silicon) of type NPN or PNP. It behaves like a triode (Bardeen and Brattain 1948) with three electrodes: the emitter, the base and the collector. It behaves as an amplifier or a switch, a function used in digital logic. Figure 1.13(b) gives an example of an implementation of logic gates, in this case, seven inverters (*cf.* § 2.1.3 of (Darche 2004)).

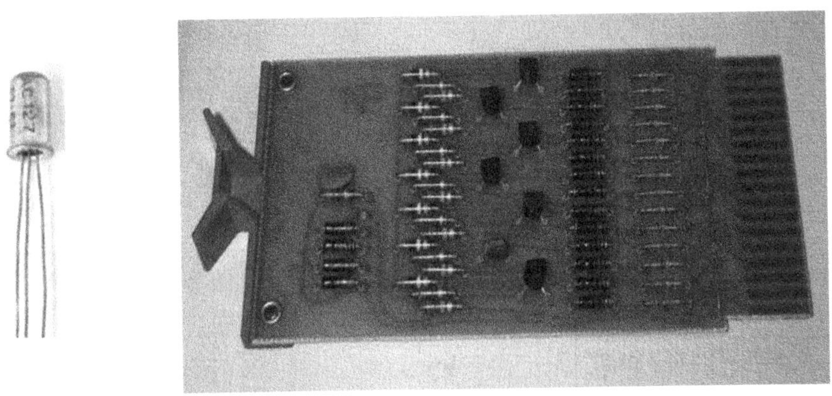

a) **b)**

Figure 1.13. *A transistor and an electronic transistor board with seven inverters from a DEC PDP-8 (source: http://www.pdp8.net). For a color version of this figure, see www.iste.co.uk/darche/microprocessor1.zip*

Table 1.3 presents the main computers of this third generation. The supremacy of the United States is notable.

Year	Name	Designer/manufacturer	Country	Key features
1960	PDP-1	DEC	USA	First minicomputer
1961	1401	IBM	USA	First electronic computer with stored program
1959	7090	IBM	USA	Transistor implementation of model 709
1963	B5000	Burroughs	USA	Battery architecture (*cf.* § 3.4.1)
1964	CDC 6600	Control Data Corporation	USA	First parallel computer
1965	PDP-8	DEC	USA	The company's iconic minicomputer

Table 1.3. *The main computers from this generation*

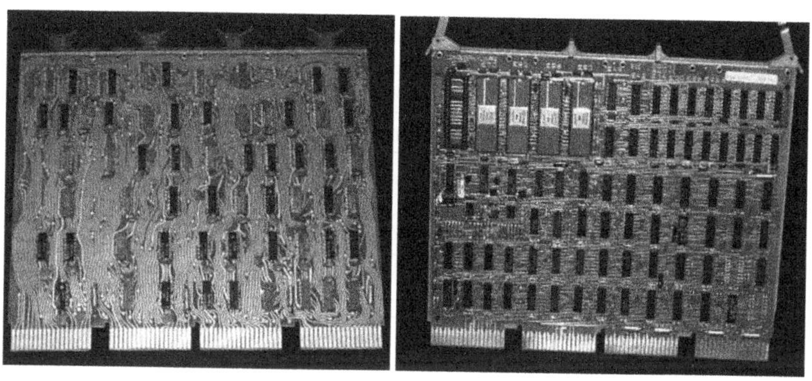

a) b)

Figure 1.14. *One of the 15 DIP integrated circuit CPU boards from a DEC PDP-11/20 and an electronic board from an LSI-11 (PDP-11/03 – 1975) (source: https://sydney.edu.au/science/psychology/pdp-11/Images/Images.html). For a color version of this figure, see www.iste.co.uk/darche/microprocessor1.zip*

The introduction of the integrated circuit marks the beginning of generation 4 (1966–1980), which saw the introduction of centralized architectures and the microprocessor. The first generations of components were called SSI (Small Scale Integration) and MSI (Medium-Scale Integration). These emerged during the period of 1966–1975. They are integrated circuits in a DIP (Dual-In-line Package) as shown on the CPU (Central Processing Unit) board in Figure 1.14. A central unit was made up of dozens of boards linked together by a backplane bus (*cf.* § V2-1.2 and V2-4.8) via edge connector Printed Circuit Board (PCB) gold fingers (bottom of the printed circuit in the photo). The encapsulation of integrated circuits was presented in § 3.3 of Darche (2004). From the 1970s, the LSI (Large-Scale Integration) generation enabled the appearance of the microprocessor (*cf.* § V3-1.1) manufactured using MOS (Metal-Oxide Semiconductor), PMOS (Positive (channel) MOS), and NMOS (Negative (channel) MOS), and then CMOS (Complementary[9] MOS), which was used in computing for the first time only in the microcomputer. The microelectronic technology used in computers was essentially bipolar (1965–1985 period) for the sake of operating frequency. The most widespread were the "standardized" families of TTL (Transistor–Transistor Logic) and ECL (Emitter Coupled Logic, *cf.* § 2.3.3 of Darche (2004)). These families were previously introduced respectively in § 2.3.2 and 2.3.3 of Darche (2004). Proprietary hybrid integrated circuit technologies coexisted, such as SLT (Solid Logic Technology) (Davis *et al.* 1964), in IBM's System/360 family. Passive and active components (Diode–Transistor Logic – DTL) were then assembled on a ceramic substrate and encapsulated.

Table 1.4 presents some models of microcomputers, minicomputers, mainframe computers and supercomputers.

Year	Name	Designer/manufacturer	Country	Key features
1964	System/360	IBM	USA	ISA concept (*cf.* § 3.5)
1970	PDP-11	DEC	USA	Iconic minicomputer
1973	Micral N	R2E	France	First computer with PMOS technology
1975	CRAY-1	Cray	USA	First super-computer
1978	VAX-11	DEC	USA	Successor to the PDP family

Table 1.4. *Primary computers in this generation*

As shown in Figure 1.15, manufacturing technology has evolved over time. Initially bipolar, it slowly evolved towards unipolar technologies – MOS, and then today, dominantly, CMOS. Two crossovers should be noted, in 1985, when CMOS technology achieved the performance level of TTL, and in 1991, when CMOS achieved results equivalent to ECL technology (Emitter Coupled Logic). This meant that unipolar technology eventually overtook these two bipolar technologies in terms

9 Technology brought together MOSFET transistors (MOS Field Effect Transistor) from the two aforementioned technologies, that is, canal p and canal n respectively, from whence this adjective stemmed.

of performance. ECL nevertheless continued to be used in the supercomputer industry until 1990 thanks in particular to its functionality as a line amplifier (transmission line driver). These technological advances had an impact on the number of supply voltages and their values, as well as on current consumption. This subject is dealt with in § V3-6.1.2.

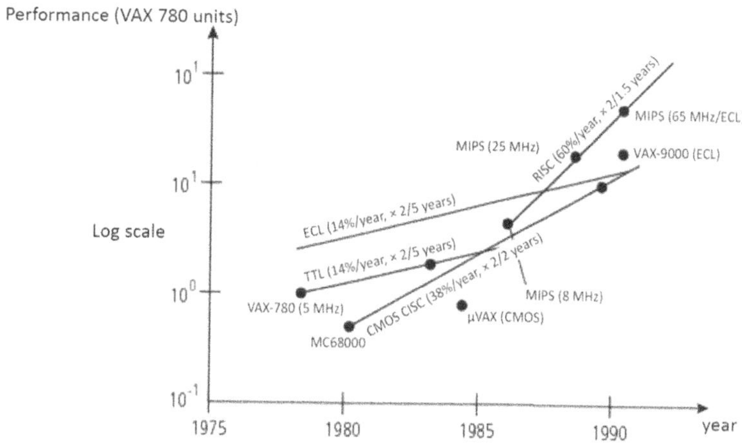

Figure 1.15. *Evolution of computing performance over time (from (Bell 2008b))*

Generation 5[10] saw the emergence of electronic computers with integrated VLSI (Very LSI) circuits in the 1980s. Seraphim and Feinberg (1981) introduce IBM's computer encapsulation technologies that were current as of the date of the article and provide an overview of the evolution. The microcomputer that still serves as a reference today, the IBM PC (Personal Computer) from the IBM Corporation, was released in 1981 (Figure 1.16).

The 21 Century has taken us to the next generation with ubiquitous or pervasive computing and integrated parallel systems. This is the era of SoC (System on (a) Chip), which is a complete, integrated computer including several so-called core processors, as well as Input/Output (I/O) controllers and RAM (Random Access Memory). This is a result of Moore's law (*cf.* § 1.5). The SoC's predecessor is the Application-Specific Integrated Circuit (ASIC), usually developed for a specific

10 An orthogonal use of the same phrase was used in Japan in 1981 when it launched the national "fifth generation" project (Moto-oka *et al.* 1982; Treleaven and Lima 1982). The associated software development used declarative languages referred to as the fifth generation. In addition, Treleaven (1981) spoke of the fifth generation to refer to spatially distributed systems carrying out decentralized computing.

client with various design styles (full custom, semicustom and programmable). These began to emerge in the early 1980s. In addition, MEMS (MicroElectroMechanical System) or electromechanical microsystems, increasingly integrated peripherals such as sensors, or even actuators, such as a micro-pump.

Figure 1.16. *PC motherboard (5150) from IBM (1981). For a color version of this figure, see www.iste.co.uk/darche/microprocessor1.zip*

Tables 1.5(a–c) summarize the different generations of integrated circuits by showing, for each of them, the number of transistors n and equivalent gates p per package, according to different authors. The equivalent gate (NAND with two inputs)[11] is independent of technology and logic type. The number of gate-equivalent circuits is a unit of measurement of the complexity of a circuit that indicates the number of gates necessary to perform a given function. There exists a correspondence between a given technology and the number of transistors per gate. Note the introduction of two generations following VLSI, called ULSI (Ultra LSI) and GSI (GigaScale Integration), the latter of which allowed for the integration of an entire system or SoC (System-on-(a)-Chip). We should also anecdotally mention the intermediate generations ELSI (Extra LSI) and SLSI (Super LSI). The range of the intervals varies from author to author. Each generation has made it possible to integrate increasingly complex functionalities. The SSI generation brought integrated gates; the MSI, simple combinational and sequential functions (for encoding, multiplying, adding, storing, counting, etc.) and the LSI, which was an entire system (Arithmetic and Logic Unit (ALU), 4–8-bit microprocessor, I/O controller, memory size < 256 Kib, etc.). The VLSI and the GSI represent the generations of 16–32-bit and 64-bit microprocessors.

11 Remember that NAND (Not AND) is a complete operator (*cf.* § 1.5.7 in Darche 2002).

Today, the purpose of this categorization is to show the hierarchy of the ideas behind these logical systems and the acceleration of the density of integration.

Generations	Year of introduction	Primary electronic technology	Number of logic gates p per package (Osborne 1980; Weste and Harris 2010)
SSI	1964	Bipolar	1–10
MSI	1968	Bipolar	10–1000 100–1000 (Osborne 80)
LSI	1971	PMOS NMOS	10^3–10^4
ELSI	–	–	–
VLSI	1980	HMOS CMOS	10^4–10^5
SLSI	–	CMOS	–
ULSI	1990	CMOS	10^5–10^6
GSI SoC	2000	CMOS	–

Table 1.5a. *Classification of generations of integrated circuits according to various authors*

Generations	Number of logic gates p equivalent per package (van de Goor 1989) (Kaeslin 2008) and TI	Number of transistors n/gates p (Lilen 1979)
SSI	1–10	< 100/1–25
MSI	10–100	$100 \leq n < 1000$ $25 \leq p < 250$
LSI	10^2–10^4	$1000 \leq n < 10000$ $250 \leq p < 2500$
ELSI	–	–
VLSI	10^4–10^6	≥ 10000 $p \geq 2500$
SLSI	–	–
ULSI	$\geq 10^6$	–
GSI SoC	–	–

Table 1.5b. *Classification of generations of integrated circuits according to various authors (continued)*

Generations	Number of transistors n/gates p (Wickes 1968)	Number of logic gates p (Siewiorek *et al.* 1982)
SSI	$n < 10$ $p < 12$	1–9
MSI	$10 \leq n < 100$ $12 \leq p < 100$	10–99
LSI	$100 \leq n < 1000$ $p \geq 100$	100–9999
ELSI	$100 \leq p < 999$	–
VLSI	$1000 \leq n < 10\,000$ $1000 \leq p < 999\,999$	10^4–99 999
SLSI	$10\,000 \leq n < 100\,000$	–
ULSI	$n \geq 10^6$ $p \geq 10^6$	$\geq 10^5$
GSI SoC	–	–

Table 1.5c. *Classification of generations of integrated circuits according to various authors (continuation and end)*

The point of this functional decomposition was to "standardize" the electronic components, thus allowing for a reduction in costs and a simplification of design. We are referring to off-the-shelf components (COTS for Commercial Off-The-Shelf). The first such components were digital electronics with simple combinational and sequential logic (gates, latches, and flip-flops), followed by more complex ones (decoders, registers, etc., *cf.* Darche (2002, 2004)). Next came the microprocessor (*cf.* V3) and bit slicing (*cf.* § V3-5.1), which were the next examples in the field.

The following table specifies the definitions used for this series of works.

Optical technology is an alternative to current (i.e. electronic) technology for obtaining a high transmission rate, lower attenuation and resistance to corrosion. It is already used in the telecommunications field in optical fiber and mass storage. Optoelectronics can be used in the interconnection of display systems and peripherals. All-optical logic gate operators exist in laboratories, aiming to achieve a higher computing speed.

Generations	Year of introduction	Primary electronic technology	Number of transistors n per package
SSI	1964	Bipolar	< 10
MSI	1968	Bipolar	$10 \leq n < 1000$
LSI	1971	PMOS NMOS	$1000 \leq n < 10\,000$
ELSI	–	–	–
VLSI	1980	HMOS[12] CMOS	$10\,000 \leq n < 100\,000$
SLSI	–	CMOS	–
ULSI	1990	CMOS	10^5 à 10^9 (Meindl 1984)
GSI SoC	2000	CMOS	$n \geq 10^9$ (Meindl 1995) $p \geq 10^6$

Table 1.6. *Classification of generations of integrated circuits adopted*

The quantum computer will undoubtedly be, if technology allows, a giant step forward from the point of view of computing performance (*cf.* § V4-3.4). Information is presented in the form of a qubit (quantum bit), which is a superposition of two basic states $|0\rangle$ and $|1\rangle$. This superposition, in association with the property of entanglement, opens the way to massive parallelization of computation. Indeed, it is possible to access all possible results in a single computation.

Bell (2008a, 2008b) defines the concept of computer class as being a set of computers with similar price, size, hardware and software technologies, computing power and field(s) of application. A hardware and software industry is associated with a class. The class determines the domain of use. The life cycle of a class, that is, the process of creation, evolution, and disappearance, evolves along four axes of cost evolution as illustrated in Figure 1.17. The class of supercomputers outstrips the others in the race for performance. There is a class at constant cost whose performance increases thanks to technological progress. There is a low-cost class. A class generates a less efficient and less expensive subclass (order of magnitude: factor of 10). A new class can supersede a previous one, as the PC did with the workstation, or it can incorporate it. The emergence phase lasts for about 10 years, triggered by new hardware technologies that enable advances in processors, buses,

12 HMOS: High-density MOS.

storage and I/O interfaces (in particular display and communications) and new software technologies (programming environment, Operating System (OS), Human–Machine Interface (HMI), etc.).

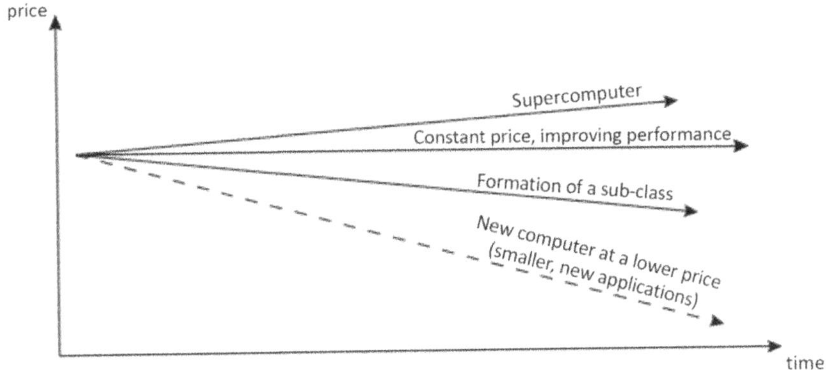

Figure 1.17. *Axes of evolution over time of the price of classes (from (Bell 2008a b) modified)*

The six main classes of computers before 2000 were, in descending order of performance, the scientific computer, the mainframe computer, the minicomputer, the workstation, the microcomputer or personal computer and the embedded system.

Scientists require intensive and time-consuming computation involving a large amount of data. This is the field of High-Performance Computing (HPC), and the associated computers are called supercomputers. This type of machine by definition has the highest computing speed, more primary and secondary storage than a minicomputer (order of magnitude: factor of 10^3 or 2^{10}). They originally had a single, ultra-fast processor. They then evolved by implementing parallelism. The representative company in this field from the 1980s is Cray Corporation with the Cray-1 (Figure 1.18), which operated in n = 64-bit format. In 1984, three classes of architecture – pipelined, vector (array processor), and multiprocessor – could be distinguished. The top countries in terms of computing performance were China and the United States (2016 data), with computers having a floating-point computing power (*cf.* § 4.2 of Darche (2000)) greater than 15,000 PFLOPS (petaFLOPS = 10^{15} Floating-Point Operations Per Second). The TOP500 project site (URL: http://www.top500.org) ranks their performance. The subclass is the mini-supercomputer (Architecture Technology Corporation 1991; Besk *et al.* 1993) like the "Crayette", a CMOS implementation of the original. This group also includes midrange systems. This type of machine, which was air cooled, consumed much less power than a supercomputer. It had vector computing capabilities and could be a multiprocessor.

Figure 1.18. *The iconic Cray-1 supercomputer referred to as the "World's most expensive loveseat?"*[13] *(Computer World 1976). For a color version of this figure, see www.iste.co.uk/darche/microprocessor1.zip*

Figure 1.19 shows the performance curve for some reference machines.

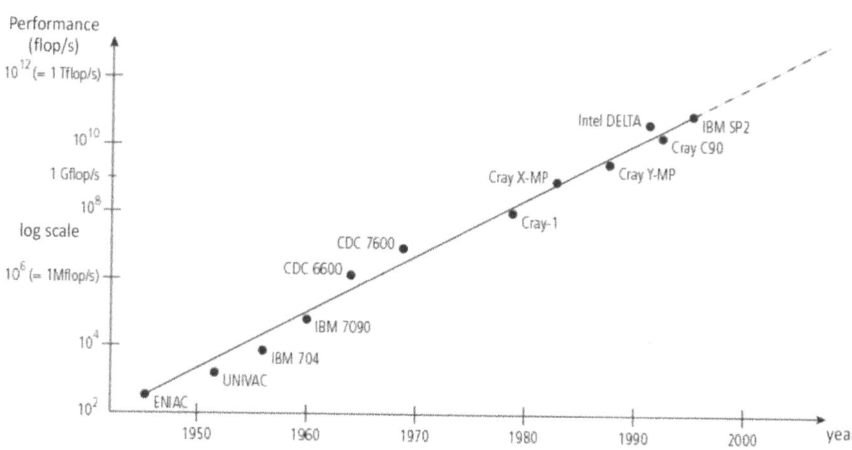

Figure 1.19. *Evolution over time of supercomputer performance (according to Succi et al. 1996)*

13 The title of the photograph in the associated article.

The term "mainframe" describes the cabinet containing the central unit and primary storage. This type of computer is characterized by sufficient computing power to support communications with hundreds of terminals and the execution of associated applications. The "mainframe" is also referred to as a "central system or central computer". It is a transaction-based system that is associated with concepts such as batch processing, Simultaneous Peripheral Operations On-Line (SPOOL), cache and devices like the hard disk Mass Storage Device (MSD). The company that is most representative of the first category is undoubtedly IBM, with the IBM System/360 (Figure 1.20) described in Pugh (2013) and the IBM System/370. In the 1990s, the IBM 3090 was a representative central computer. This type of computer could be cooled by a heat transfer fluid other than air, such as water (see Ellsworth *et al.* (2008) on this subject).

Figure 1.20. *IBM System/360 mainframe computer*

The minicomputer, abbreviated mini, is a lower-level class. It is therefore sometimes called a departmental computer[14] as opposed to the centralized view of the mainframe. A minicomputer is a central computer of reduced size and power.

14 That is, for use by a group of people. But this name is not discriminative, because a parallel computer like the cydra 5 (Rau *et al.* 1989) is referred to as a departmental machine.

However, it is based on a similar philosophy and is more powerful than a microcomputer. The first minicomputer was the PDP-8 (1965) from Digital Equipment Corporation (DEC). The precursor machines were the Bendix G-15 (1956), the LGP-30 (1956) and the LINC (1962), which is considered the first minicomputer. The representative models were the PDP (Programmable Data Processor) line, with the PDP-11 as a reference machine; the VAX-11, with the VAX-11/780 as the reference machine for DEC and the AS/400 from IBM (Figure 1.21). From this class, a derived subclass with superior performance was developed. These machines were called super minicomputers. A super minicomputer had a working data format two to four times greater than the basic version of a given generation. It was equipped with hardware accelerators or coprocessors for computation of vectors or floating-point numbers. Two representatives were the VAX 6000 series (Sullivan *et al.* 1990) and the 8000 series (Burley 1987).

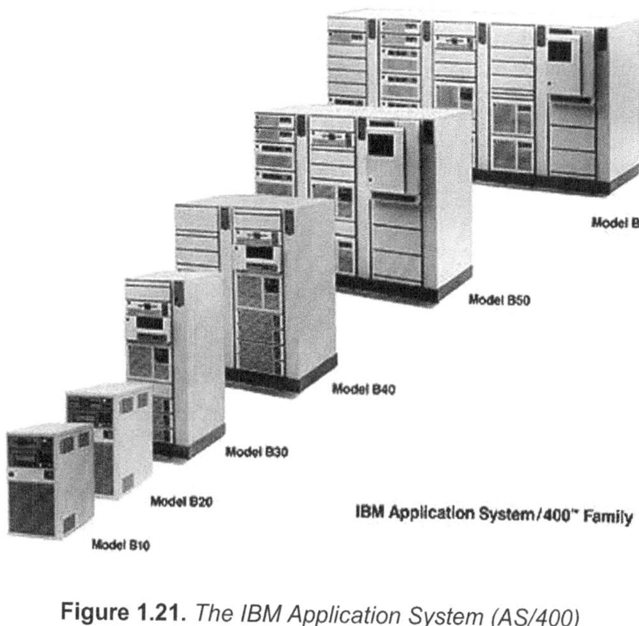

Figure 1.21. *The IBM Application System (AS/400) family of minicomputers*

Bell (2014) divides the evolution of this sector into three periods: the establishment of the associated industry (1956–1964, in green in Figure 1.22), the "triumph" (1965–1974), which overlaps with the period of cohabitation with the first (V)LSI microprocessors (1971–1984), and the decline (1985–1995, in red on this same figure). The advent of the 8-bit and especially 16-bit microprocessor generations made it possible to introduce low-cost, entry-level versions (low end).

Examples include DEC's LSI-11 (DEC 1975, 1976) chipset for its PDP-11 and the MicroNova mN601 (Godderz 1976) microprocessor or MPU (Godderz 1976) from Data General Corp. (compatible with the Fairchild F9440 Microflame™), equipped with mN606 4 Ki × 1-bit RAM and the mN603 I/O controller; these product lines provided 8- and 16-bit architecture respectively.

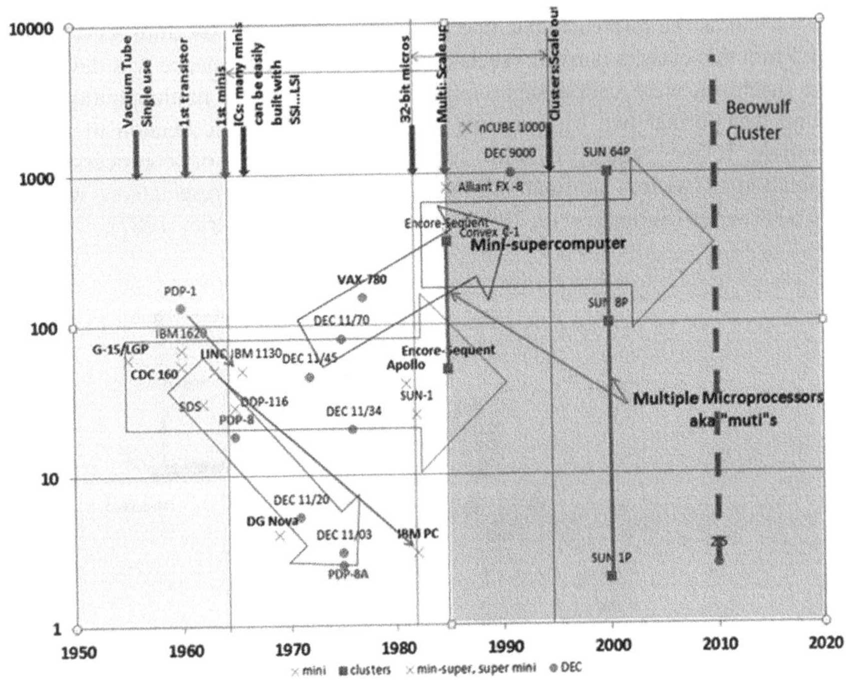

Figure 1.22. *Evolution over time of the prices of minicomputers (in thousands of $) (Bell 2014) © IEEE. For a color version of this figure, see www.iste.co.uk/darche/microprocessor1.zip*

The decline in minicomputers was due to advances in the integration of electronic technology that led to the appearance of the microprocessor, which replaced it. The impact of this component on the market in this sector has been studied in particular by Schultz *et al.* (1973). In 1973, the microprocessor had a memory access time slower by a factor 1/2 to 1/3 compared to a mid-range minicomputer.

The (personal) workstation is a powerful single-station computer built initially around a 16-bit microprocessor (the MC68000 from Motorola), mainly using the multitasking UNIX OS and connected to an Ethernet-based Local Area Network

(LAN). The goal was to break away from the classic computer-terminal system for individual use of interactive applications. The work environment was to be shared (files, for example) and distributed over a network. It offered high-resolution graphics capacity, eventually including color. The preferred fields of application were Computer-Aided Design (CAD), Computer-Aided Drawing (CAD) and HPC. Other fields included computer graphics, video processing and 3D (three-dimensional) image synthesis. The initial idea dated from the 1950s, with prototypes in the 1960s using a more powerful computer (mainframe) connected to a graphics terminal. The first prototypes appeared in the early 1970s with graphic terminals connected to mini or autonomous computers such as the Alto PARC (Xerox Palo Alto Research Center) in 1973. Mature products emerged during the next decade. Apollo (since bought by HP Company), Silicon Graphics (now SGI), Sun Microsystems (since bought by Oracle Corporation) and Xerox were the four representatives of this class with their first machines respectively the Domain DN-100 (1981), the IRIS 1400 (1984), the Sun-1 (1982) and the Xerox STAR (1981). We should also mention IBM's RS/6000 (January 15, 1990). We began to refer to 3M and 5M machines. RFC (Request For Comments) 782 (Nabielsky and Skelton 1981) specified that a 3M machine had at least one MB (i.e. MiB) of memory, a screen with a resolution of at least one Megapixel, and computing power of one Million Instructions Per Second (MIPS). In addition, it should not cost more than one "Megapenny" ($10,000 at the time). The term 5M referred to *Megabyte memory, Megapixel display, MIPS processor power, 10+ Megabyte disk drive,* and *10 Megabit/s network*). Bell (1986) and Nelson and Bell (1986) paint a portrait of this type of machine and trace its evolution. It appeared thanks to the development of local networks. The price range was $\$10^3$–$10^4$. The systems used 32-bit RISC (Reduced Instruction Set Computer)-type microprocessors because of their computing power. Today (2010), 64-bit Intel microprocessors are used. Figure 1.23 shows a modern workstation.

Figure 1.23. *An Octane graphics workstation from Silicon Graphics, Inc. (SGI). For a color version of this figure, see www.iste.co.uk/darche/microprocessor1.zip*

The microcomputer[15] is a self-contained computer whose central unit is a microprocessor. It is a general-purpose computer, personal, inexpensive, and with limited computing capacity, in comparison with the above categories. It was invented in France, with the Micral N, which was patented in 1974 (Gernelle 1974) (Figure 1.24(a)). It was intended in particular for use in real-time applications. The first model sold in kit form in 1975 was the ALTAIR 8800 (Roberts and Yates 1975a b) from the American company MITS (Figure 1.24(b)). Before these, there were evaluation kits (*cf.* § V5-2.1.1) for implementing a given microprocessor. The first generation (1971–1976) is considered to include the pioneers. The second generation (1977–1990) saw the introduction of home microcomputers. The first machines were built around an 8-bit microprocessor and natively included BASIC (Beginner's All-purpose Symbolic Instruction Code) ROM (Read-Only Memory). An audio cassette player provided mass storage (*cf.* § 7.2.2 in Darche (2003))! These computers include the iconic Apple II, the Commodore PET (Personal Electronic Transactor) 2001, the Tandy TRS-80[16] from Tandy RadioShack, the BBC (British Broadcasting Corporation) Microcomputer System (1981) from Acorn Computer, and the ZX Spectrum (1982) from Sinclair Research Ltd. Libes (1978) describes this generation's technology. These machines naturally evolved towards a 16-bit architecture. With the appearance of the Floppy Disk Drive (FDD, *cf.* § 7.2.2 in Darche (2003)) in the mid-1970s, these machines became equipped with a simple OS such as CP/M (Control Program for Microcomputers, Digital Research, Inc.). The microcomputer was de facto standardized with the Personal Computer[17] (PC) from IBM, which had a microprocessor with a 16-bit internal architecture (although the external interface was in 8-bit format) from Intel. The first laptops that were not self-sufficient in terms of power were released in 1983 (the Compaq Portable) and 1984 (the IBM[18] Portable PC 5155 model 68). In the 1990s, a representative computer used by large companies was the IBM PS/2. Today, the battery-powered laptop has an energy autonomy of less than 10 hours. The microcomputer is available as a touchscreen tablet PC, which first appeared in 2001, and the associated phablet telephone (phablet is a contraction of the words smartphone and tablet), which appeared in 2010. Doerr (1978) describes this period.

15 This is called the "micro" for short.

16 TRS stands for Tandy RadioShack.

17 This name was popularized with this machine, but the term has multiple origins (Shapiro 2000). One source was the magazine Byte, which published an editorial by Helmers in its May 1976 issue. An older source can be found in an advertisement for the HP 9100 in the journal Science on October 4, 1968 (HP 1968).

18 This company was the first to commercialize the (trans)portable computer in 1975, the 5100. It was not designed around an MPU, but a custom controller called the PALM (Put All Logic in Microcode).

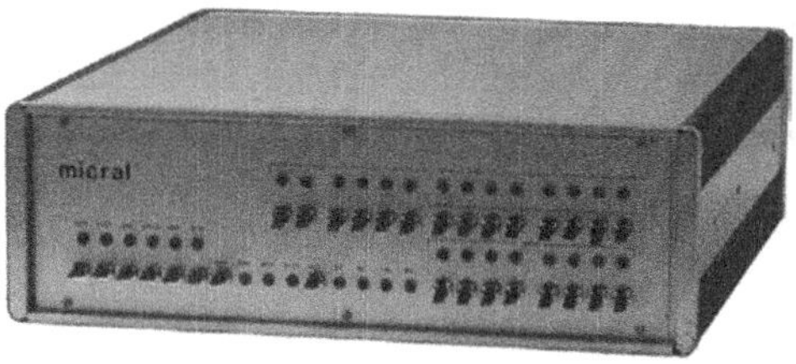

a)

b)

Figure 1.24. *The first microcomputers: the Micral N from R2E and the ALTAIR 8800 from the American company MITS (source: unknown). For a color version of this figure, see www.iste.co.uk/darche/microprocessor1.zip*

Single-Board Computers (SBC) were a variant of the microcomputer used for process control and automation. These are complete MPU computer systems on a single printed circuit, sometimes in an OEM (Original Equipment Manufacturer) version. One of the first companies to offer this type of equipment was DEC with the LSI-11 series (Doerr 1978, Stiefel 1978). They were mainly intended for the industrial market, although there was also a market for individuals (i.e. hobbyists). These boards generally had a standardized form factor (*cf.* § V5-3.4.1) and communicated via an industrial bus (*cf.* § V2-4.8). There were also versions for embedded systems, such as those from the PC/104 consortium.

Another type of computer is the embedded or on-board system. These systems contain a dedicated management system. It therefore consisted of an electronic system with autonomous software from an operating point of view. The software is built-in. The algorithms implemented are generally complex and require a powerful microprocessor. They often involve a real-time concept. Etiemble (2016) thus distinguishes, on this last criterion, between on-board systems, which are mobile with real-time constraints, and embedded systems, which are fixed and without real-time constraints, although the term "embedded" is generally considered to encompass both definitions. Autonomous energy systems impose thermal and current consumption constraints. Examples of applications are computer peripherals like the printer, automated systems like industrial controllers and mobile devices like the mobile phone. They are widely used in the transportation sector (car, train, rocket, etc.). And similarly to what was said in the previous section, after 2010, the line between the on-board system and the microcomputer becomes increasingly blurry for certain devices like the mobile phone (smartphone).

Advances in microelectronic technologies, mainly CMOS, have enabled advances in the fields of storage and communications, allowing space-saving (corresponding form factors: SFF for Small Form Factor), low current consumption and communications-based devices to emerge. We are referring to Cell-Phone-Sized Devices (CPSDs). As illustrated in Figure 1.25, digital systems equipped with one or more microprocessors or microcontrollers (MCU for MicroController Unit, *cf.* definition in § V3-5.3) are becoming ubiquitous. In everyday life, they control, for example, washing machines (1), cars (2) and cameras (3). In healthcare, they manage heart rate monitors (4) and control artificial hearts. They are found in network interconnection equipment such as the router (6), the gateway and the Internet modem. They are used in entertainment electronics, for example, in game consoles (7) and sound/video players (PAD for Personal Audio Device, PVD for Personal Video Device, PA/VD for Personal Audio/Video Device). They are used in mobile devices such as the mobile phone (5), the Personal Digital Assistant (PDA), and the portable microcomputer (8). The server (9) and the mainframe (10) perform computation even faster thanks to the microprocessor. They have become ubiquitous in connected objects, with one commercially available example being the connected watch (11). They are also embedded in devices such as the connected electric meter (12). Since the early 1990s and the beginning of this century, Wireless Sensor Networks (WSN) and the Internet of Things (IoT) have opened up a wide field of applications. The 21 Century will undoubtedly see the rise of robots (13). The boundaries between all these categories are increasingly blurry or non-existent. Today (2000), servers are often structured like microcomputers with more powerful technical characteristics including computing power and the size of primary and secondary storage. The same goes for the workstation.

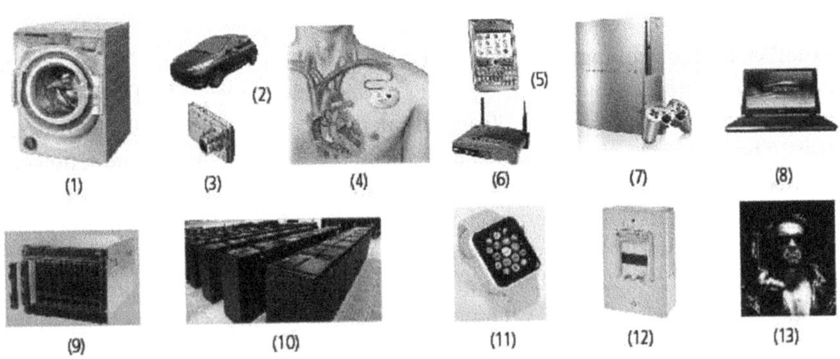

Figure 1.25. *Increasingly blurry boundaries. For a color version of this figure, see www.iste.co.uk/darche/microprocessor1.zip*

As of 2010, the microprocessor is the foundation for all classes, from the supercomputer to the Internet of Things (Figure 1.26). It is gradually eliminating the notion of classes! This trend was symbolized by the expression "killer micro" popularized by Brooks (1989), which refers to CMOS-based microprocessors, which were going to gradually replace the mainframe computers, minicomputers, and super-computers.[19] Belak (1993) illustrates its applications. Figure 1.26 shows the evolution of these classes over time. Michael Burwen (Architecture Technology Corporation 1991) divides classes into three categories of large, medium, and small systems. In the first, we find super computers, central computers with vector computing capability, and parallel computers. The midrange systems category includes mini super computers, classic mainframe computers, servers and super minicomputers. Small systems include servers, conventional and graphical workstations, and other systems. They merge into a single category, namely, multiprocessor systems. We can also add two other categories for microcomputers and small-form factor systems.

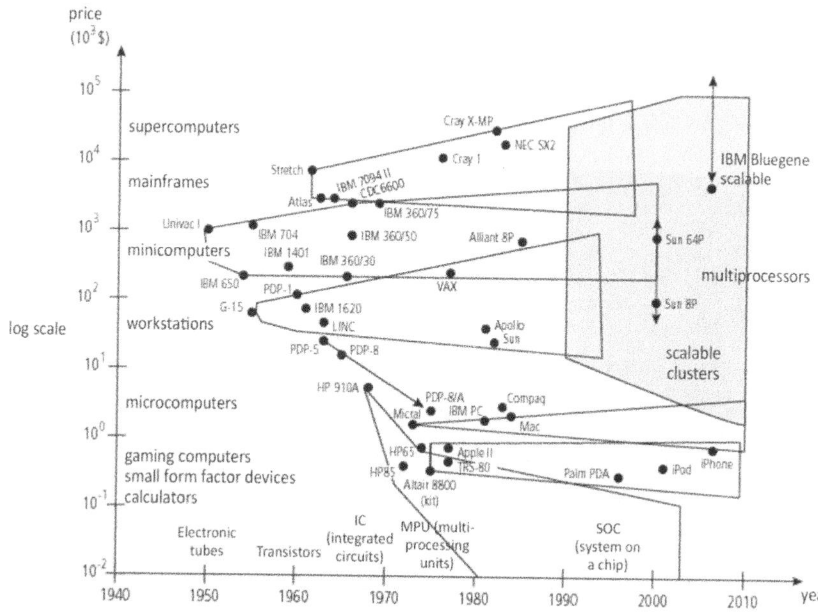

Figure 1.26. *Categories of computers (according to Bell (2008a))*

Thanks to the development of communication networks, the server offers services to connected clients such as the sharing of applications or storage. These

19 "No one will survive the attack of the killer micro!"

computers have powerful computing, storage and communication capabilities (Figure 1.27).

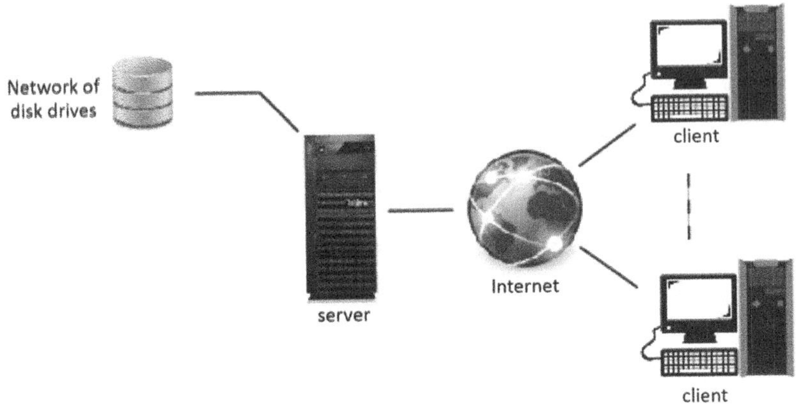

Figure 1.27. *The client–server model. For a color version of this figure, see www.iste.co.uk/darche/microprocessor1.zip*

Figure 1.28. *A blade server. For a color version of this figure, see www.iste.co.uk/darche/microprocessor1.zip*

Its modern form is the blade server. Several blades are mounted in a chassis that supplies them with power and cools them with air, as illustrated in Figure 1.28. This pooling of electronic sub-assemblies (power supply, cooling system, communication elements and even storage systems) makes it possible to achieve a compact format. The alternative solution is the server rack, which is a cabinet that accommodates servers with standardized dimensions (unit: U = 1.75"). Another form factor is the tower. Haghighi (2001) describes this architecture.

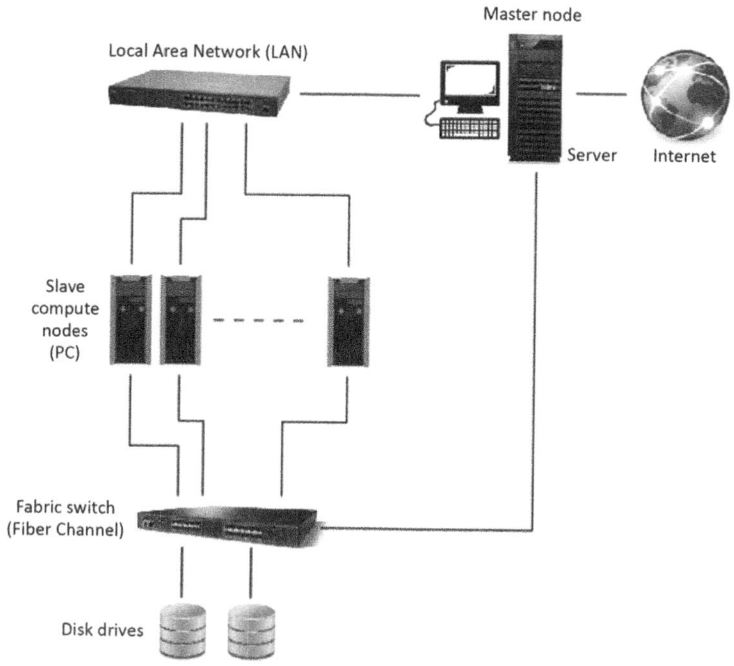

Figure 1.29. *Example of a Beowulf server architecture. For a color version of this figure, see www.iste.co.uk/darche/microprocessor1.zip*

Today, in order to increase computing power, the computer has become parallelized. This means that it is made up of several computing units (parallelism of execution) and that the data is shared. Access occurs simultaneously (data parallelism). Computing and data resources can be distributed geographically, and access must be transparent. Thanks to the development of communication networks and these types of parallelism, three types of computing resources have appeared, namely, compute farms, grid computing and cloud computing. The term cluster designates a set or cluster of a dozen servers at most, also called a compute farm. Each node in the cluster is a commercially available computer, and these nodes are identical in terms of hardware and OS (property of homogeneity). Figure 1.29 shows an example of a Beowulf cluster (Sterling *et al.* 1995). For a workstation, we speak of NOW (Anderson *et al.* 1995) for a Network Of Workstations, or COW for a Cluster Of Workstations. The nodes communicate via a broadband network such as Infiniband. The cluster appears externally as a single computer, with the user connecting securely via a front-end server. This organization facilitates the hardware management of the different computer components (processor, primary and secondary storage, communication interfaces, etc.) and the software. It allows for easy scalability. From the point of view of fault tolerance, it increases availability. One possible use is HPC. For more information on the subject, see Pfister (1998).

A computational grid is a heterogeneous hardware and software infrastructure that is geographically distributed (i.e. delocalized) and allows virtual organizations (individuals, institutions, etc.) to solve problems and share data (Foster *et al.* 2001). This term was chosen by analogy to the electrical network, which supplies energy pervasively. This virtual computer system thus offers extensible and transparent access to distributed resources. A node in the grid can be a supercomputer or a cluster. These resources can communicate via any type of network, including LAN, Metropolitan Area Networks (MAN), or Wide Area Networks (WAN) like the Internet. Originally, this Information Technology (IT) infrastructure was implemented in response to the scientific community's needs (particle physics in particular) for distributed computing (computational grid) and data storage (data grid). A desktop grid is a variant where weakly coupled standalone computers participate in global computation in their spare time. For more information on the subject, see Foster and Kesselman (2003) and Shiva (2006).

Cloud computing is a paradigm that enables a user to relocate computing and storage resources, which can then be accessed via a network, generally a metropolitan or wide area network like the Internet. The two earlier infrastructures can be incorporated. These hardware and software resources are delivered as services. Table 1.7 summarizes the main differences between farm, grid and cloud computing. The main advantages of these architectures are their scalability thanks to their modularity and their high power/cost ratio thanks to the standardization of hardware and software components.

Depending on the level of service, cloud computing can provide Infrastructure-as-a-Service (IaaS), Platform-as-a-Service (PaaS) and Software-as-a-Service (SaaS). The first offers a virtualization solution for servers, networks and data storage. The second also provides middleware. The latter, also known as the "ASP model" (Application Service Provider), offers software functionality over the Internet where the application, in whole or in part, is run on remote servers.

Characteristics	Computing farm	Computing grid	Cloud computing
Homogeneity/Heterogeneity	Homogenous	Heterogeneous	Either/or
Hardware and OS characteristics	Identical hardware and OS	Different hardware and OS	Computers managed by the OS in physical units
Allocation	Works as a single unit with no use of external computing resources	Can call on "idle" PC computing resources	Several applications executed in parallel
Geographical distribution	One location	Distributed over local, metropolitan, and wide area networks	Distributed primarily on metropolitan networks
Resource management	Centralized	Independent nodes with own-resource management	Independent nodes
Centralization	Centralized and tightly coupled	Decentralized and loosely coupled	Dynamic infrastructure
Task and scheduling management	Centralized	Decentralized	Minimal management or self-managed platform
User interface	Appears as a single system	Appears as a dynamic and diversified system	Self-service use
Application domain	Education, research, engineering	Simulation and modeling, Computer-Aided Design (CAD), Research	Banking, insurance, weather forecasting, SaaS

Table 1.7. *Comparison of characteristics between computing resources (from Suri and Sumit Mittal (2012))*

1.3. Analog approach

The beginning of the history of computers is generally dated from the appearance of calculating machines (*cf.* § 1.1), but we must not forget analog calculating machines. The first known analog calculator is the Antikythera mechanism (Figure 1.30) dated around 90–60 BC. It described the movements of the moon and the sun in order to predict an eclipse.

Figure 1.30. *The Antikythera mechanism (left) and a reconstruction (right), by Michael Wright (source: unknown). For a color version of this figure, see www.iste.co.uk/darche/microprocessor1.zip*

An analog computer, unlike the digital version, uses analog quantities proportional to the calculation values (Truitt and Rogers 1964). The precision of the result depends specifically on the measurement of the result. The underlying technology was hydraulic, mechanical, then electrical and electronic. These computers could be for general use, such as the slide rule, or they could be dedicated. They were primarily used to perform simulations of physical phenomena because they were able to compute the four basic arithmetic operations (+, -, etc.) or more complex functions like integration or derivation. An example of mechanical technology is Vannevar Bush's differential analyzer (1931; 1945). Data entry was done using an entry table that looked like a plotter. Figure 1.31 shows an electronic implementation, the PACE (Precision Analog Computing Element) 231R-V analog computer from the leading company of the time, Electronic Associates Inc. (EAI). The output device could be a galvanometer, an oscilloscope or a paper recorder. These devices were used by industries including aeronautics and space for simulation and systems control purposes. Variants were the hybrid computer (logic/analog combination) and the high-speed analog computer. Its industrial decline in the late 1970s was due to the predominance of digital electronics, which became cheaper, faster and more precise with standard components like the microprocessor. For a historical introduction, see Small (2001).

Figure 1.31. *The PACE 231R-V analog computer system from EAI (EAI 1964)*

1.4. Hardware–software relationship

It is now necessary to position software (SW) in relation to computer hardware. Figure 1.32 shows a layered view with hardware and software examples. The lowest layer is the hardware layer (HW). The microprocessor component of the computer is the subject of this work. Primary storage has been described in Darche (2012). I/O interfaces were discussed in Darche (2003). Above, a first low-level software layer called firmware[20] (FW) tests the hardware, initializes it, and loads the operating system. Designated by the term BIOS (Basic Input/Output System) in the PC (Personal Computer) world, it includes a set of software routines executed in interrupt mode (*cf.* Chapter V4-5). The third software layer is the OS (operating system software), which manages hardware and software resources for the whole. It is responsible in particular for security in the broad sense. The execution of applications (last layer, application software) relies on the latter. Between each layer, an interface allows the upper layer to use the services of the one below. In

20 In contemporary usage (*cf.* § V5-3.5.1), this is a program stored in ROM, as opposed to one stored in mass storage (secondary or tertiary memory), which is referred to as software.

particular, a virtual machine is a software layer located either below the OS (System Virtual Machine) or above it (Process Virtual Machine), which emulates another architecture and its associated computing model (within the meaning of Chapter 3). On this last subject, Smith and Nair (2005) provide an excellent reference.

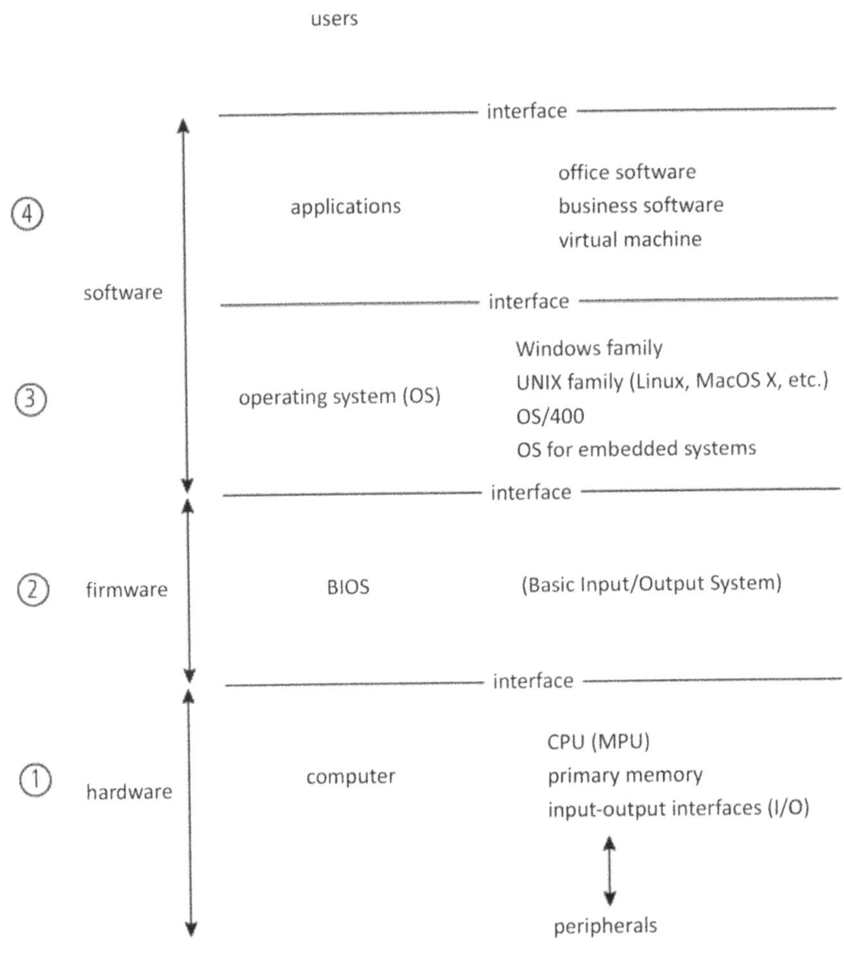

Figure 1.32. *Layered view of software infrastructure*

The technological generations within the meaning of § 1.2 provide support for software concepts such as programming languages and operating systems. As noted by Denning (1971), this classification is also linked to technological advances in the software field. In addition, they characterize the entire computer system. Thus, the term "generation of computers" encompasses both hardware and software technologies, as summarized in Tables 1.8(a) and 1.8(b).

	Generations of electronics	
Characteristics	**1st**	**2nd**
Period	1946–1955	1956–1965
Electronics		
Electronics components	vacuum tube	transistor
Cycle time	0.1–1 ms	1–10 μs
Primary storage		
Components	Delay line Electrostatic tube Magnetic drum (start)	Magnetic drum Magnetic core
Access time	1 ms	1–10 μs
Secondary storage	Punched tape Punched card Delay line	Punched card Magnetic tape Magnetic disk Magnetic drum
Programming languages	Machine language Assembly language (start)	Assembly language High-level language (HLL)
Hardware concepts	Arithmetic units	Floating-point units microprogramming (concept) interruption I/O processor
Software concepts	-	Batch processing monitor
Hardware examples	ENIAC IAS Princeton UNIVAC IBM 650/701	IBM 7090–7094 CDC 1604 CDC 6600

Table 1.8a. *Generations of computers and main features*

	Generations of electronics		
Characteristics	**3rd**	**4th**	**5th**
Period	1966–1975	1976–1989	1990–202X
Electronics			
Electronics components	Integrated circuit (SSI-MSI)	Integrated circuit (LSI-VLSI)	Integrated circuit (ULSI-GSI)
Cycle time	0.1–1 μs	0.1–1 μs	1 μs–1 ns–0.1 ns
Primary storage			
Components	Magnetic core Other magnetic media	Solid-state memory	Solid-state memory
Access time	0.1–10 μs	0.1 μs	100 ns–< 1 ns
Secondary storage	Same as 2nd generation Extended core storage Mass core storage	Same	Magnetic hard disk Solid-State Disk (SSD)
Programming languages	High-level languages	High-level languages Concurrent programming	
Hardware concepts	Microprogramming Pipeline cache Pagination (Virtual memory) Code translation	Microprocessor (1971) Microcomputer (1973)	Instruction-Level Parallelism (ILP) Thread-Level Parallelism (TLP) (multicore) Massively Parallel Processing (MPP) Heterogeneous environment
Software concepts	Timesharing Segmentation (virtual memory) Multiprogramming	Multiprocessor OS Windowing	
Hardware examples	DEC PDP-8 IBM System 360/370 ILLIAC IV CDC 6600 TI ASC Cray 1 Cyber 205 (Control Data)	IBM PC VAX 9000 IBM 3090 Cray X-MP	Cray MPP Fujitsu VPP500 TMC CM-5 Intel Paragon

Table 1.8b. *Generations of computers and main features (continued)*

ADDITIONAL CONCEPT.– We classify languages by increasing levels of abstraction. Generation 0 was machine language. The next generation includes Assembly Languages (AL, *cf.* § V5-1.3). These are low-level languages. The first high-level qualified languages that characterize the third generation appeared in the 1950s. These include FORTRAN (FORmula TRANslation, 1957), ALGOL (ALGOrithmic Language, 1958) and COBOL (COmmon Business Oriented Language, 1959). The designation "4th Generation Languages" or 4GL characterizes languages that are close to natural language. They facilitate programming by offering, for example, easy access to databases and a better Human–Machine Interface (HMI). Some enable automatic generation of lower level code. They are generally specialized for a particular field such as mathematics or management. The subcategories are query languages, data reporting and code generators.

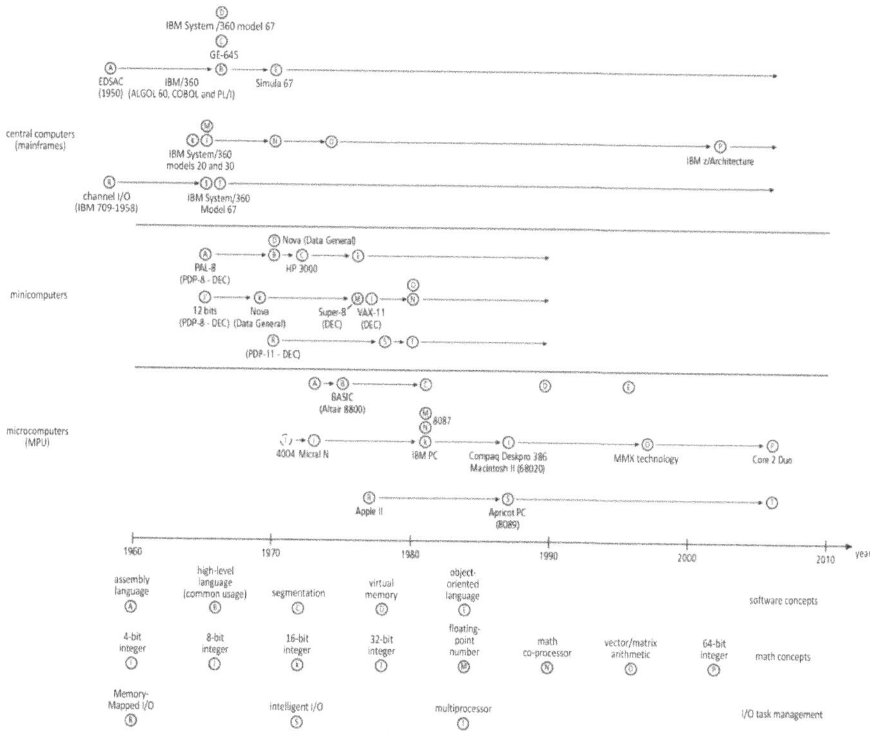

Figure 1.33. *Historical timeline of the evolution of concepts for the families of computers (inspired by Burger et al. 1984)*

A new class of computers is benefiting from advances in technology and integrating earlier hardware and software concepts as soon as technically possible, as shown in Figure 1.33. An example is the Virtual Memory (VM) mechanism that appeared in MPUs only in 16-bit versions with segmentation in the 8088/8086. Thus computer concepts shift from class to class when necessary and when the technology allows. Innovations, initially much more spread out in time, saw their rate of appearance intensify with the invention of the MPU. The 'I'' mark is just a time marker to indicate the release of the first MPU, the 4004.

As soon as computing power becomes sufficient, new applications can be supported, as illustrated in Figure 1.34 for the multimedia field.

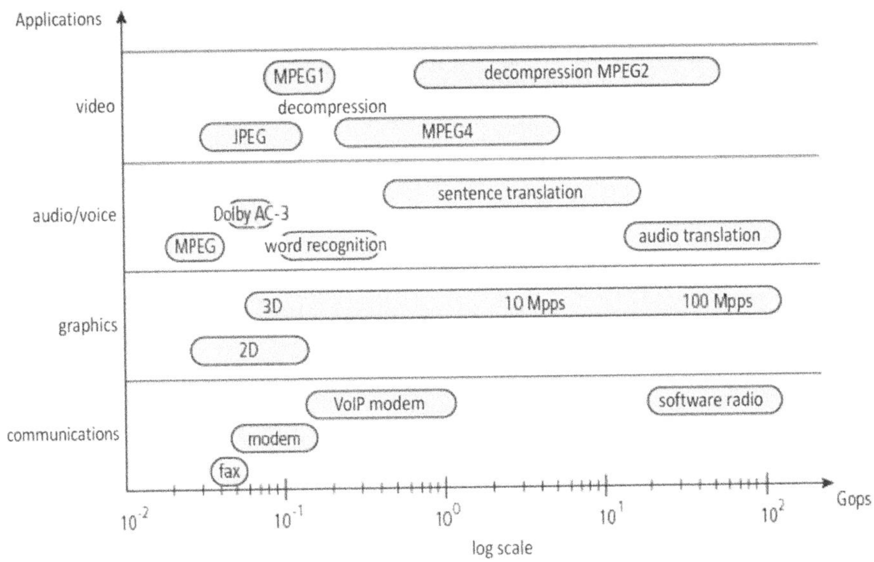

Figure 1.34. *Need for computing for multimedia applications (based on 2003 ITRS document)*

Finally, it should be noted that the notions of operator/programmer/user were initially nested. As shown in Figure 1.35, the operator was first responsible for executing the programs written by the programmer/user. Later, the concept of user was detached from that of programmer to be attached to the operator. These changes are due to progress in both hardware and software.

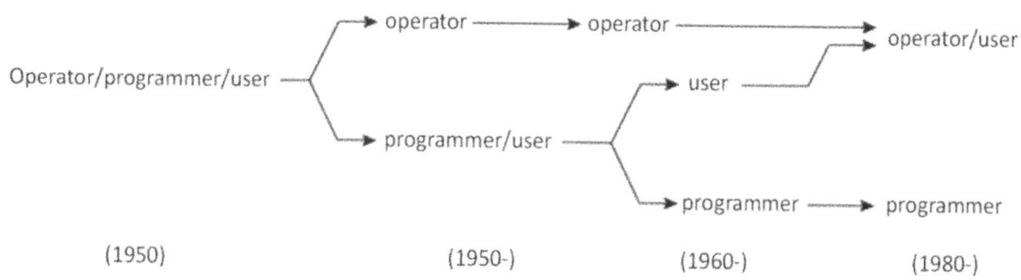

Figure 1.35. *Evolution of computer roles (from Nelson and Bell (1986))*

1.5. Integration and its limits

Electronics, with the three aforementioned active components (diode, transistor and integrated circuit), represented a major technological development that marked the computer industry. Continued advances in microelectronics have increased the functional density of integrated circuits and the speed of information processing. An observation made by Intel co-founder Gordon Moore that bears his name, Moore's Law, was that the number of transistors integrated on a microchip would double every 18 months (Moore 1975). This value has varied over the years from 24 (Moore 1965) to 12 months, eventually stabilizing at the aforementioned value. Figure 1.36 shows the evolution of the number of transistors for our topic. The dominant manufacturing technology, initially essentially bipolar, is today unipolar, namely, MOS and, more precisely, CMOS.

Bell (2008a b) gives the equation for the growth in the number of transistors n per chip as a function of the year t, which is:

$$n = 2^{t-1959} \text{ (for } 1959 \leq t \leq 1975) \quad [1.1]$$

$$n = 2^{16} \times 2^{\frac{t-1975}{1,5}} \text{ (for } t \geq 1975) \quad [1.2]$$

A professional association, the International Technology Roadmap for Semiconductors (ITRS), representing the main regional professional associations in the sector, publishes a report every two years detailing the future of the semiconductor industry. Current technologies for manufacturing primarily CMOS-based integrated circuits are reaching their limits. There is what specialists call the red brick wall first predicted in 2001 to occur in 2005–2008 (ITRS 2001), which is the physical limit for etching.

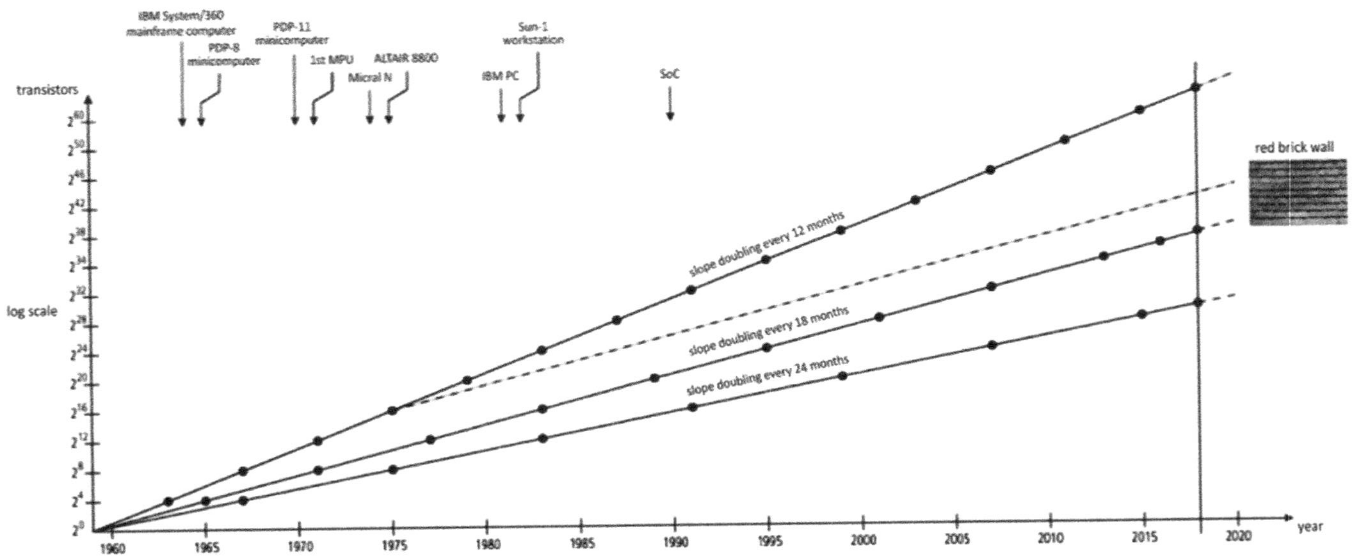

Figure 1.36. *Evolution over time of the number of transistors of an integrated circuit. For a color version of this figure, see www.iste.co.uk/darche/microprocessor1.zip*

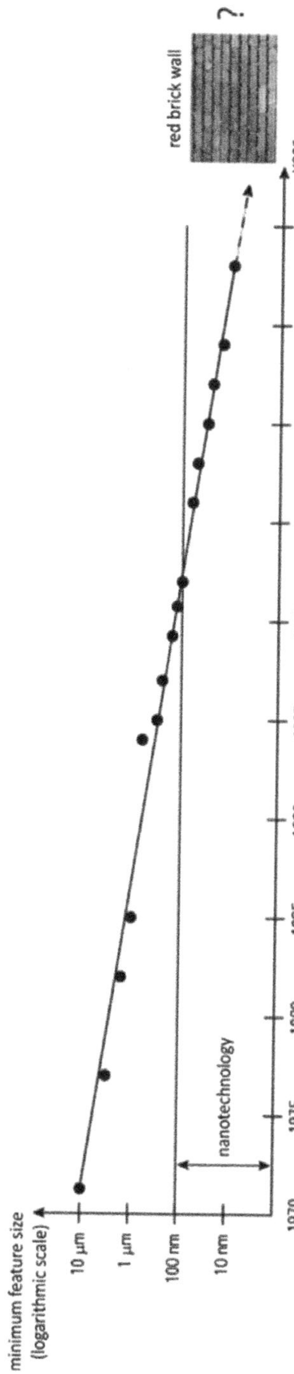

Figure 1.37. *The fineness of etching of integrated circuits over the years (technological node). For a color version of this figure, see www.iste.co.uk/darche/microprocessor1.zip*

The evolution in etching for integrated circuits depends on physical and technological parameters, as well as, of course, economic constraints. For example, as the width of the channel of the unipolar transistor decreases, the mobility of the electrons also decreases. Figure 1.37 shows its change over time. This controversial metric, used by the industry (*cf.* (Arnold 2009)) and withdrawn by the ITRS in 2005, is called the technology node, also referred to as the process, technology or manufacturing node, or simply the node or generation. Depending on the case, this is the length of the gate of a Field Effect Transistor (FET) in MOS technology or the minimum distance[21] between two lines of metal or polysilicon. For storage, we speak of a half-pitch. This improvement in technology (minimum feature size and diameter of the wafer) then allows for greater integration and an increase in clock speed. Greater integration can mean an increase in the number of functional blocks of the CPU, or even a multiplication of processors for parallel processing. It also makes it possible to integrate an entire system (SoC approach).

Another wall is the power wall, which refers to a chip's maximum energy dissipation.

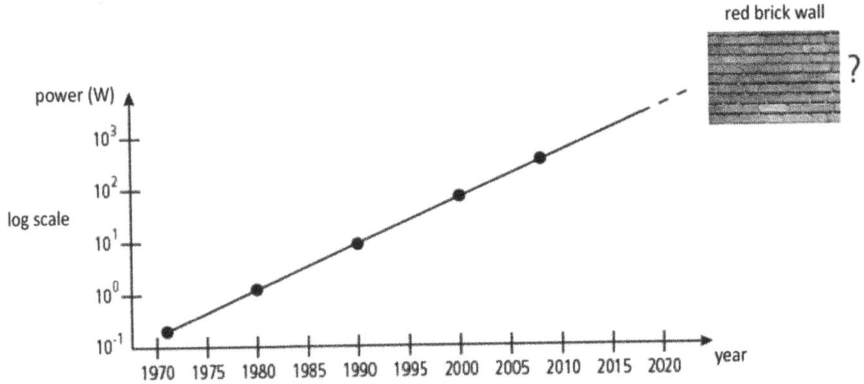

Figure 1.38. *The energy wall (from Xanthopoulos 2009 on data from ISSCC). For a color version of this figure, see www.iste.co.uk/darche/microprocessor1.zip*

Figure 1.38 shows the evolution of the power dissipation per unit area which continues to increase with the different generations of MPU. In this graph, power doubles every 3.5 years, going from 0.2 W in 1970 to 200 W in 2005. Considering that a chip has an area of 1 cm^2, the most extreme value to compare is the power density of a nuclear reactor, for example with pressurized water, which is around 300 W/cm^2. Feng (2003) performed the same study, but with Intel circuits.

21 Another term is "feature size", which is the minimum width that can be etched in silicon.

Dissipating more calories therefore requires increasingly efficient cooling. This requires the use of a better thermal conductor (i.e. with lower thermal resistance), for example ceramic or metal, or the implementation of forced circulation of a gaseous heat-carrying fluid (air) or liquid.

Another physical limit is the signal propagation speed wall. This is linked to the operating frequency of the logic. The propagation delay does not decrease, even with ever-finer etching. Matzke (1997) has shown that the more the technological node decreases, the less it is possible to reach distant logical subsets (Figure 1.39).

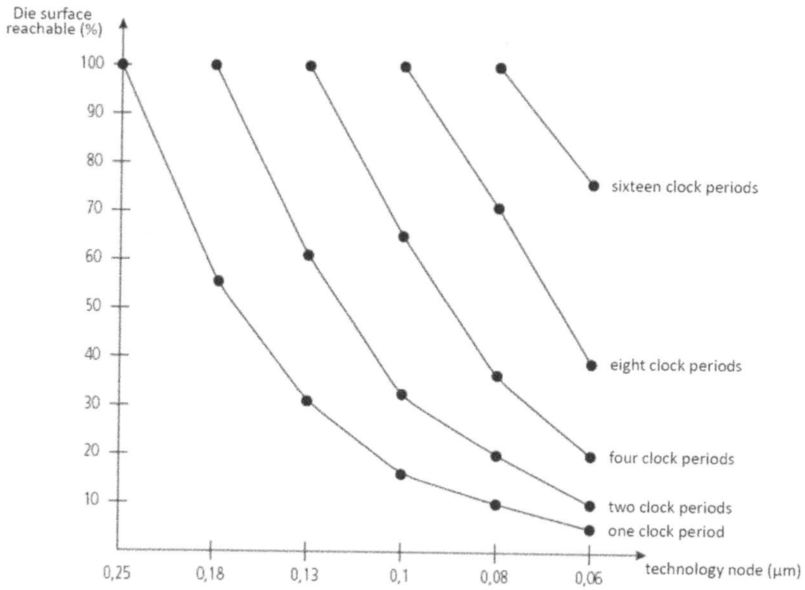

Figure 1.39. *Chip area achievable with progress in integration (according to (Matzke 1997), modified)*

1.6. Conclusion

Two inventions have enabled advances in the field of computing. These are the concepts of the stored program (*cf.* section 3.2.3) and the transistor (Patterson 1995). We must add a third, that of the integrated circuit, which, with VLSI and subsequent generations, enabled the emergence of complex integrated circuits like the microprocessor. Without them, the microcomputer and the democratization of computing would not exist. The evolution of computers is characterized by increasing generalization. Initially specialized for scientific computing, they have now invaded all fields thanks to the microprocessor. The latter destroyed the notion of computer classes.

2

The Function of Memory

Storage is one of the computer's most important functions. It is omnipresent. It is found in the main memory and obviously in the cache hierarchy, but also in the processor, Input–Output (I/O) interfaces and peripherals. The main memory is made up of integrated electronic components designed for memorization, which are usually soldered onto one or both sides of a small multilayer Printed Circuit Board (PCB for Printed Circuit Board), the whole called a memory module. Memory can also be a functional subset of a more complex chip such as a microprocessor or a microcontroller. It can be present in the form of registers or memory areas of larger size such as a cache or a small main memory chip. In this case, it is referred to as "embedded memory" (*cf.* V2, a continuation of Darche (2012), forthcoming). It is also found in I/O controllers in these two formats (i.e. register or cache) or in the form of a buffer that manages the flow of information according to the "First In, First Out" (FIFO) policy. A peripheral such as a printer or a Hard Disk Drive (HDD) can also have FIFO or cache-type buffer memory. Solid-state memory, initially in discrete form and then in integrated form beginning in the 1970s, has never stopped increasing in capacity. Manufacturing technologies have evolved over the past 40 years, but the principles of memorization and its internal structure have hardly changed, paradoxically. These technologies form the basis of one of the largest markets for integrated circuits, but have low profit margins.

NOTE.– This chapter only provides a review; the subject was thoroughly addressed in Darche (2012).

2.1. Definition

Memory is mainly characterized by its total storage[1] capacity C as well as its organization, the method or policy of memory access, the type of access or operation, its operating speed, permanence (or non-volatility) of the information and its cost.

The unit of measure of capacity C is the bit. In Table 2.1, we present the vocabulary relevant to a set of bits. The term byte actually originates from the word "bite", but its spelling was changed because of its similarity to the word "bit" (Buchholz 1962, 1977). It defines a group of bits. In the 1950s and 1960s, computers used bytes of 1 to 6 bits (Buchholz 1956). Today, the byte is 8 bits. With the advent of 16-bit microprocessors (1980s), a *word* came to represent 16 bits. The term *double word* was introduced for 32-bit microprocessors. The next generation brought about the term *quad word*. We sometimes also speak of density, which refers to the number of bits stored per unit area (in.^{2} or mm^2).

English terms	Format n (bits)
bit (b)	1
nibble	4
byte (B)	8
word *dualoct*	16
double word quadlet quadoct	32
quad(ruple) word *octlet* (IEEE 1996) *octbyte*	64
octaword (vocabulary VAX)	128

Table 2.1. *Vocabulary describing a packet of bits (Darche 2012)*

1 This term generally describes a storage peripheral with direct or sequential access, such as respectively a hard disk drive or magnetic tape, while the term "memory" is used for components such as random access memory.

But beware: the term “word” can sometimes apply to any format depending on the context and the manufacturers, not necessarily limited to a multiple of the byte. So the word “word” can mean a different format *n*, which generally changes as a result of technical evolution. Thus, for the VAX (Virtual Addressed eXtended) minicomputer from Digital Equipment Corporation (DEC), n = 16, and for MIPS (Microprocessor without Interlocked Pipeline Stages) microprocessor, n = 32. Figure 2.1 provides the vocabulary associated with the format of a binary word of n = 32 bits, which has been adopted for this work (*cf.* § 1.1 of Darche (2012) for details).

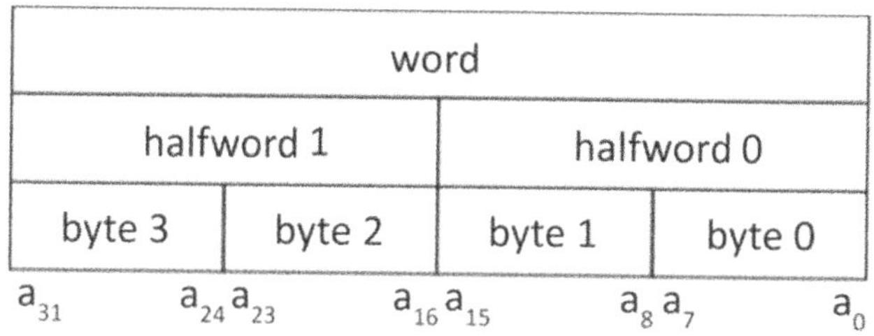

Figure 2.1. *Vocabulary for binary formats*

Table 2.2 specifies the symbol and prefix (or name) for multiples of the bit. To differentiate the International System’s (SI) kilo prefix (10^3) from the kilo units used for memory size, the capital letter K is usually used. For example, we have 1 Kb (kilobit), which represents 1024 bits, and 1 KB (kilobyte), which represents 1024 bytes. A term of art is the kilobinary. However, for the other prefixes (i.e. mega, giga, etc.), it was necessary to eliminate the ambiguity[2] because the symbols all started with a capital letter and only the context made it possible to distinguish their value (i.e. $2^{10 \times k}$ or $10^{3 \times k}$, $k \in \mathbb{N}^*$). Thus, the IEC (International Electrotechnical Commission; in French, the Commission Electrotechnique Internationale – CEI), an international standardization body, approved a new name for these powers of 2, the kilobinary, with the symbol Ki and the short name kibi[3] (IEC 2000). Self (1999) describes this aspect. The IEEE (Institute of Electrical and Electronics Engineers), an American technical professional organization, then standardized it (IEEE 2002a, 2002b).

2 This confusion has always existed. As an example, see the definition of the prefix “giga” in the glossary in DEC (1983).

3 The second syllable “bi” is pronounced like the word “bee”.

Symbols and prefixes standardized by the IEC	Origin	Factors	Examples	Symbols and prefixes standardized by SI (review)
Ki, kibi	*kilobinary*	2^{10} (= 1 024)	1 Kib, formerly 1 Kb	k (kilo) = 10^3
Mi, mebi	*megabinary*	2^{20} (= 1 048 576)	1 Mib, formerly 1 Mb	M (mega) = 10^6
Gi, gibi	*gigabinary*	2^{30}	1 Gib, formerly 1 Gb	G (giga) = 10^9
Ti, tebi	*terabinary*	2^{40}	1 Tib, formerly 1 Tb	T (tera) = 10^{12}
Pi, pebi	*petabinary*	2^{50}	1 Pib, formerly 1 Pb	P (peta) = 10^{15}
Ei, exbi	*exabinary*	2^{60}	-	E (exa) = 10^{18}
Zi, zebi	*zettabinary*	2^{70}	-	Z (zetta) = 10^{21}
Yi, yobi	*yottabinary*	2^{80}	-	Y (yotta) = 10^{24}

Table 2.2. *New prefixes of measurement units for memory*

The memory cell is the smallest subdivision (atomic entity) of memory for which it is possible to read or write data. A memory cell or word has a format or width w or n (width of a register) or a size. Some authors speak of length (Meinadier 1971, 1988; Ciminiera and Valenzano 1987), from which come declarations in programming languages of variable types such as long int. This term is not used here because it is reserved for the number of words.

Organization refers to the physical arrangement of cells in memory. From the overall size, it allows us to specify the distribution between the format n of the memory cell and the number L of cells. We are talking about data input–output organization with length L × width n, for example 16 Ki × 16 bits. In cases where there are several internal memory banks (*cf.* § 2.3.2 in Darche 2012), we speak of bank organization B × length L × width n, where B is the number of banks, for example 8 × 2 Ki × 16 bits. The total memory capacity C is then equal to:

$$C = B \times L \times n \quad [2.1]$$

The access strategy (management strategy or policy) specifies how memory is accessed. These are ranked in Figure 2.2. In access by address, random[4] access means that any memory cell can be accessed via its address with identical access time. In the case of serial or sequential access, memory cells or records are accessed in a pre-determined order defined by the policy. The Shift Registers (SR) SIPO (Serial In Parallel Out) and PISO (Parallel-In Serial-Out) operate at the bit level and allow for multiplication or division depending on the direction of shift. They are also used in I/O interfaces. Example of other policies are "first in last out" (FIFO) for the queue and "Last In First Out" (LIFO) for the stack. These should not be confused with serial localization, such as a magnetic stripe, which is not semiconductor-based memory. Data is accessed sequentially, and the headers are read to determine which data is being requested. In the case of access by content, data is accessed by partial correspondence, as would be done with a telephone directory where the name of the correspondent is used to retrieve his number (Belady *et al.* 1981). The data must therefore contain a key or an identifier. This type of policy is well suited to information retrieval. Content-Addressable Memory (CAM) is often used in network devices and in the cache (*cf.* V2 on memory, forthcoming). Associative addressing is a generalization of content addressing because it does not require an exact match (Chisvin and Duckworth 1989). Components generally implementing these various policies are called specialty memory or application-specific memory (ASM).

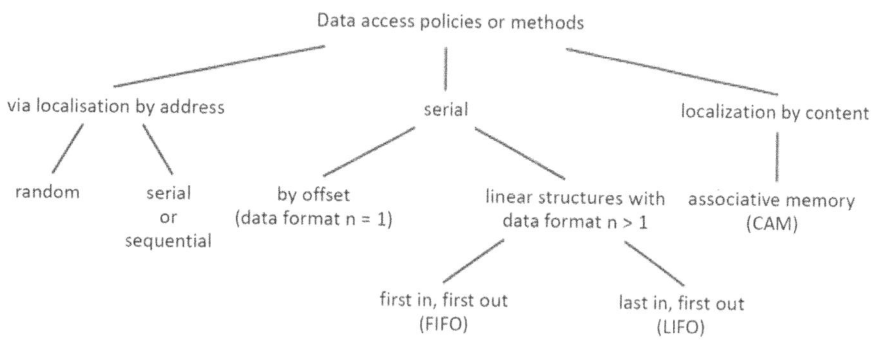

Figure 2.2. *Memory access policies*

4 Direct access may also be used as a synonym. It is in fact reserved for defining one of the addressing methods for a memory location by a processor (microprocessor or microcontroller). For a Hard Disk Drive (HDD) type mass storage, we also speak of direct addressing but you should know that the access time is then a function of the location of the information, unlike a semiconductor memory.

In the case of location-based or coordinate addressing, the memory cell is accessed using an address. If we number each cell in memory from 0, then the cell address is this number or digit (Figure 2.3).

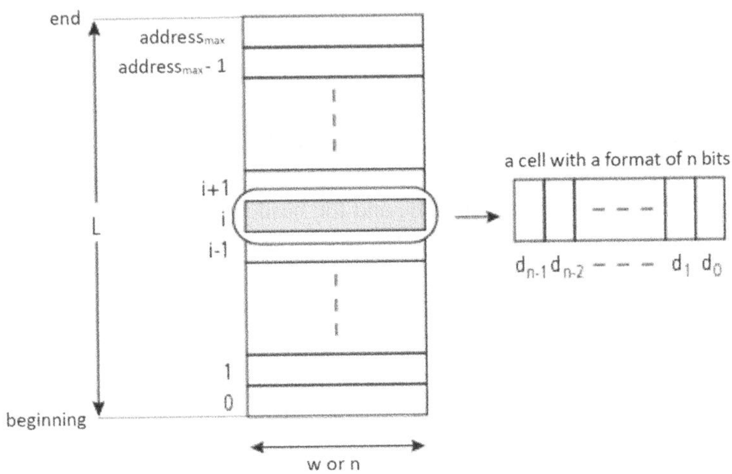

Figure 2.3. *Memory organization and addressing*

The access type specifies the requested operation, which can be Read (R), Write (W), Read-Write (RW), or Read-Modify-Write (RMW). Read-write means that it is possible to read the stored data and then to store other data at the same address during the same cycle. The last operation is a special case in which the data read is modified and then stored at the same address, always within the same cycle. This last type of access is useful, for example, for the detection and correction of errors (ED(A)C for Error Detection (And) Correction, ECC for Error-Correcting Code, *cf.* § 2.6.4 in Darche (2012)).

To characterize memory temporally, the read access and cycle times are specified. The access time t_a is the time elapsed between the presentation of the address and the presentation of the data output from the component. The cycle time t_c is the overall time for a read or write operation. This cycle time can be differentiated based on the operation to be performed with a write cycle time (t_{WC}) and a read cycle time (t_{RC}). It should be noted that t_a is usually less than t_c. In the case of Random Access Memory (RAM), we should add that these two times are independent of the memory cell's position.

At the level of the module or of the component itself, other times are used to refine the temporal characterization. They depend on the type of memory and the organization selected. They are therefore detailed in Darche (2012).

Operating speed for memory is measured primarily at the macroscopic level using two parameters, which are latency and bit rate.

For successive accesses, also called access by block or burst mode (*cf.* § 4.4.5 and 5.5.2 in Darche (2012)), the flow rate must be considered. Flow breaks down into input–output flow (I/O rate) and data flow (Chen and Patterson 1993). The first, measured in number of accesses per second, is used when the number of bytes transferred per access is low, for example in the case of requests (transaction processing). This definition applies to a storage system such as a hard disk mass storage unit or HDD. In this work, we will distinguish between two types of flow: the overall flow, or (raw) data rate, and the useful flow, or throughput. The overall flow is the maximum flow that the component is capable of providing at the hardware level. The useful bit rate is the average bit rate that the requester, generally a memory controller or a processor, will receive. The data rate is measured in number of bits or multiples of the bit (the byte, usually) transferred per unit of time. It is a function of the data format n. The basic unit is therefore bits per second (bits/s). Multiples of the flow are powers of 10. Thus a speed of 1 kb/s (note the lowercase k, following the SI standard) represents 1000 bits/s. For semiconductor-based memory, the raw bit rate can be expressed in b/s/pin (bpspp), that is, for n = 1 bit. If the data transfer format is higher, the total bit rate is obtained by multiplying this bit rate by n. The flow is the reverse of t_c. Access is generally done in blocks to maximize throughput. This is called burst mode access.

Another important parameter is latency, which is the total time elapsed between the presentation of the address and the availability (read) or recording (write) of the data. It is the sum of all the delays in the data path. It is an upper boundary. In the case of block access, latency concerns access to the first element. We must therefore, as before, consider the flow. This depends on the speed of the memory (access time for reading and cycle time for writing), the speed of the subsystem (organization, controller) and the exchange rate between the memory subsystem, the bus and the processor. For the bus, this is determined by its access protocol, in particular its arbitration, its operating frequency and its width. For the processor, this is determined by its protocol and its cycle time. Latency and bitrate(s) are the two most frequently used parameters to evaluate the performance of a memory subset. A rule of thumb from Patterson (2004, 2005) is that bandwidth grows at least by the square of the improvement in latency. More specifically, with regard to secondary storage using magnetic disks, Gray and Shenay (1999) provide some rules of thumb concerning the evolution of the computing performance of technologies for processor, memory/storage, and communication interfaces. Notably, storage capacity increases by a factor of 100 every 10 years, and bandwidth increases by a factor of 10.

Data permanence indicates whether, when the power supply is interrupted, the information is erased or remains stored. In the latter case, it is necessary to specify the storage duration. Data permanence is characterized by data retention time. Memory that loses its stored information when the power is lost or because of the properties of the storage material is called “volatile”. In the latter case, it is necessary to specify the duration of information retention.

2.2. Related concepts

Two concepts that relate to primary memory are the order of storage and alignment. They have consequences in particular for information exchange.

2.2.1. *A story of endianness*

The order in which information is stored is a story of endianness according to Cohen (1981) (*cf.* § 2.6.2 in Darche (2012)). This problem arises when the CPU’s information transfer rate is faster than that of the bus and the slave, memory, and I/O controllers. Big Endian (BE) storage, that is, most significant byte first in the ascending direction of addresses, is more natural for reading a memory dump listing or an assembly result file. Microprocessors from Motorola (the 68xx and 68K families) were based on this model, as have been the processors in many computers, including the IBM System/360 and/370 families (Amdahl *et al.* 1964; Gifford and Spector 1987), the PDP-10 from Digital Equipment Corporation (DEC) (Bell *et al.* 1978) but also many RISC microprocessors (*cf.* V2) such as the SPARC from Sun. The 80x86 family of MPUs from Intel, however, rank data in Little Endian (LE) order. DEC PDP-11 computers and the VAX family also used the latter. Modern microprocessors like the PowerPC handle the two orders indifferently (BiE for Bi-Endian). These aspects were studied in § 2.6.2 of Darche (2012). The order affects performance, such as in the time to compute an address (*cf.* § V4-1.2.3.4).

2.2.2. *Alignment*

A word of k contiguous bytes can be stored in an arbitrary position in memory organized in the form of a byte, referred to as arbitrary byte boundary storage. For the sake of access time, when the data bus format is the word, it is necessary to operate at the word border to avoid repeat accesses. This is called alignment. A generalization is made in § V4-3.1.2. See also § V2-1.2.

2.3. Modeling

Memory as a component or subsystem can be modeled by three subsets, which are the storage medium or memory area, the controller and the interface (Figure 2.4; see also Figure 9.1 in Darche (2012)). The latter two can perform complex operations. The storage medium can be removable, as in the case of a CD-ROM (Compact Disk Read-Only Memory), or fixed. At the interface level, information can be exchanged bit by bit (serial interface) or by words of n bits (n > 1) in a single exchange (parallel interface). This exchange can be synchronous, that is, an external clock is necessary to clock the operation (*cf.* the concept of clock in § 3.1.2 and 3.1.4 of Darche (2002)). Otherwise, it is asynchronous, that is, it is performed in a bounded time frame. The control signals group comprises at least one signal specifying the type of access (R/#W or #WE for Write Enable) and, generally, a memory selection signal (#CE for Chip Enable or #CS for Chip Select). The latter controls the component's standby. In a synchronous approach, a clock signal Clk is present. The controller generates the internal control signals from the external control signals.

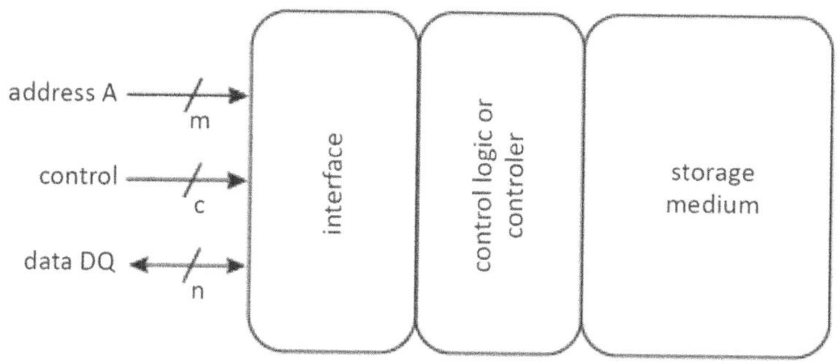

Figure 2.4. *Memory area*

Also, to decrease average processor access times for instructions and data, several storage technologies have been added to the data path. These different types of memory have been modeled as a "memory hierarchy". This abstraction presents them vertically by levels or layers according to a technical characteristic (Multi Level Memory (MLM) hierarchy). The hierarchy is generally represented by a triangular, even pyramidal, shape (Nakagomi 1993). Figure 2.5(b) presents a classic hierarchy. At the top is the flip-flop, an elementary storage component (i.e. one bit capacity). This is followed by the register, the internal cache on the MPU (on-chip cache), the external cache (off-chip cache), the main or central memory (primary memory, main memory) and secondary and tertiary storage, also known as backup (tertiary memory system, off-line back-up storage, or backing store (Handy 1998)). Not shown, archival memory is used to store information over dozens of years. These Mass Storage Systems (MSS) are composed of a library of several hundred cartridges with a magnetic tape or optical disks manipulated by robotic arms to insert them into the read/write peripherals. Local memory is the memory built into the processor, that is, registers, on-board memory and internal cache memory. Since the technologies used for manufacturing are heterogeneous, each level therefore has its own technical characteristics, the value of which increase or decrease in a discrete manner, that is, in stages (Figure 2.5(a)). The surface or base of the trapezoid is intended to represent the order of magnitude of the values. In general, we are only interested in four characteristics, which are the total storage capacity, the cycle times, the access time in reading and the bit rate. A fifth, the cost of storage per bit, is also to be considered. It decreases when capacity increases. The memory hierarchy makes it possible to offer the largest amount of memory at the lowest price while providing the fastest possible access. The utopian goal of any architect is to design memory with the highest possible capacity and the lowest cost (lowest level) operating at processor speed (highest level).

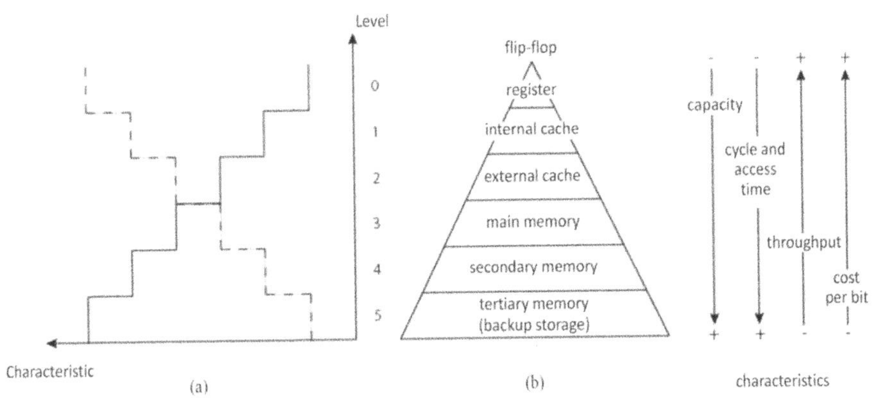

Figure 2.5. *Memory hierarchy*

Today, the technology is electronic, magnetic or optical. But the current trend is towards the elimination of moving components (motors, plates, arms, etc.). Secondary memory is starting to use flash-type reprogrammable read-only memory (dotted line in Figure 2.6, *cf.* V2). Each of these three technologies corresponds to a level of the memory hierarchy, as shown in Figure 2.6.

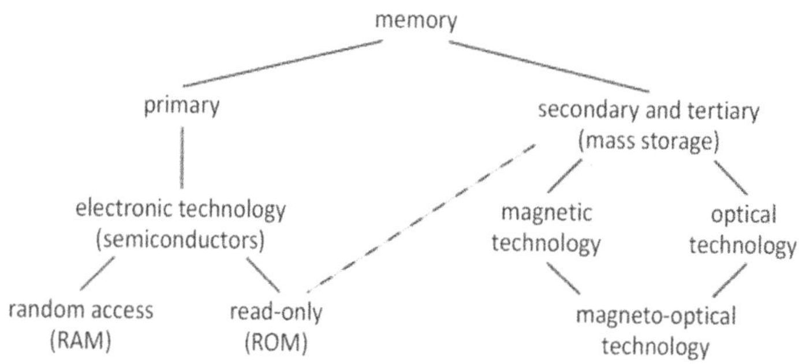

Figure 2.6. *Types of storage technologies in modern computers*

2.4. Classification

Classification of semiconductor memories is very difficult since there are many types and the technology is evolving very quickly. We have classified random access memory according to its volatility (Figure 2.7). Two large families exist: random access memory (RAM) and permanent memory. The first loses its information when the power supply to the chip stops, hence it is also called "volatile memory". Permanent memory (NVM for Non-Volatile Memory) has, depending on the type, an information retention period generally equal to 10 years (programmable read only memory), equal to the life of the component (hidden read only memory), or with energy source autonomy (BBSRAM for Battery-Backed SRAM). Among the kinds of random access memory, we distinguish Static Random Access Memory (SRAM) and Dynamic Random Access Memory (DRAM). The static model stores data by sustaining its logical state. The dynamic model stores electrical charges in stored-charge memory. It originally used a clock (synchronous model) but soon became asynchronous in 1971. Since 1996, dynamic random access memory returned to synchronous operation for reasons of speed with synchronous cycle communication (SDRAM for synchronous DRAM) and packet communication models. This category requires a periodic refresh (T_{ref} period = 64 ms) of the information stored to prevent memory loss. It is carried out by specialized logic, which is usually external. When this logic is integrated with the memory chip, we speak of Pseudo-Static RAM (PSRAM).

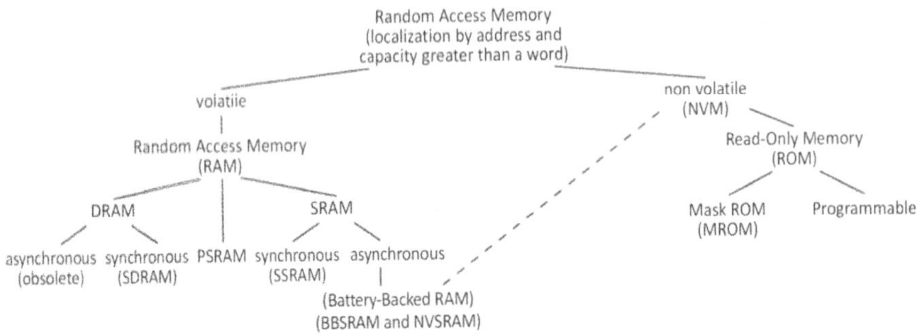

Figure 2.7. *Simplified classification of random access semiconductor memory*

Figure 2.8 shows a classification of non-volatile memory. Read-Only Memory (ROM) was originally simply that. It then became programmable with the release of UV (UltraViolet) EPROM (Erasable Programmable ROM) in 1971. Today, it is also accessible in programming as random access memory but with a much higher cycle time. In this category, we can also cite MROM (Mask ROM, Mask-programmed ROM, or Mask-programmable ROM), PROM (Programmable ROM), EEPROM or E^2PROM (Electrically Erasable PROM) and FEEPROM (Flash EEPROM). These models will be detailed in the forthcoming Volume 2 of this series, a continuation of Darche (2012).

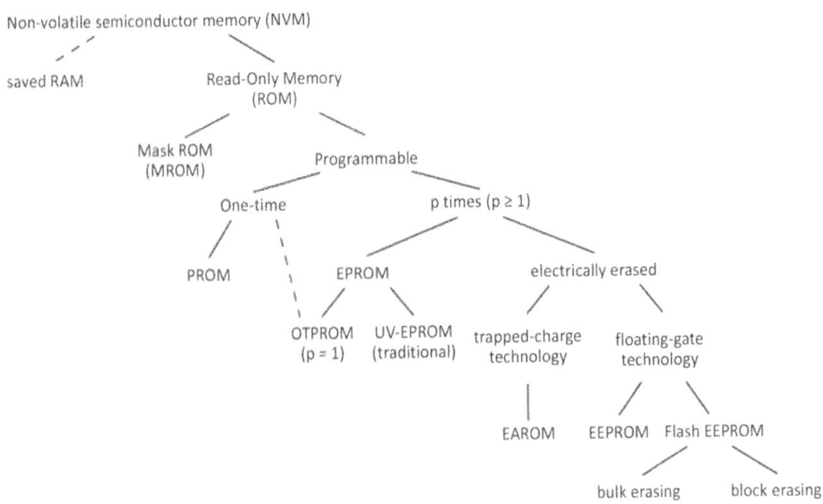

Figure 2.8. *Detailed classification of permanent semiconductor memory*

All these kinds of memory, originally manufactured using bipolar technology, today use unipolar technologies, with CMOS (Complementary Metal-Oxide Semiconductor) being dominant, or mixed technologies such as BiCMOS, for Bipolar and CMOS. Each generation brings its share of innovations to improve performance (access time, throughput, power consumption, etc.). Today, the market is mainly segmented into three parts: SDRAM for main memory, SSRAM for the cache and EEPROM in flash version (FEEPROM) for mass storage (SSD and USB keys). Random access memory was examined in Darche (2012).

2.5. Conclusion

Storage is one of the computer's essential functions. The choices made by the designer for the memory hierarchy directly impact the performance of the computer system as a whole. As proof, one third to one half of the chip surface in modern microprocessors is occupied by cache memory.

3

Computation Model and Architecture: Illustration with the von Neumann Approach

A user working today in front of his or her microcomputer workstation hardly suspects that he or she is in front of a machine whose operation is governed by principles described by the mathematician John von Neumann in the 1940s[1] (Ceruzzi 2000). This remains the case when modern terms such as “superscalar architectures” and “multicore” or accelerating mechanisms like the pipeline, concepts discussed in the forthcoming Volume 2, are mentioned. Before studying the functioning of the microprocessor, we need to clarify the theoretical concepts of the computational model and computer architecture. The so-called von Neumann approach, which still governs the functioning of computers internally despite all the progress made since it was developed, is described by presenting the basic execution diagram for an instruction. This architecture has given rise to variations, which are also presented. Finally, the programmer needs an abstraction of the machine in order to simplify his or her work, which is called the “Instruction Set Architecture” (ISA). It is described before the basic definitions for this book, which complete this chapter.

NOTE.– In this book, the term CU for “Central Unit” (or CPU for Central Processing Unit) is taken from the original word, that is, the unit which performs the computations, and not from the microcomputer itself. It most often describes the

1 The roots of the idea of a stored-program computer are commonly attributed to him. However, as is generally the case in the sciences, it was the result of collaboration with a team, including engineers J. Presper Eckert and John W. Mauchly. John von Neumann was rather the first to formalize this architecture. On this subject, see Stern (1980).

microprocessor also referred to as an MPU (MicroProcessor Unit) or μP for short, which is a modern integrated form of the CU. We are also adapting the level of discourse to the component's scale. However, we do not include main memory, as do some definitions, which generally rely on the vocabulary of mainframes from the 1960s.

3.1. Basic concepts

Definitions of the fundamental concepts of the Model of Computation (MoC) and of architecture have evolved over time and vary from author to author (Reddi and Feustel 1976, Baer 1984). The same is true for associated terms such as "implementation" or "achievement". Before presenting them, the concepts of program, control and data mechanisms and flows must be clarified.

3.1.1. *The idea of a program*

A program is a static sequence of high-level statements or constructions broken down into simple and structured instructions. It is written by a programmer or produced by a language translator, for example, a compiler (*cf.* § V5-1.1.2) or an assembler (*cf.* § V5-1.2.1). During its execution, the processor triggers a sequence of actions from the static sequence of instructions that make up the program.

Control structures make it possible to control the instruction flow, which is historically sequential[2]. High-Level structured programming Languages (HLL) use three main types, which are concatenation, selection and repetition. Concatenation or sequentiality specifies instructions in linear order. For its declaration, we use the opening and closing braces of C or the *begin_end* declarations of Pascal. Selection allows you to make a decision, that is, to take another branch in a program. There is, for example, the structure *if_then_else* or the multiple *switch* selection in C. We can also anecdotally mention "*goto*" from Fortran. Finally, repetition or iteration occurs in two forms, loops and recursion, which make it possible to repeat a block for either a determinate or indeterminate number of times (depending on a test). We can mention the *for_do*, *while_do* and *do_while* structures in C. A less common type of structure is the exception (e.g. in Ada), which allows an error to be addressed by escaping (*cf.* § V4-5.1).

2 Operating principle of the von Neumann machine (*cf.* § 3.2).

3.1.2. *Control and data flows and mechanisms*

The central processing unit manipulates instructions and data to perform computations. The execution of a program is a dynamic process that can be abstracted using the notion of flow. A particular execution must be distinguished from the whole or from a subset of the possible executions. There will be three flows characterized by the type of information concerned. These are the flows of instructions, control and data[3].

The instruction flow is the continuation of the executed instructions, that is, the path taken by an execution in the program's code. The execution path is a succession of program points that characterize this instruction flow, a program point identifying a location in the code. By default, the instruction flow in a computer is sequential, but it is possible to control (or alter) this flow using specialized instructions called control flow statements, as well as using an interrupt or signal mechanism (*cf.* Chapter V4-5). The instruction flow graph shows all the possible flows.

The control flow or flow of control is the succession of path selections for an execution. The control flow is explicit in an imperative programming language[4], and it is implemented, in particular, in the form of jump instructions (*cf.* § V4-2.4-1). This is what distinguishes this type of language from declarative programming languages. The Control Flow Graph (CFG) shows all the possible control flows. In an imperative language, a node in this graph will be a basic block, that is, a set of contiguous instructions without branching or that are not the target of any branching, and an arc represents a possible branching. A sequential control flow means that there is only one control thread moving from instruction to instruction in an implicit manner. A sequential control flow can be transformed into a parallel flow, for example, by introducing parallel-type operators such as *fork-join*. An Exceptional Control Flow (ECF) can be defined when this type of event is detected (Bryant and O'Hallaron 2016).

The data flow is the path that the data takes during an execution. It should be noted that Johnson (1990) breaks down the data flow into two categories, register data flow and memory data flow.

---

3 The definitions in the next two § are based on Martlet (2011).

4 The adjective "imperative" stems from the fact that the machine is controlled by a series of instructions. Imperative languages are based on Turing's computation model.

It is now possible to define two mechanisms associated with instruction and data flows that are respectively control and data mechanisms (Treleaven 1981). Furthermore, instead of considering the instruction, it is possible, as proposed by van de Goor (1989), to introduce a higher level of abstraction, the computational unit, which can be a simple instruction or a more complex function.

The control mechanism specifies how the computation is executed and how one instruction causes the execution of another. It defines the relationships between the instructions, for example, when the computation begins and the what operation(s) will follow. Treleaven and Lima (1982) distinguishes between control-driven, data-driven, demand-driven and pattern-driven executions. In the first case, an instruction is executed when it is selected by the control flow. Its execution will make it possible to designate the following instruction. In the second case, the statement is executed when all of its arguments are available, hence the moniker "availability-driven" execution. With demand-driven execution, also called execution by necessity or by need, an instruction is executed if its result is necessary for the execution of another that is already being executed. This is referred to as lazy evaluation. For the latter, the execution of the instruction is conditioned by the correspondence of certain patterns, also called a goal statement. In all cases, this means that the execution of a unit of computation takes place if conditions are satisfied (i.e. are true).

The data mechanism specifies how an instruction obtains its operands and how the result is communicated to others or, more generally, exactly how computational units exchange data. A distinction must be made between shared memory and message passing. In the first case, a main memory stores a single copy of the information available for computation. Data is shared and accessed by reference. This is the most common mechanism in today's computers because it is the simplest. In the second case, a copy of the operands is sent to each unit of computation. Here, the data access mechanism is by value[5]. Table 3.1 brings together the eight possible cases of these two mechanisms. The intersection of control and data mechanisms defines a type of execution model referred to by acronym. The most common architectures implement the instruction-driven execution model with a shared data computational model (COSH).

5 It should be noted that there is a third data mechanism, which is passing by literal where the argument is known at compilation and where a copy is provided to each instruction that uses it.

		Data mechanisms	
		Shared data (SH) (access by reference)	**Passing messages (ME) (access by value)**
Control mechanisms	**Control-driven (CO)**	COSH control flow (von Neumann)	COME control flow (communicating processes)
	Data-driven (DA) (controlled by availability)	DASH	DAME data flow
	Demand-driven (DE) (controlled by need, lazy evaluation)	DESH graph reduction	DEME chain reduction
	Pattern-driven (PA)	PASH logic	PAME actor

Table 3.1. *Runtime models and computer categories (Treleaven and Lima 84, van de Goor 89)*

3.1.3. *Models of computation*

A computation model is a high-level abstraction (i.e. formal system) which explains how computations are carried out. It specifies the basic entities for the computation, the possible operations and the execution and data models. Sima *et al.* (1997) also adds the problem description model. Representative examples are the Turing and von Neumann models (by control flow, *cf.* § 3.1.2), object and actor oriented, by data flow, application or based on the predicate logic.

The Turing model of computation, named after its inventor (Turing 1937a b), makes it possible to know whether a function is computable. The base entity is a set of symbols belonging to a ribbon (or strip) of infinite length divided into cells (or boxes). A state transition function allows you to manipulate these symbols. The description of a problem is procedural. The Turing machine M is formally described by the tuple $(Q, \Sigma, \Gamma, \delta, q_0, F)$, where:

– Q is a finite set of states;

– $\exists$ a symbol #, is the empty symbol filling the band outside initial data; there are also two sets of symbols or alphabets:

Σ is the finite input alphabet, excluding the blank symbol #,

Γ is the finite alphabet in the ban such that $\Sigma \subseteq \Gamma$ and $\# \in \Gamma$;

– $\delta: Q \times \Gamma \rightarrow Q \times \Gamma \times \{\leftarrow, \rightarrow, \uparrow\}$ is the transition function;

– $q_0 \in Q$ is the initial state;

– $F \subseteq Q$ is the set of accepting or final states.

The Turing machine is an Infinite State Machine (ISM, Minsky 1967). For more information, Turing and Girard (1995) describes the machine's historical and theoretical aspects.

Communicating Sequential Processes (CSP) is originally an algebra allowing for the specification of parallelism in a computer system (Hoare 1978). The latter is broken down into a set of entities called processes that interact concurrently. It is a distributed computation model.

Table 3.2 summarizes the characteristics of the previously described models. The procedural programming style that includes the imperative style is based on the concept of procedural calls.

	Main computation models		
Characteristics	**Turing**	**Control flow (von Neumann)**	**Control flow (communicating processes)**
Basic elements of the computation	Symbols of a finite alphabet on an infinite band Applying a transition function on them	Data rows in named entities (variables) Operations performed on this data	Process sending (a)synchronous message between processes
Execution semantics	State transition	State transition	State transition
Execution model	CO	CO	CO
Data model	SH	SH	ME
Programming style	Procedural	Procedural	Procedural
Example languages	–	C, Fortran, Cobol	Occam (Inmos)
Execution model	Sequential model	Sequential model	Parallel model

Table 3.2. *Characteristics of the main models of computation (according to Sima et al. (1997))*

The object-oriented computational model (Dahl and Nygaard 1966; Nguyen and Hailpern 1986) uses the object as the basic entity. The latter encapsulates the attributes (i.e. variables) and the methods (i.e. functions) that will be applied to the former as directed by messages. The problem description model can be seen as a series of passive messages sent to the objects. In the actor computation model (PAME model), which is derived from the previous model, the message is active. This paradigm has been defined in Hewitt *et al.* (1973) and Hewitt (1977). This model is inspired by social organization models. An actor is an autonomous and cooperating or expert active entity that communicates with his or her fellows and with themselves via message. The actor respects the principle of encapsulation of the object paradigm, with the added notion of activity (Masini *et al.* 1990). Its behavior is expressed in the form of a script. Agha's computation model (1985, 1986) can be considered as a concurrent and distributed computation model with an object-oriented approach. There are other competing models. Among the most well-known models are synchronous reactive (SR; Edwards 1997), time-triggered (Kopetz 1998), event-driven and dataflow process networks (Kahn 1974). Table 3.3 summarizes the characteristics of the last models.

	Main computation models	
Characteristics	**Object**	**Actor**
Basic elements of computation	Objects manipulated by messages Sending messages to these objects	Active objects Sending asynchronous messages to each other
Execution semantics	State transition	State transition
Execution model	CO	PA
Data model	ME	ME
Programming style	Object oriented	Actor oriented
Example languages	C ++, Java, Smalltalk	Act1, Act2
Competition	Sequential model	Parallel model

Table 3.3. *Characteristics of the primary computation models (according to Sima et al. (1997))*

The dataflow computation model is a data-driven execution model with message passing (DAME model). The basic entity is the data to which operations will be applied. The instructions produce data consumed by other instructions. The availability of all the operands of an instruction will trigger its launch. The control is driven by the data itself (data-driven control). The description of a dataflow computing program is done using an oriented graph called a dataflow graph; the example shown in Figure 3.1 calculates the factorial of n (i.e. n!). Each instruction expects the operand(s)[6] necessary for its execution in the form of a data token, which can be a partial result. As soon as all the operands are available, execution is requested and the node in turn provides a result in the form of an outgoing token. The description model is also procedural. Parallelism is specific to the model. The associated architecture is called a dataflow architecture (Ackerman 1982). There are variations of the basic model. Examples include the static (Dennis 1980), synchronous (SDF for Synchronous Dataflow; Lee and Messerschmitt 1987a b), structured and dynamic (DDF for Dynamic Dataflow; Buck 1993; Buck and Lee 1993) models. Shiva (2006) gives details on this computational model and the associated languages and architectures.

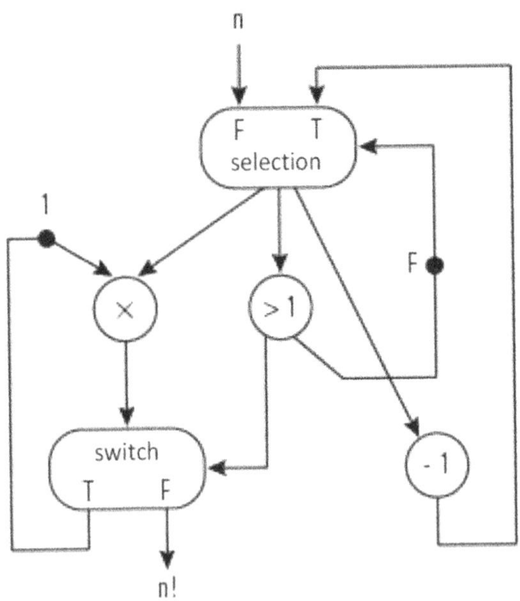

Figure 3.1. *Description of the computation of a factorial via dataflow graph*

Computation models that are not based on the change of state over time are called declarative. We can mention the lambda-calculus (or λ-calculus) or the interpretation of Horn[7] clauses as examples. Languages based on λ-calculus are called functional or application languages. The computation mechanism of λ-calculus is reduction (DESH or DEME execution model). Languages based on Horn clauses are said to be logic-oriented.

6 An operand is a variable or a constant on which an operation is carried out.

7 Horn clauses are a subset of predicate calculus (Kowalski 1979).

The application computation model uses the argument as the basic entity to which functions will be applied for evaluation. The problem description model is a set of function definitions. The description style is declarative. The application programming style is based on the application of functions and on the recursive definition of functions. Parallelism is implicit. Execution is demand-driven. In reduction-based computers, the need for a result triggers the execution of the instruction that will generate the result (execution on demand). The principle of reduction is based on a replacement of expressions based on predefined reductive rules, also called rewrite rules, based on an iterative process until this is no longer possible. In other words, the execution of the instructions is based on the recognition of reducible expressions and their transformation, that is, their replacement by others, the end condition being the obtaining of a constant expression (Treleaven *et al.* 1982). The expressions are nested with an evaluation that starts with the outermost (i.e. the program). Thus, the main function with its arguments (main expression) is rewritten iteratively by replacing the sub-expressions according to these rules. For the called functions, the operation of substituting effective parameters in place of formal parameters is applied to the definition of these functions referenced before reduction. A reducible expression is also referred to by the abbreviation "redex", and its replacement is called a reduction step. The order in which the rules are applied is called an "evaluation or reduction strategy", which can be serial or parallel. The resulting expression (constant expression) is expressed in its normal form. There are two main types of reduction – graph and chain reductions. They are distinguished by the way the instructions share the data (Treleaven 1983) and by the way in which the program is represented in memory. Graph reduction architectures use a data-sharing (update in place) mechanism optimized for large graphs (i.e. passage by reference). Chain reduction architectures have a data mechanism by message passing (i.e. separate copy, passing by value) which is simpler than the previous method.

The predicate logic-based computation model is based on a set of objects to which predicates are applied. A predicate is a property or attribute of an object. The control mechanism is of the "pattern-driven" type, and the data mechanism is of the shared data type (PASH model). In the framework of the logic of first-order predicates reduced to Horn clauses, the execution mechanism is a Selective Linear Definite clause (SLD)-type resolution, that is, a linear resolution with selection function (SL) with defined clauses. The computation consists of filtering (pattern matching). The initial goal is iteratively rewritten using the resolution mechanism until it is satisfied or there is no possibility of unification.

Table 3.4 summarizes the characteristics of the three models described above.

	Main computation models (continued)		
Characteristics	**Data flow**	**Application/λ-calculus**	**Logic**
Computation elements	Data stored in named entities (variables) Operations performed on this data	Arguments Functions applied to arguments	Elements of predicate sets declared on these elements
Execution semantics	Data flow	Reduction	SLD resolution
Execution model	DA (Immediate evaluation (Eager evaluation))	DE (Delayed or lazy evaluation)	PA (Defined by the goal processing and the computation rule)
Data model	ME	SH (chain reduction) ME (graph reduction)	SH
Programming style	Procedural	Declarative (application style)	Relational or declarative (predicate logic)
Example languages	ID, Lucid	Lisp	PROLOG (PROgramming in LOGic)
Competition	Parallel model	Parallel model	Parallel model

Table 3.4. *Characteristics of the main computation models – continued (based on Sima et al. (1997))*

Finally, there are other computational models, for example, those inspired by biology (biology-inspired computing) such as neural models, a subject beyond the scope of this work.

3.1.4. *Architectures*

To function, the computation model relies on a computer architecture and on a programming language (Figure 3.2(a)). The main language types are procedural imperative, object oriented, functional or logical. Respectively associated examples are the C, Ada, Lisp (LISt Processing) and PROLOG (PROgramming in LOGic) languages. Another way to look at the computation model is shown in Figure 3.2(b), where the model is executed on the abstract machine that should be implemented.

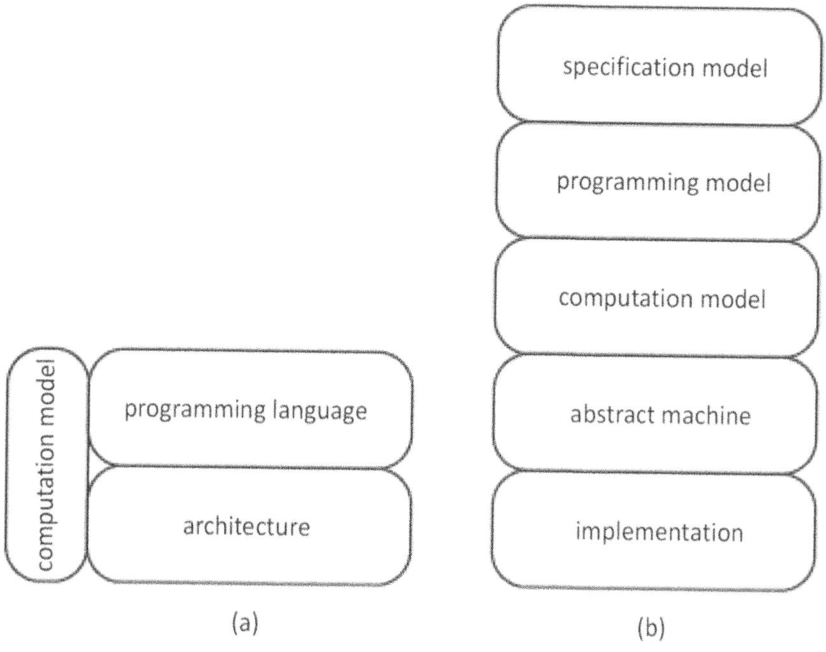

Figure 3.2. *Positioning of the computation model in relation to the architecture*

Originally, the architecture concerned only buildings. Architecture is the art of imagining, designing and constructing buildings based on a set of rules. An architect will, for example, be concerned with the appearance and functionality of a building from the user's point of view, without being concerned with the details of the construction. Today, it is not only a question of buildings but also of works such as bridges and ships. The outline is undoubtedly the basic descriptive document. Another part of the definition is that "architecture designates the corpus of all the buildings constructed, that is to say their classification and their study" (Wikipedia definition). These two definitions also apply to the IT (Information Technology) field.

The origin of the term "architecture" can be found in Amdahl *et al.* (1964)[8], designers of the IBM System/360, who define it as "the attributes of the system seen

8 Consider the premises of a definition in Buchholz (1962) presented as part of the description of the Stretch project, begun in 1961, mentioned in Blaauw and Brooks (1996).

by the programmer, that is, the conceptual structure and the functional behavior", based on a computation model and on its programming language(s). The architecture defines the Instruction Set (IS) with, among other things, the format for the instructions, their operation code and their addressing modes (*cf.* respectively § V4-1.1 and V4-1.2). It specifies the representation of the operands, that is, the type of data, their number and their format n (i.e. the number of bits, *cf.* § I-1.2 in Darche (2000)). It describes storage, that is, the registers and the management of the main memory. For the latter, it specifies whether the words must be aligned in memory (memory alignment) and the order in which the bytes are stored (little or big endian order, *cf.* § 2.6.2 in Darche (2012), also § 2.2 of this work for these two concepts). There may also be a mechanism for Virtual Memory (VM) with paging and segmentation (*cf.* V2 on semiconductor memory, forthcoming) or structured memory (Treleaven *et al.* 1982). If we set aside mass storage for backup (i.e. tertiary memory, *cf.* § 7.2 in Darche (2003) and § 1.3 in Darche (2012)), then the memory hierarchy can be seen as an address space provided to the software architect. It is therefore a tangible component of the hardware architecture. The Input–Output (I/O) mechanisms are also specified, as well as the interrupt diversion mechanism (*cf.* Chapter V4-5). This means we are examining the interface between hardware and software.

The term "architecture" also refers to the study and classification of computers. A family of computers can be characterized by a single basic instruction set and with backward compatibility (*cf.* § V4-3.3.3). One consequence will be that a family of computers with the same architecture will be able to run the same programs. Two notable examples are the IBM System/360 computer and the Intel x86 microprocessor architecture. The economic benefit is obvious. The counterpart is that this is a major constraint on potential technical progress.

Intel (1981) defines several computer architectures. Each of them is defined at the boundary between two conceptual levels (Figure 3.3). An architecture provides the interface with the lower layer by providing a functional abstraction of the latter for the upper layer. Brooks (1975, 1995) defined it as the complete and detailed specification of the user interface. In this definition, the term "user" is a function of the level being considered. The level most commonly recognized and accepted under the term "computer architecture" is that of ISA (Instruction Set Architecture, *cf.* § 3.5).

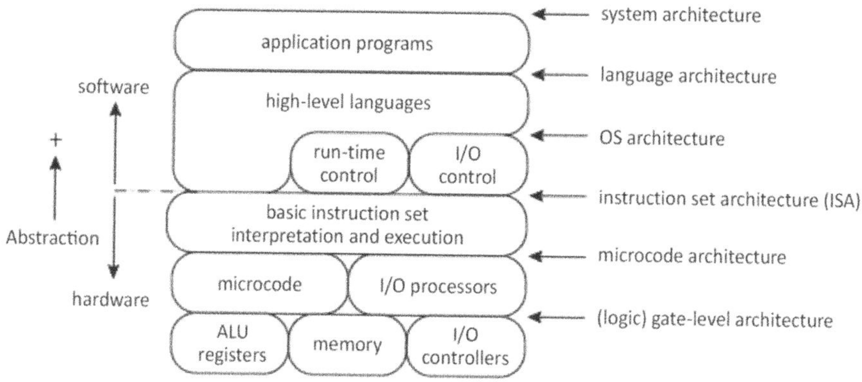

Figure 3.3. *Multi-level architectural concepts*

Blaauw and Brooks (1996) consider three levels in computer design, namely architecture, (abstract) implementation and production (Figure 3.4-a). The architecture does not describe the design (i.e. the combinational and sequential logical operators) or the physical implementation (i.e. the electronic components). Not considering these technological aspects allows us to consider progress in electronics in terms of components (vacuum tube, transistor, then integrated circuit) and, subsequently, integration (SSI for Small-Scale Integration, MSI for Medium-Scale Integration, LSI for Large-Scale Integration, VLSI for Very LSI, ULSI for Ultra LSI, etc., *cf.* § 1.2) without this having any effect. It is therefore an abstraction, that is, an idealized view, making it independent of the material (i.e. electronic) aspects. The (abstract) implementation or organization (as it is called in some works) concerns functional organization, also referred to as the logical structure of the architecture or microarchitecture. The organization or structure refers to the operational units and their interaction (i.e. relationship) that performs the specifications designated by the architecture. Static and dynamic aspects can be distinguished. Thus, the structure refers to the arrangement of the elements, while the organization concerns the dynamic interaction between them. Here, we primarily focus on describing the control unit and the data path, but other functional units can be included. The physical implementation concerns the electronic and mechanical domains at the level of basic components. This layer embodies the implementation. It is linked to the technology used at a time t. We will speak, for example, of static or dynamic logic (carried out in unipolar (*cf.* § 2.2.2 of (Darche 2012)) and bipolar technologies. An important concluding remark is that the same architecture can have several possible organizations. An equivalent view is that of Figure 3.4-b. The architecture here boils down to ISA (*cf.* § 3.5), which defines among other things the instruction set (*cf.* Chapter V4-2) and its characteristics, such as the addressing modes (*cf.* § V4-1.2). The microarchitecture describes the data path and the control path with two sub-layers, the RT (Register Transfer)-type description written in RTL (RT Language) and the firmware (*cf.* V2, forthcoming) if this approach is chosen. The concepts of architecture and implementation can be grouped under the concepts of exo- and endoarchitecture (Figure 3.4(c)). The exoarchitecture provides only the information necessary for the system programmer or the compiler designer. It describes the logical structure and behavior of the system, hiding unnecessary details. Endoarchitecture is interested in the hardware layer by describing its logical structure, its behavior and its control in relation to the upper layer (Dasgupta 1990). We also find the designation of external and internal architectures (Figure 3.4(d)).

(a)	(b)	(c)	(d)	(e)
architecture	ISA	exoarchitecture	external architecture	behavior
(abstract) implementation	microarchitecture	endoarchitecture	internal architecture	structure
implementation	implementation	implementation		implementation

Figure 3.4. *Computer design layers based on Blaauw and Brooks (1996)*

These views can be compared with Figure 3.4(e), where each layer is an axis of the diagram in Y (*cf.* Figure 2 in Gajski and Kuhn (1983)). The latter is a descriptive model that represents the design stages of a VLSI circuit like the microprocessor with three fields of description: behavioral (or functional), structural and physical (Figure 3.5).

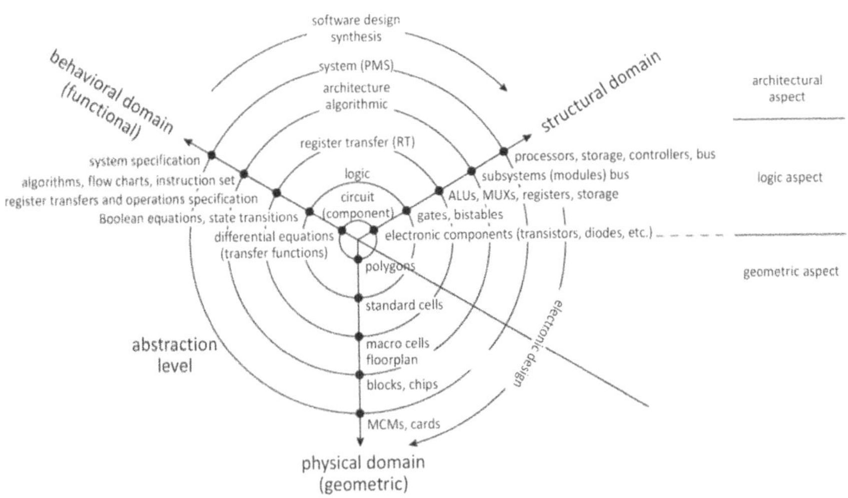

Figure 3.5. *Y-diagram (Gajski and Kuhn 1983)*

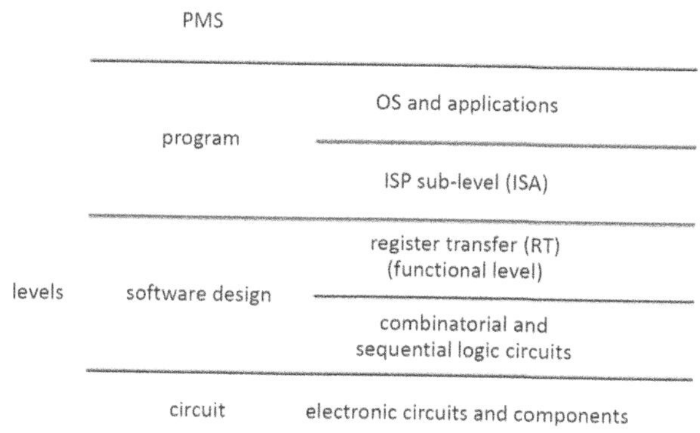

Figure 3.6. *Hierarchical structure of a computer*

Another way to structure a computer system is that of Bell and Newell (1970, 1971), who proposed two notation systems to describe a computer in a hierarchical form (Figure 3.6) using the PMS (Processor, Memory, Switch) and ISP (Instruction Set Processor) descriptive systems. There are the PMS, the programming or program level, the logic level and the circuit level. The first level describes the links between computers. The second is the level of the program. The next is that of logical design. It is necessary to distinguish the level "transfer by register" (RT) from the lower level of the basic and complex logical, combinatorial and sequential operators (in the sense of Darche (2002)). This first sub-level algorithmically describes the transfer of information between registers using a specialized language called RTL. The last level concerns implementation, with, for electronic technology, discrete, passive and active components and integrated circuits.

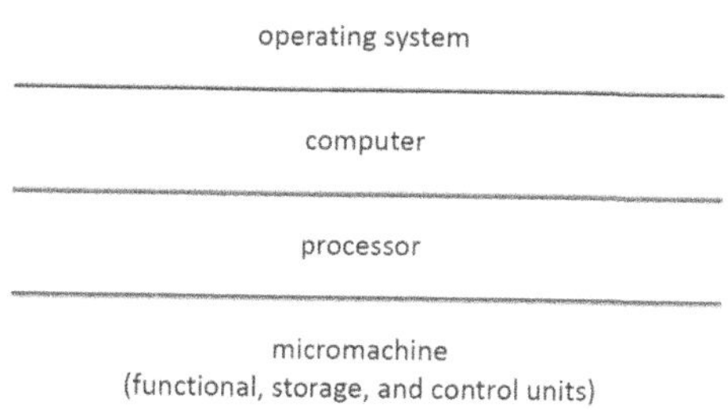

Figure 3.7. *Different levels of abstraction of computer architecture based on Sima et al. (1997)*

Sima *et al.* (1997) provides another, more hierarchical, architectural view that is more interesting because it covers all of the computer's systems (Figure 3.7). Each level is an abstraction of the lower level. Several computation models can run on the same architecture simply by changing the programming language or using a virtual machine. The more specialized the architecture, the higher the performance in terms of processing speed. The Digital Signal Processor (DSP) is an example (*cf.* § V3-5.2).

At each architectural level, we must consider both abstract and concrete features, whether logical or physical (Figure 3.8). The abstract view is that of the black box. For example, a computer is made up of processors and memory. Microarchitecture is the concrete view of a processor. The functional units are the registers, the micro-instruction sequencer. The components at the concrete level are logic gates and flip-flops.

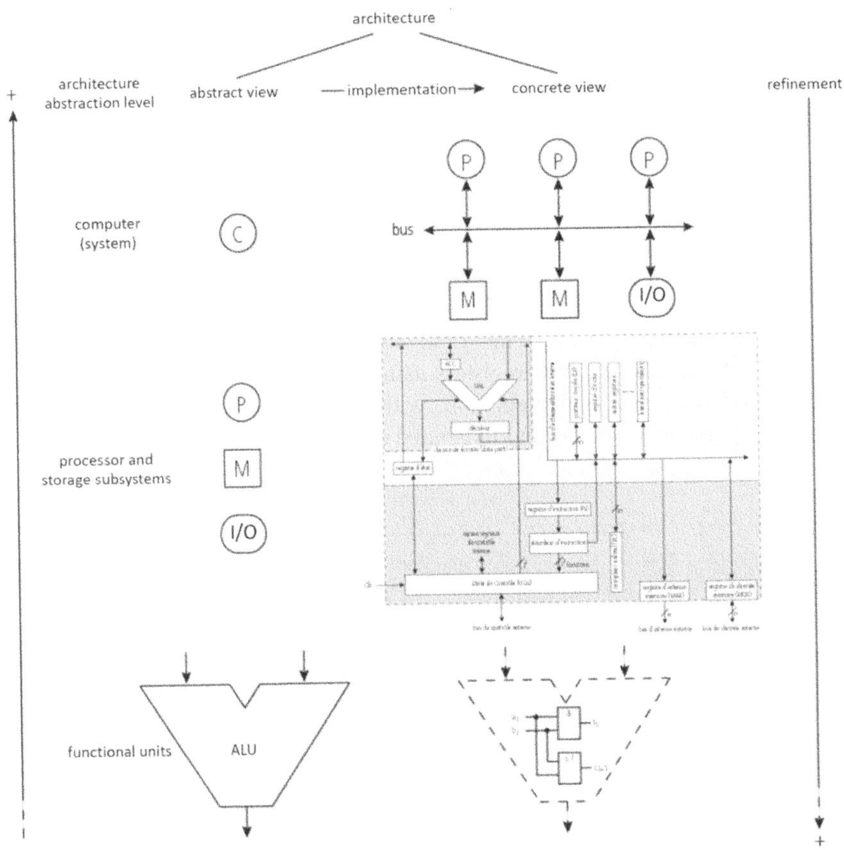

Figure 3.8. *Abstract and concrete hierarchical aspects of an architecture*

A computer architecture A_i is described at an abstraction level i, by an associated computation model C_i, a functional specification S_i and an implementation I_i of the architecture responding to S_i (Figure 3.9). This can be written as:

$$A_i = (C_i, S_i, I_i) \qquad [3.1]$$

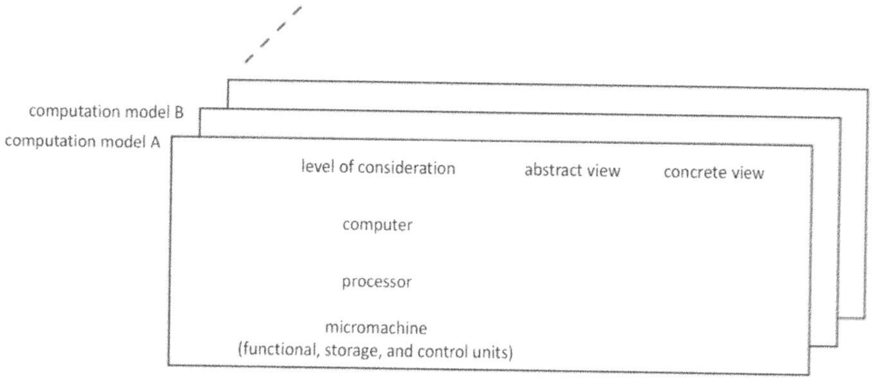

Figure 3.9. *The concept of computer architecture according to Sima et al. (1997)*

Finally, Sima *et al.* (1997) propose integrating these lower levels into the architecture and considering all the levels as summarized in Figure 3.10. Thus, the low-level hardware aspects are not eliminated from the description of an architecture, but rather encapsulated. The design of a computer will consist of carrying out an iterative process, generally under constraints, which consists of breaking down a system into subsystems until the result corresponds to the requirements expressed, usually in the form of specifications. However, the level of detail changes. In the beginning (1960–1985), this was a question of microarchitecture, which describes internal functioning with hardwired or microprogrammed approaches. This then passed to the processor level (1985–2015) with the progress of integration (solid line arrow on the figure). In the near future, it will move to the next level, with the computer as the building block of a distributed system. The functioning or behavior of these elements will be described respectively by the primitives (i.e. system calls) of the Operating System (OS), the instructions, the Hardware Description Language (HDL, *cf.* § 2.2.3 in Darche (2012) for an example and § 4.4 in Darche (2004)), the Register Transfer Languages (RTL), Boolean equations and electric equations. The design of an architecture must meet several objectives such as performance in terms of computing power, minimization of energy consumption and the ability to run applications programmed in a high-level language. The performance measure concerns, for example, the number of instructions per second and the memory bandwidth (*cf.* § V4-3.4 for a development of this feature).

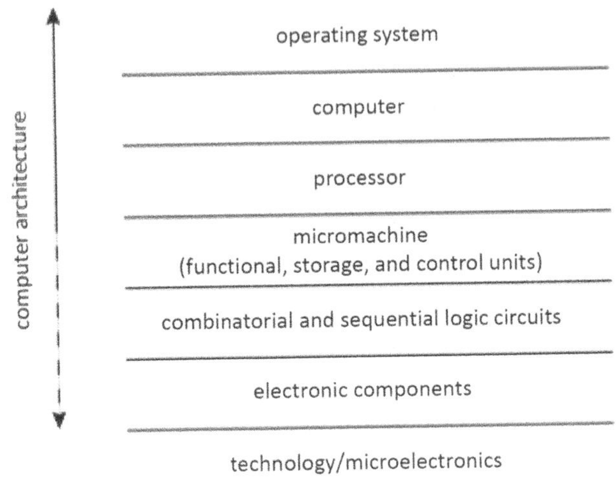

Figure 3.10. *Layered design of a computer*

For more details, the excellent synthesis in Sima *et al.* (1997) studies the historical evolution of the concepts of computational model and architecture from the work of Backus (1978), Treleaven and Hopkins (1981), Treleaven *et al.* (1987), Dally and Wills (1989) and Treleaven (1990). Another reference work that conceptualizes computer architecture is Blaauw and Brooks (1996).

3.1.5. *The semantic gap*

The semantic gap is the difference between the High-Level programming Language's (HLL) computation model and the architecture that must support the execution of programs written with them. This is closely linked to the organization of memory. The manipulation of information in a computer can be done by value, reference or literal. It is stored in memory. For example, a multi-dimensional array is implemented by adding management code, thus increasing the management time. Figure 3.11 situates the semantic gap between the different architectural approaches that will be discussed in this work, particularly in § 3.4.3.1.

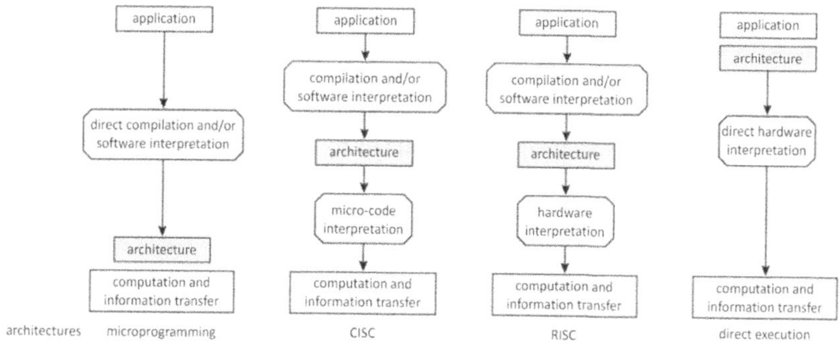

Figure 3.11. *Positioning of architecture for four historic architectures (Corporaal 1995)*

3.2. The original von Neumann machine

This section describes the computation model and the architecture of the von Neumann machine.

3.2.1. *von Neumann's computation model*

The von Neumann computation model that gave birth to the current computer has been the reference model since its origin (von Neumann 1945). The base entity is data implemented as a variable in computer languages. The problem description model is procedural, a sequence of instructions executed on an incoming flow of data and producing an outgoing flow of data that is the result of computation. Here, we can see the execution of a program and the definition of the latter, which is an ordered sequence of instructions executed on a data set. The centralized execution model is based on a semantics of state transition. It is "control-driven", with a shared data mechanism (COSH model, *cf.* § 3.1.2), the most commonly encountered model in computers. The stream of instructions executed on data stored in memory is unique (single-instruction stream).

This architecture is capable of supporting different computation models and programming styles. Let us cite as an example the functional and application models of computation and their associated programming styles. However, imperative and procedural programming styles are specific to the historical model of computation.

3.2.2. *von Neumann's (machine) architecture*

The result of the EDVAC (Electronic Discrete Variable Automatic Computer) project (von Neumann 1945), this architecture is at the heart of all current processors, even if new mechanisms are added to accelerate computation time or data access speed, such as the pipeline (*cf.* § 4.5.1 in Darche (2012)), cache memory or prefetching of instructions or data (*cf.* V2, forthcoming).

3.2.2.1. *von Neumann's report*

In his report, von Neumann compared the functioning of the computer to the brain, and its various components to neurons. He theoretically describes the subsets in the form of a network of E-elements, an E-element being a formal model of a neuron, Pitts and McCulloch's binary model (McCulloch and Pitts 1943). Therefore, this approach allows him to step away from implementation and therefore from technology.

The version corrected and described by Godfrey and Hendry (1993) broke down the computer into six parts (Figure 3.12): the control unit (CC for Central Control), the processing unit (CA for Central Arithmetical or Central Arithmetic logic unit), Memory (M) and Input (I) and Output (O) units. The visible part of the device is the external storage area for information in transit R (External Recording medium for the device). The program currently running is stored in primary memory (stored-program computer). The memory is said to be unified because it contains both the instructions and the program data. The memory is read sequentially, but only the state of the machine at the time a word is fetched from memory makes it possible to determine its type (i.e. instruction or data). The CC is responsible for fetching, decoding and executing the instruction. To do so, a Program Counter (PC), not shown in the figure, points to the next instruction to be executed. The CA performs the computation from the operands stored in the I_{CA} input register and then transferred to J_{CA}. The result of the computation is added to the existing contents of the O_{CA} register, hence the name "accumulator" for a register, referring to this function (*cf.* § V3-3.1.2). This means that the result of an instruction is added to the contents of this register (i.e. $O_{CA} \leftarrow O_{CA}$ + result). The two input registers work in a stack, I_{CA} being the top of the stack. The R subset allows for interaction between humans and computers. There we see the input–output devices, which at the time were various types of perforated media players and perforators, playing the embryonic role of secondary memory.

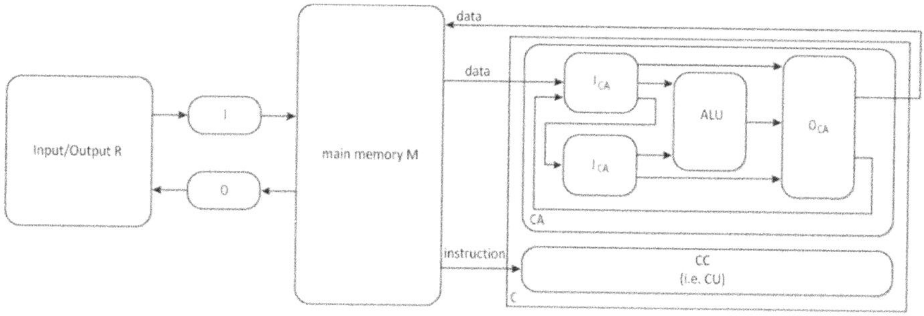

Figure 3.12. *Architecture according to von Neumann (1945)*

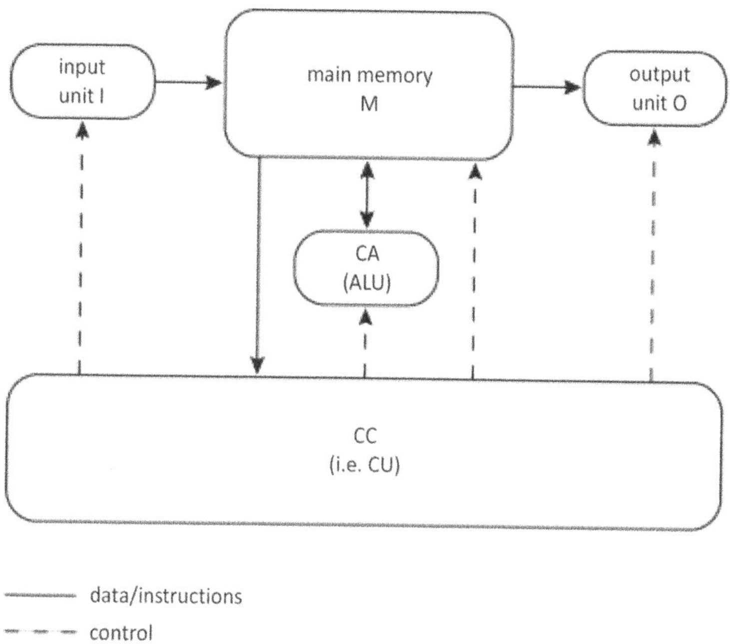

Figure 3.13. *Von Neumann machine with its five functional units*

By not taking into account the realm of external (i.e. mass) storage, this architecture is reduced to five functional units, which are the computation and control units, the main memory and the input and output exchange units. Through the input unit, an unlimited number of instructions and associated operands are read. The control unit receives the instructions to be executed. The arithmetic and logic unit performs the computations under the control of the control unit. The results are sent to memory or to the output unit. The memory stores all information (instructions and data) in its cells. Each of these is associated with an address for its location. I/O units, in addition to providing the basic interface between the computer and the outside world, have two subsidiary functions: buffering[9] and converting information. Buffering makes it possible to adapt the speed and provides synchronization. An example of conversion is a conversion from binary base to base-10 so that a human will be able to read the results. Figure 3.13 presents its information path. In computer architecture, the term "path" characterizes the set of functional units that participate in storage and transformation, in this case of information. We can divide information into data and instructions and their associated paths, the data path and the instruction path.

3.2.2.2. *The IAS*

These ideas were implemented in an electronic vacuum tube-based machine at the IAS (Institute for Advanced Study), and the architectures that were based on this machine were called von Neumann architecture, or preferentially, Princeton architecture, due to the location of this institute. It is described in Burks *et al.* (1946–1947). It contains all of the modern aspects of computer architecture. Internally, the machine uses a binary numbering system (represented in fixed-decimal mode in sign and module with the complement at 1 for signed numbers). Figure 3.14 shows its functional organization. We can see four subsystems. The main memory M contains the program and the data:

> "*Conceptually we have discussed above two different forms of memory: storage of numbers and storage of orders. If, however, the orders to the machine are reduced to a numerical code and if the machine can in some fashion distinguish a number from an order, the memory organ can be used to store both numbers and orders.*" (Burks *et al.* 1946–1947)

The Data Processing Unit is responsible for carrying out the four basic arithmetic operations with the help of an adder and three registers, two of which are shift-type registers:

> "*Inasmuch as the device is to be a computing machine there must be an arithmetic organ in it which can perform certain of the elementary arithmetic operations. There will be, therefore, a unit capable of adding, subtracting, multiplying and dividing.*" (Burks *et al.* 1946–1947)

9 That is, temporary storage.

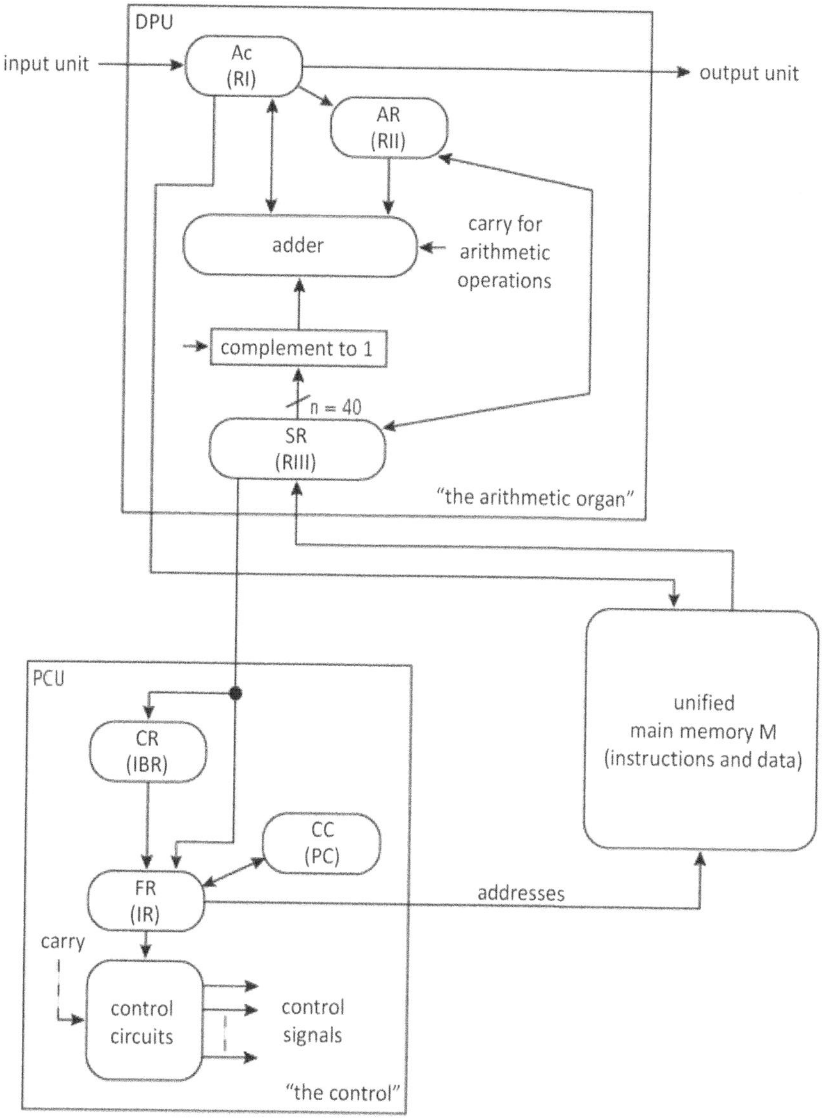

Figure 3.14. *Simplified functional organization of the IAS machine*

Three registers with the format n = 40 bits, named RI, RII and RIII, store information in the DPU. RI is a shift register, referred to as an accumulator register (Ac), because it receives the results of an addition. It will receive the resident number (i.e. the implicit operand or cumuland (augend)). To store a number, the accumulator must be previously set to zero, because the number will be added to its current value. It can also be dedicated to storing the partial product (the most important part), the dividend or the partial remainder. This register also makes it possible to store a value in memory. It therefore plays the role of a memory (general-purpose) data register (*cf.* below).

RII is also a shift register. It was initially called the Arithmetic Register (AR). It stores the multiplier, the partial product (the less important part) or the quotient. RIII is called the Selectron Register (SR) because it receives information from memory. The latter was originally composed of Selectron tubes (*cf.* § 1.3.1 in Darche (2012)) from RCA (Radio Corporation of America). Subsequently, during implementation, the Selectrons used in the prototype were replaced with Williams tubes (Kilburn 1948; Williams and Kilburn 1949, *cf.* § 1.3.1 in Darche (2012) for an introduction) with an individual capacity of 1,024 bits; 40 tubes were used (Estrin 1952, 1953) for availability reasons. This decision leads to structural changes. Specifically, the FR and CR registers (*cf.* below) were removed because RIII could serve this role. This is what was done during reading of a Memory Data Register (MDR) (*cf.* below). Contrary to its two predecessors, it did not have a shift function. It received a random number (*cf.* the explicit operand of the addition, that is, the addend, the multiplicand and the divisor). Before being used, an operand can be complemented to carry out an algebraic addition (i.e. Signed, *cf.* § 3.1.1 in Darche (2000):

> "*It should be a parallel storage organ which can receive a number and add it to the one already in it, which is also able to clear its contents, and which can transmit what it contains. We will call such an organ an Accumulator.*" (Burks *et al.* 1946–1947)

This unit is controlled by the Program Control Unit (PCU) responsible for executing the program. An SR word contains a pair of instructions, because it has a large size. The first code is sent to the FR register (for Function table Register), which will be the Instruction Register (IR). The second is sent to the control register (CR), also called the Instruction Buffer Register (IBR), which serves as temporary memory (buffer). The FR is so named because it controls the function tables, that is, in modern terminology, the binary decoders concerned with memory addressing (*cf.* § 2.1 and 2.2.6 in Darche (2012) and the determination of which operation to execute (*cf.* § 3.3.2). A table contains n inputs and 2^n outputs, with only one active at a time; hence, it is referred to as a decoding or many-one function table. Once the instruction is decoded, the control circuits generate control signals for the two units and the memory. A 12-bit address counter called Control Counter (CC), which will be the future Program Counter (PC), makes it possible to access all memory addresses. Contrary to a modern program counter, it contains the address of the last pair of executed instructions, and not the address of the next instruction to be executed. In addition, FR plays the role of the future MAR for reading:

> "*If the memory for orders is merely a storage organ there must exist an organ which can automatically execute the orders stored in the memory. We shall call this organ the Control.*" (Burks *et al.* 1946–1947)

To overcome the obstacle of sequential execution, a conditional jump instruction makes it possible to change the address of the next instruction to be executed in the CC:

> "*We introduce an order (the conditional transfer order) which will, depending on the sign of a given number, cause the proper one of two routines to be executed.*" (Burks *et al.* 1946–1947)

The CPU is made up of the DPU combined with the PCU. To conclude, the input and output equipment, the paper tape reader and paper tape punch respectively make it possible to access memory serially via the accumulator, whose structure makes shifting possible. It is notable that the central role of the DPU in the circulation of information can become a bottleneck (*cf.* § 3.3.4). Burks *et al.* (1946–1947) describe the logical features of this machine, and Goldstine and von Neumann (1947–1948) describe the programming features.

The preceding functional organization is shown in Figure 3.15.

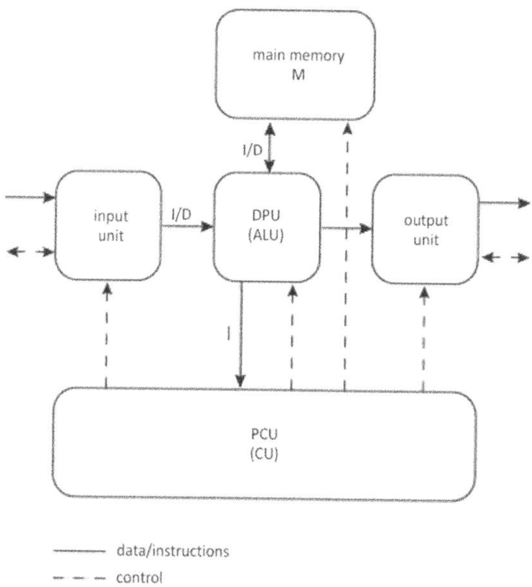

Figure 3.15. *Functional organization of a von Neumann machine*

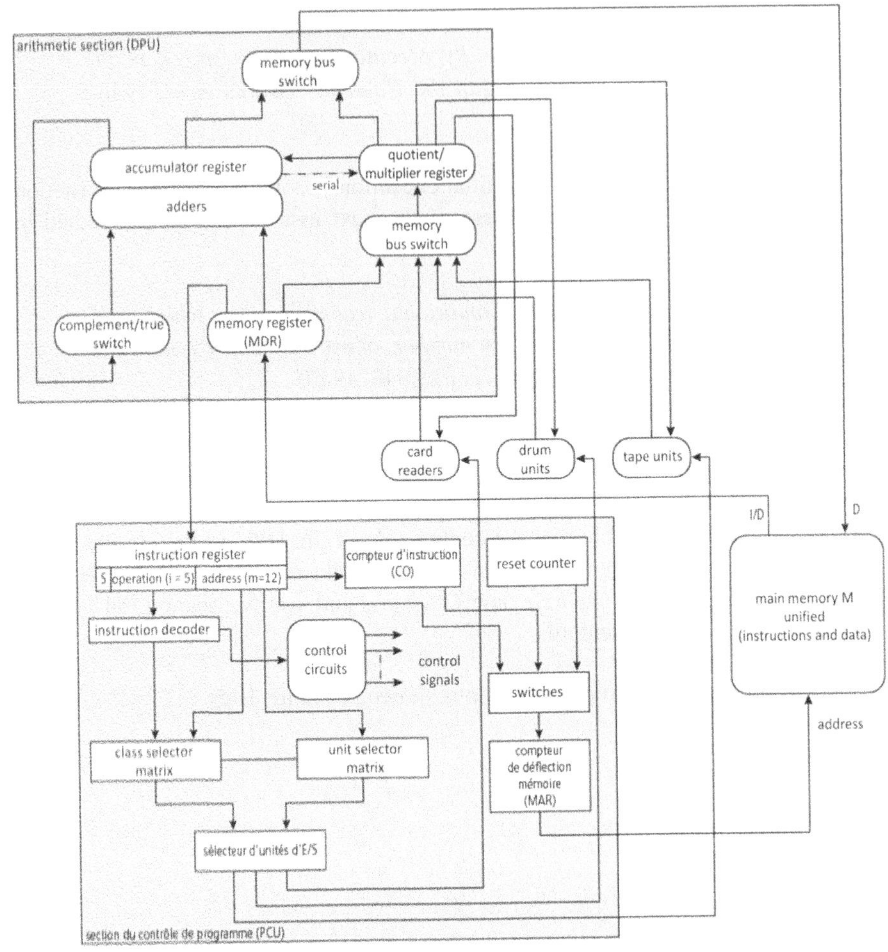

Figure 3.16. *Functional organization of the IBM 701 (based on Frizzell (1953), modified)*

3.2.2.3. *The IBM 701*

This architecture gave rise to the production of several dozen computers. The IBM 701 is a commercial example of the results of the preceding ideas. All of the functional units in modern computers are found here, as illustrated in Figure 3.16. The four main management registers are (M)AR ((Memory) Address Register), (M)DR ((Memory) Data Register), IR (Instruction (opcode) Register) and PC (Program Counter). The first two allow the CPU to communicate externally. The memory deflection register[10] is the address register, or MAR. The address either comes from the instruction counter, also known as the Sequence Counter (SC, also known as the Program Counter (PC)), or from the renewal counter for refreshing memory, such as for DRAM (Dynamic Random Access Memory). The accessed information (instructions and data) enters through the (M)DR data register. In the case of an instruction, its code is transmitted to the instruction register (IR). The operation code is decoded for execution. Data is transmitted to the accumulator. The CPU executes instructions sequentially. Two important data registers are the accumulator (Acc) and the Multiplier-Quotient register (MQ). The latter communicates with the input/output (I/O) peripherals. More information about this machine is given in Buchholz (1953) and Ross (1953).

3.2.2.4. *Execution cycle*

The execution cycle for an instruction is a graph that represents the different states for executing an instruction. It also indicates the execution time. On first impression, it can be broken down into two parts, the code fetch in main memory and actual execution (Figure 3.17). During the first phase, the address contained in the PC is presented to memory via the MAR. After it is read, the instruction code is stored in the MDR. Then, it is transferred to the IR to be decoded. The control unit can then begin the second phase, during which the actual execution occurs. A description of the cycle is given in § 3.3.2.

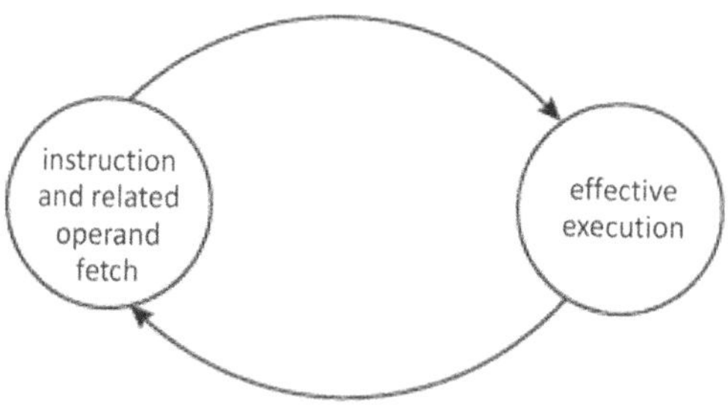

Figure 3.17. *Infinite two-phase execution cycle*

3.2.3. *Control*

The fundamental principles underlying the modern general-use computer rely especially on the stored-program concept. According to the progress as described by Metropolis and Worlton (1980), the control of the first computers was manual, with

10 The name of the era is based on the use of electrostatic memory made up of Williams tubes.

instruction input using a terminal keyboard called a teletypewriter, an example of which is the complex calculator developed by Bell Labs (1940). Then, the sequence to be calculated was entered using either a perforated 35 mm film reader for the Z3[11] electromechanical computer (1941) or punched tape for Harvard's Mark I (1944). The ENIAC (Electronic Numerical Integrator And Computer) at first (1946) employed internal hardwired controls, using cables with jacks plugged into plugboards and by positioning interrupters. Then, the principle of memory-based control (decoding matrix associated with read-only function tables) was implemented in 1948. Finally, the BINAC (BINary Automatic Computer, 1949) and the EDSAC (Electronic Delay Storage Automatic Calculator, 1949) were the first two machines to implement program storage in read-write memory, the concept having emerged from the EDVAC (1946–1951). The historical details have been described by Goldstine (1993) and Rojas and Hashagen (2000). See also Hartree *et al.* 1948) along with Nature (1948) and Williams and Kilburn (1948).

3.3. Modern von Neumann machines

This architecture has been extended over time to offer additional functionality in high-level languages and to increase processing speed. Thus, the idea of a stack (*cf.* § V4-4.1) made it possible to implement the concept of a procedure that encapsulates that of function. This made recursive computation possible. New kinds of data were able to be used, such as Binary Coded Decimal (BCD), real numbers coded in fixed and floating-point representations and character strings (*cf.* Darche (2000) for more details on representation). Modes of address became more complex, with modes such as indexing and indirection (*cf.* § V4-1.2.3). The former facilitates the use of tables. The latter makes it possible to introduce the concept of the pointer and dynamic entities. The capacity of main memory was increased using the concept of virtual memory, which led to the mechanisms of pagination and segmentation. Access times were improved with mechanisms such as interleaving (*cf.* in Darche (2012)) or the implementation of memory hierarchy with the addition of a cache to minimize traffic between main memory and the processor. I/O exchanges were facilitated using mechanisms such as Direct Memory Access (DMA, *cf.* § 1.2 and 4.1.3 in Darche (2003)) or using specialized I/O processors, freeing up the central processor for other tasks. Parallel computation was introduced by multiplying the functional units externally (the idea of the co-processor, *cf.* § V3-5.4) and then internally, for example, in superscalar architectures and by implementing the pipeline structure (*cf.* V2). Today, microprocessors internally execute computations in parallel using cores, with each core being a basic processor (*cf.* V3).

11 The idea had already been used in Konrad Zuse's Z1 (*cf.* § 1.2).

3.3.1. *Abstraction level*

It is possible to functionally present a computing system in hierarchical form. We must therefore distinguish between two levels of abstraction – the computer and the processor.

3.3.1.1. *Computer-level abstraction*

From an organizational and modern perspective, it is no longer necessary to distinguish between the three subsystems that make up the central unit or processing unit, in other words, microprocessor P for a microcomputer, memory M, called central, primary, or main, and the input–output (I/O) exchange units, and the communication system called the interconnection bus, which enables communication between the three subsystems (Figure 3.18). A bus consists of a number of tracks or electrical wires shared by the connected units (*cf.* V2 and § V3-1.1). The peripherals D (for Device) are connected to the exchange units, which enables the central process to receive and transmit information. The main memory is made up of semiconductor-based Random Access Memory (RAM) and Read-Only Memory (ROM). This is a master-slave-type model. The process is always the master in exchanges (active entity). The memory and the input–output exchange units are passive entities, and therefore referred to as slaves[12].

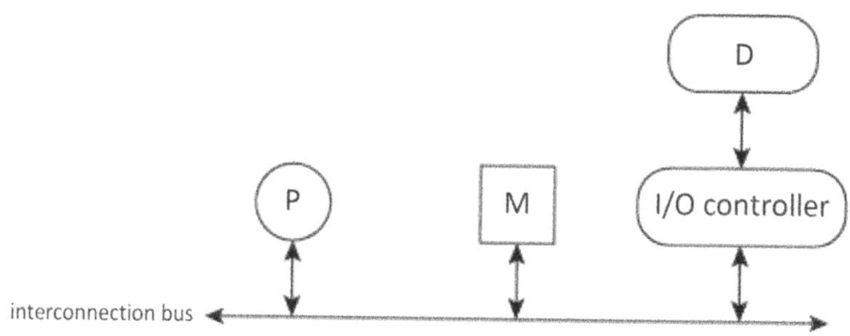

Figure 3.18. *Modern view of a von Neumann computer*

This communication medium is generally composed of three buses. A bus is a set of communication paths in which information circulates, in the most general sense. There are buses for data (exchange), addresses and control. As their name may or may not suggest, the first carries data, as well as instruction codes, the second carries addresses and the third enables control of exchanges between the

12 This term needs to be qualified, because these entities can be active. For example, a process can be integrated into the memory chip, which becomes Intelligent RAM (IRAM). For more information on this topic, see Patterson *et al.* (1997a, 1997b, 1997c, 1997d).

various subsystems and can also carry state information (Figure 3.19) for each of them in the format respectively of n, m and c bits. To use a "postal" analogy, when the central unit wants to communicate with the memory or the I/O interface or exchange units, it does so via an envelope labeled with an address and containing information (instruction or data). The study of buses is the subject of the following volume.

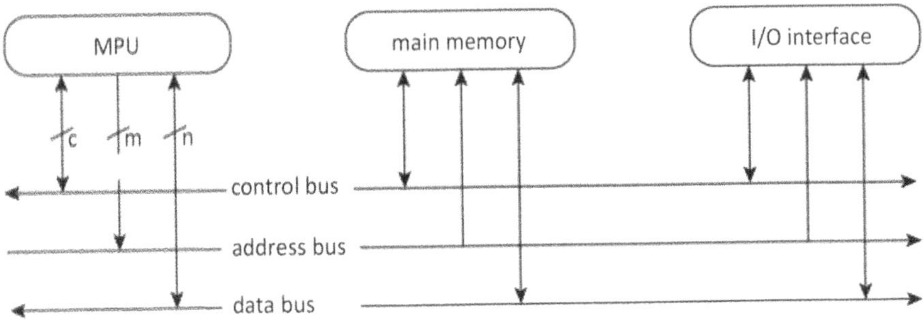

Figure 3.19. *The three communications buses*

3.3.1.2. *The processor level of abstraction*

At this level, we find the analysis of von Neumann's central unit (i.e. CC and CA). Thus, as illustrated in Figure 3.20, the processor is made up of an Integer Processing Unit (IPU), controlled by a (Central) Control Unit ((C)CU). To these functional units must be added a storage subsystem composed of registers R.

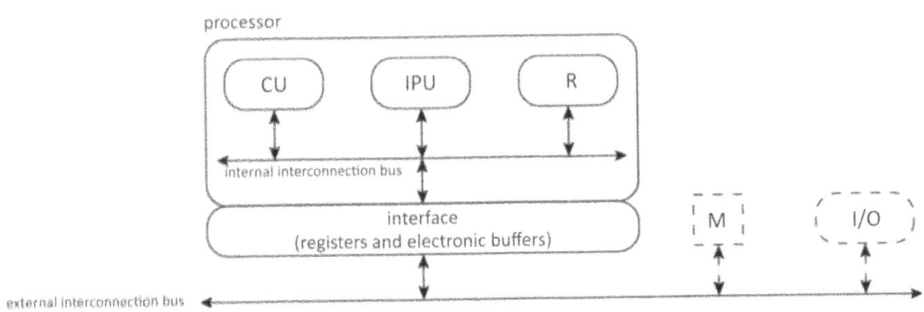

Figure 3.20. *The three functional units of a microprocessor*

Figure 3.21 presents the internal information flow. A program being executed is stored in main memory. It is an ordered sequence of instructions. The control unit (command portion) accesses information (i.e. machine code or data) by presenting its address on the address bus, first internally, then externally. It must also indicate whether it is a read or write access. After decoding the instruction, it asks the processing unit (operating portion) to execute the instruction.

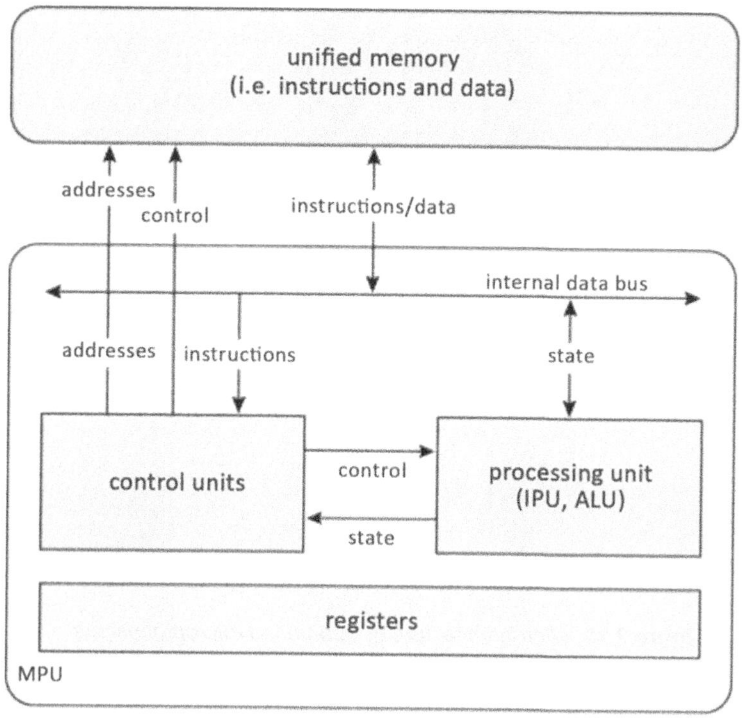

Figure 3.21. *Internal circulation of information inside a microprocessor*

We can examine the previously described diagram in Figure 3.22. Some registers can be used by both units, such as the status register, while others, such as the instruction register, cannot. Some registers can be accessed by the programmer: they are part of the ISA, in other cases, only internal units have access, such as for the previously mentioned registers. Carter (1995), who uses the vocabulary promulgated by AMD, distinguishes three subsystems in the microprocessor, the CCU (Computer Control Unit), the PCU (Program Control Unit) and the ALU (Arithmetic and Logic Unit). The Control Unit defined in this work is made up of the first two units.

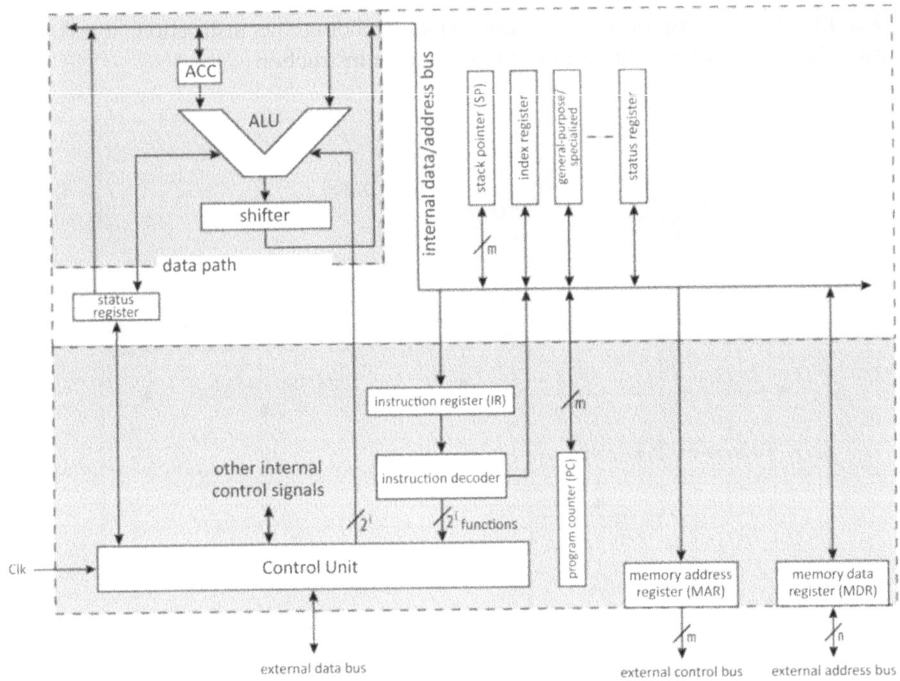

Figure 3.22. *Microarchitecture of bus-based microprocessors*

3.3.1.2.1. Integer processing unit

Henceforth, we will refer to the integer processing unit as the ALU (Arithmetic and Logic Unit). In effect, its role is to execute fundamental logical and arithmetic instructions.

With regard to arithmetic operations, addition and subtraction are always implemented. Note the specific cases of incrementation and decrementation, operations for which one of the operands is a constant, usually 1. Subtraction makes it possible to implement comparisons (*cf.* Exercise E3.2). Multiplication and division can also be implemented. Historically, the latter were added much later to second-generation microprocessors because the technology offered enough room on the chip. For other, more complex, operations, such as an elementary function (i.e. logarithmic, exponential, trigonometric, etc.), there is an alternative, which is either to add hardware or to emulate the desired instruction in software. In the first case, one solution can be the use of a specialized circuit, which we will call the mathematical co-processor. This co-processor is today integrated with the process (in the case of the Intel Pentium). In the second case, a subprogram will replace the execution of this specialized instruction (software solution). These specialized functions belong to mathematical libraries. More generally, if the hardware does not implement the desired operation, there is a software alternative. Of course, this emulation will be computationally expensive, because it requires the execution of several other replacement instructions for each requested instruction.

Logical operations are the classical Boolean functions AND, OR, XOR (eXclusive OR) and NOT, a combinatorial operator (*cf.* § 2.2 in Darche (2002)), and the functions for logic or arithmetic shift, and for rotation (*cf.* § V4-2.3.2.3), classes that are typically sequential but have been implemented in combinatorial logic to increase execution speed (*cf.* § V3-3.3). They are described in § 3.5 in Darche (2002).

The operations can be unary or binary, that is, there can be one or two operands. As an example, logical NOT only uses one operand, while addition requires two operands to execute. The ALU may set binary indicators called flags to confirm the validity of the result (*cf.* § V3-3.1.5). This is primarily the case for most instructions, which are arithmetic. The constructor's information indicates the state of each instruction after execution.

The Data Path (DP) is the set of components or logical subsystems participating in computations on data, in other words the components responsible for storing and transferring data and carrying out arithmetic and logical operations on the latter. It is characterized by its format or width, which is generally expressed in powers of 2, beginning with 2^2, that is to say 4, 8, etc., for accounting purposes. There are exceptions, such as among DEC minicomputers, which used 18 for PDP-1, 24 for PDP-2 and 36 for PDP-3 and PDP-6. This path is made up of functional units, storage elements and steering logic. The functional units generally employ combinatorial logic for maximum processing speed. They perform operations on the data path (*cf.* § below). The primary such unit is the IPU. The storage components are registers, including register files, latches, Flip-Flops (FF) and memory. The interconnection logic is made up of (de)multiplexers and buses. It is programmed using register transfer language (RTL). In general, the data path is used to describe a microprocessor, since the control component is hidden.

3.3.1.2.2. Control unit

The control unit is also referred to as the command unit or the Instruction Control Unit (ICU). This is what manages the overall processor. It is made up of the CCU and the PCU.

The CCU is the sequencer, in other words, the Finite State Machine (FSM, *cf.* § 3.7.3 in Darche (2002)). Timing is provided by the clock signal generator, in the case of a hardwired version (Figure 3.23). It exclusively uses the instruction register (IR), which is occasionally referred to as order memory (Profit 1970). From an instruction accessed and stored in main memory, this unit decodes the required information and implements a series of basic commands. The circled levels indicate the location of the three basic steps in the execution of an instruction, respectively fetch, decoding and execution proper, as presented in § 3.3.2. The sequencer may be guided by status register flags, also referred to as Processor Status Registers (PSR, *cf.* § V3-3.1.5). The size of this subsystem is a function of the number of instructions and addressing options provided to the programmer. The controller/sequencer can be hardwired or microprogrammed. In the former, a timing generator creates sequencing signals. The microprogrammed version, invented by Wilkes (1951), is also a state machine controlled by a microprogram (*cf.* V2).

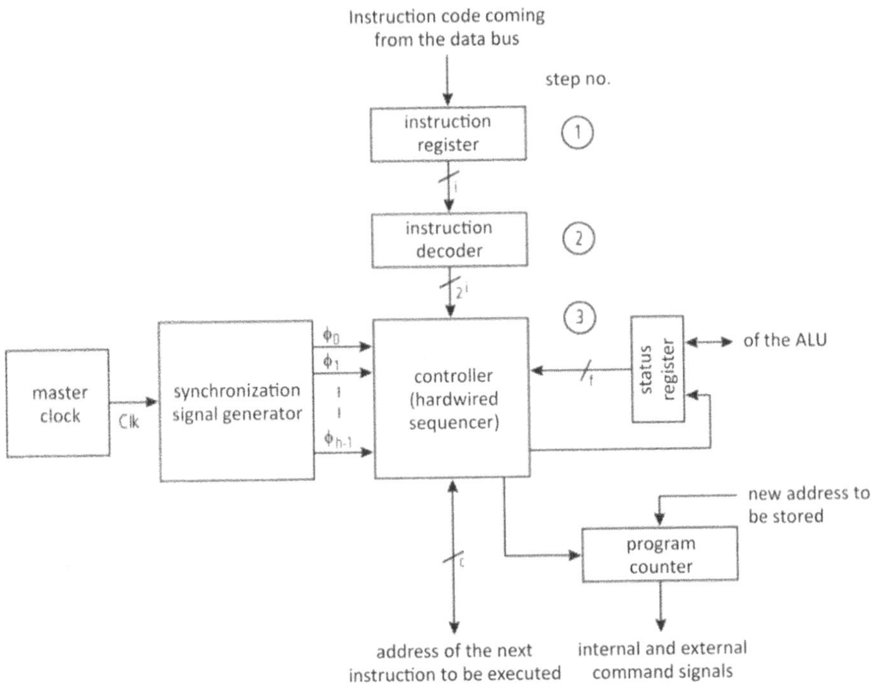

Figure 3.23. *Decoding of an instruction by a hardwired sequencer*

The PCU carries out (external) addressing at the processor level. This unit provides access to unified memory. It is made up of a Program Counter (PC), a Stack Pointer (SP) and the MAR and MDR register interfaces. It has an incrementer and, for some kinds of addressing such as relative addressing (*cf.* § 1.2.3.2), an adder. It manages the stack with a stack pointer and may use an internal stack, such as in the Am2930 circuit.

All of these logical operators belong to the instruction path, which is occasionally referred to as the Control Path (CP), which is the set of components or logical subsystems (i.e. functional unit), which participates in the fetching, decoding and execution of an instruction and, therefore, commanding the DP. As for the data path, we are not taking the bus into account.

3.3.1.2.3. Registers

A register is fast memory with storage capacity for a binary word in n-bit format that operates at the speed of the component[13] or logical subsystem into which it is integrated. For pedagogical reasons, registers are shown in Figure 3.20 separately from the other two units. In fact, some registers are dedicated to a unit. The processor can also provide a generic storage area to the programmer. The register can be implemented in static or dynamic logic (*cf.* § 2.2.1 in Darche (2012) on these kinds of logic. It can be composed of flip-flops (*cf.* § 3.4 in Darche (2002)), each storing a bit. More details on the use of registers are given in § V2-2.7.1.

3.3.2. *Base execution outline*

Main memory contains the instructions in machine code[14] and the data on which the operations will be carried out. Two approaches are taken in microprocessors: instructions and data can have the same address space (in the case of the 1st MPU), or they can be distinct. The latter is the case in the Harvard architecture or when the memory is segmented. Thus, in the segmentation[15] mechanism used in the x86 architecture, the data and the machine code are contained in separate segments. The value of this approach is to be able to share a program among multiple users such that each user has his or her own data storage area.

The command unit gives orders to the ALU in order to carry out the requested instruction. However, as illustrated in Figure 3.24(a), it plays this role in three successive stages or steps, which are the Instruction Fetch (IF) stage, the Instruction Decode (ID) stage and the Execute (EX) stage, referred to as the Fetch-Decode-eXecute cycle (FDX), the Fetch-Decode-Execute cycle (FDE) or the fetch-and-execute cycle.

---

13 Initially a subsystem.

14 Machine code is also called *hard code* (*cf.* Bell (1973)) in reference to the instructions permanently set in the hardware (hardwired or microprogrammed).

15 A segment is a set of contiguous memory words with specialized contents. This mechanism will be introduced in Volume 2.

During the instruction fetch phase (no. 1), the instruction code pointed by the program counter is transferred from main memory to an inaccessible register by the user, which is the instruction register IR.

During the second stage, decoding, the type of operation requested and the operands to be used are determined. If necessary, the processor will fetch the operand(s) to execute the instruction (stage 2 in Figure 3.24(b)). During this stage, the program counter is incremented by a value k such that it contains the address of the next instruction to be executed. This value k will depend on the location in memory occupied by the instruction being executed:

> "*The function table just described energizes a different output wire for each different code operation.*" (Burks *et al.* 1946–1947)

Finally, the last stage involves the execution of the operation. The execution unit may provide information about the properties of the result, particularly its validity (i.e. whether the result is correct), via the intermediary of the status register's indicators or status flags (CC for Condition Code, *cf.* § II-3.4 in Darche (2000) and § V2-2.7.1.5). For example, for the 8086, the instruction `xor ax,ax` (*cf.* exclusive OR on the same register) sets the indicator Z to 1, since the result is 0. On the other hand, a transfer instruction `mov ax,0` (i.e. resetting of a register to zero) does not set any indicators. The result may be stored (Write Back (WB)) in main memory.

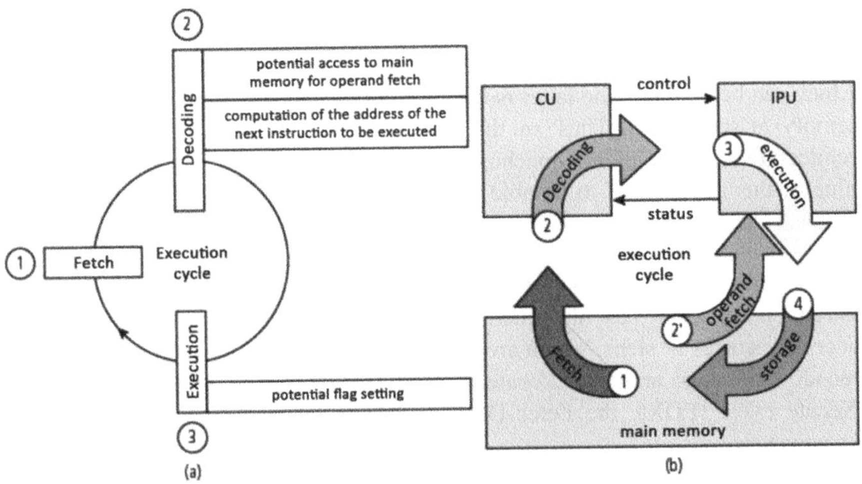

Figure 3.24. *Basic steps of the basic execution cycle*

Figure 3.25 shows the execution cycle in the form of a flowchart. To simplify, the request and management of interruptions (*cf.* Chapter V4-5) are not included. By convention, at initialization, for example, when the power is turned on, for example, the first word the microprocessor fetches will always be an instruction code. It should be noted that the execution cycle can be incorporated into an interpreter's loop. This will be developed in the second volume.

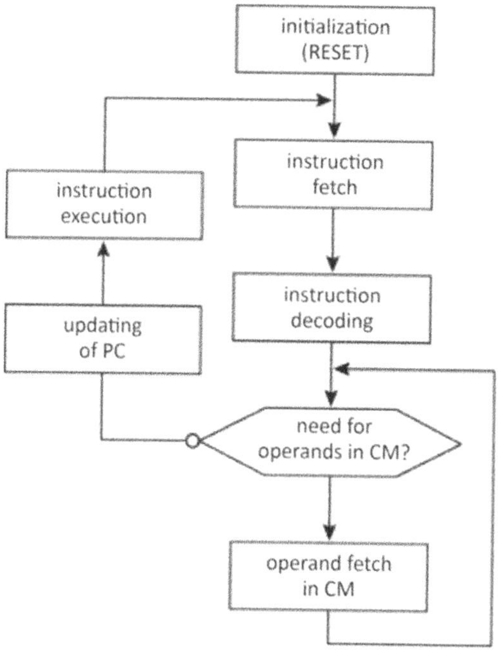

Figure 3.25. *Execution cycle flowchart*

Fetching one or more operands in memory that are required for execution and storage of the result can be carried out in separate cycles. This then leaves us with a five-stage cycle: IF, ID, OF, EX and WB. Fetching an operand will require computation of its address. A processor can be studied from a functional point of view. It is thus possible to break down the MPU into five functions, as shown in Figure 3.26, which are procurement of instructions, their decoding, procurement (if necessary) of associated operands and the effective computation and storage of the result. Computation of an address can be requested at several steps. These steps can provide a reference for the concept of a pipeline (*cf.* V2).

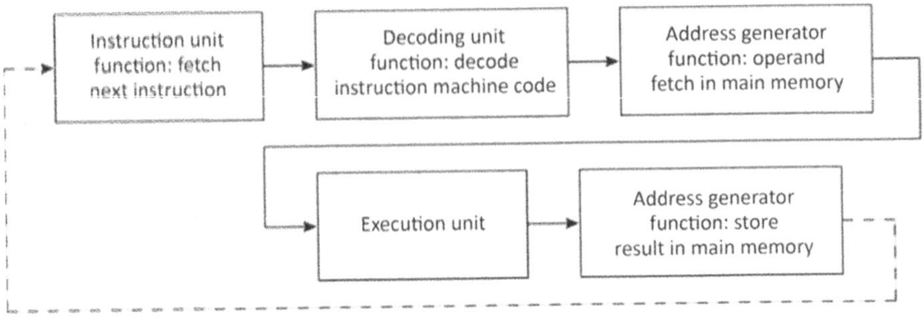

Figure 3.26. *Functional steps to execute an instruction*

Figure 3.27 summarizes the preceding remarks by describing the various steps of an execution cycle with, in addition, an operand fetch and an operand storage in main memory. The dotted lines indicate an optional execution path.

The duration of an execution cycle for an instruction is a function of, among other things, the period of the timing or clock signal. Sections V3-1.4 and V4-3.2.1 describe the temporal features of execution.

3.3.3. *Possible transfers*

The von Neumann architecture is characterized by the sequentiality of the operations. Moreover, the memory data path is unique. If we consider the registers and the memory, this of course has consequences on the types of transfers that are possible. Traditionally, there are three directions of transfer: from register to register (example: `mov ax,bx`), register to memory (examples: `mov [memo],ax` or `mov [bx],bx`) and memory to register (example: `mov dl,[memo1]`). To this, we must add the two transfers connected to immediate addressing, immediate value to register (example: `mov cx,4`) and immediate value to memory (example: `mov [memo],0FFFFh`). Memory to memory transfer cannot take place because it would violate what we can call the golden rule of transfer in the von Neumann model for architectures with one or two buses (*cf.* § 3.4.1). Some processors will have different instructions depending on the direction (`load` and `store`), while others have one undifferentiated instruction (`mov`). Of course, there are exceptions to this rule, in which memory-to-memory transfers can take place. This occurs for stack manipulation instructions, such as `push [memo]`, and character manipulation instructions, such as `movsb`. These features are studied in detail in the first two chapters of Volume 4.

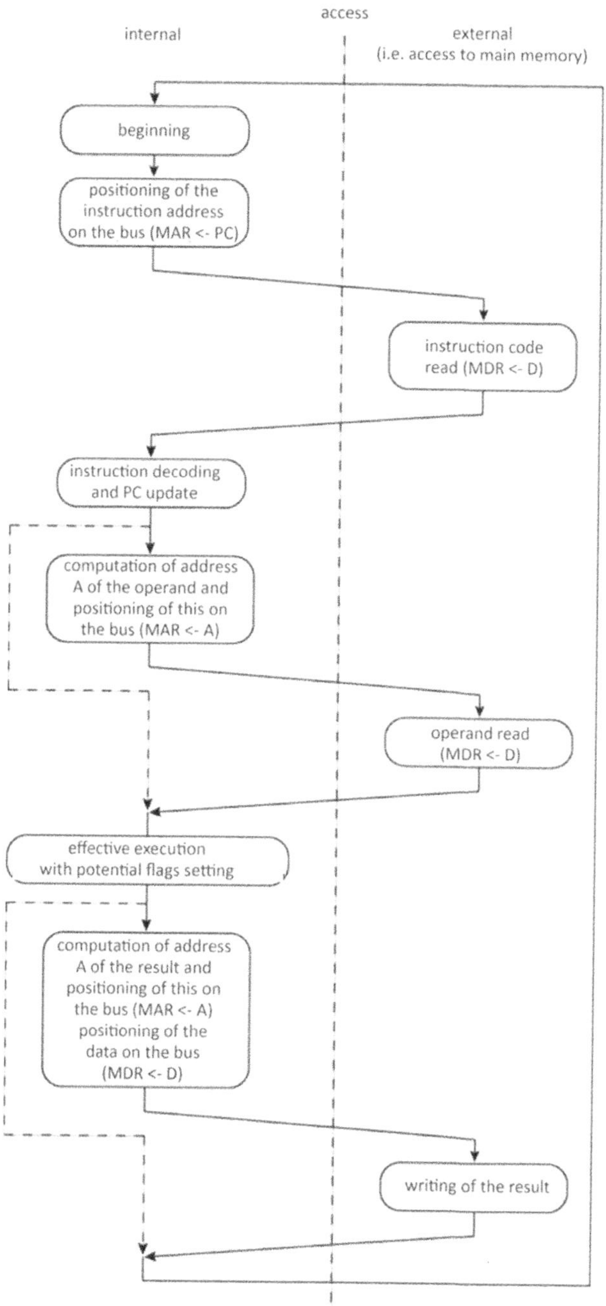

Figure 3.27. *Execution cycle described with different forms of access*

3.3.4. *Summary: advantages and disadvantages of this model*

This model is the most widespread. It is the basis for the modern computer. The three main subsystems in the von Neumann architecture are:

– a single main memory made up of a linear organization of memory cells of fixed size that contain instruction codes, data and address or pointers (unified memory);

– a single computation component, integer processing unit (IPU or ALU), controlled by the control unit (CU), with the whole forming the processor (Figure 3.28);

– an I/O system enabling communication.

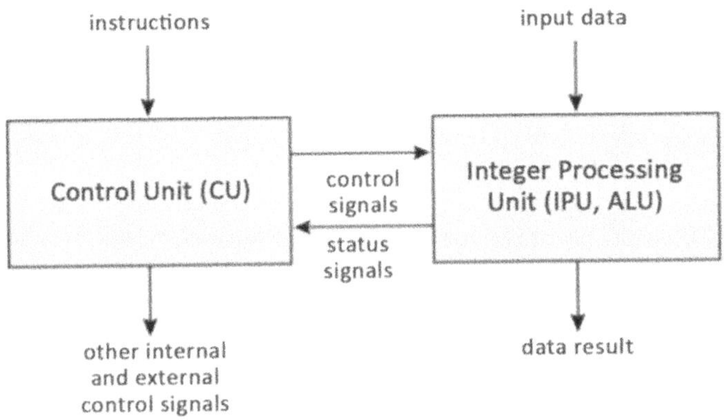

Figure 3.28. *Information flow in a processor*

To this, we must add the following characteristics. There is a low-level language called "machine language" to program the processor. Control of execution is centralized and sequential. The CPU executes instructions sequentially. The address[16] for an instruction is therefore implicit during execution. All machines execution status is represented by all or some of the registers (*cf.* § V3-3.4.1). The processor possesses a linear address space with cells on a single level. The data, the basic component in the computation model, is stored in a memory cell or a register. It is addressed by reference or literally (Treleaven 1981). Instructions and data are

16 An address is a numeric designation (*cf.* a natural or relative integer) for a location or a memory cell.

stored in a single memory and processed homogeneously (i.e. access and transport), which justifies the use of the term "unified memory". The distinction between the two is made via the machine state. After initialization, the first information read is an instruction.

This architecture possesses intrinsic disadvantages. The main one is called the von Neumann bottleneck or tailback, a term introduced by John Backus during an Association for Computing Machinery (ACM) conference (Backus 1978). It refers to the fact that information transfer between processor and memory is only done in a unitary manner using a sequence "address sent to memory/transfer of the word" via a communication system referred to by Backus (1978) as a connecting tube. The traffic between the first two subsystems does not only concern useful data but also instructions and addresses. This limits computation speed to the flow rate. In modern computers, the communication system is a bus shared by all of the communicating subsystems. All information is required to be transmitted over the bus. This is another bottleneck. An analogy is traffic congestion during the holidays, when all of the vacation-goers find themselves on the road at the same time at the beginning or end. Solutions for this problem have been proposed in other architectures, such as the Harvard[17] architecture (Moore 4199), for example, with the separation of data and instructions. This architecture was subsequently modified. Modified Harvard architectures are characterized by specialized memory, one for instructions and the other for data. They are shown in § 3.4.2. Besides, the centralization of data exchange means that the processor is also a bottleneck because it slows down communication. An exchange between memory and an I/O exchange unit is required to take place via the microprocessor, which executes the transfer via one of its registers. With improvements such as Direct Memory Access (DMA), the control of exchanges can be shared among multiple masters, the processor and the DMA controller. In addition, in a parallel architecture, that is, one with several processors, memory becomes a new bottleneck, as does shared I/O, although to a lesser extent.

From this physical bottleneck, Van de Goor (1989) distinguishes a conceptual bottleneck. He is referring to the fact that high-level entities are precisely based on the machine's low-level entities, which introduce restrictions. For example, variable memory refers to a memory cell or to a register. Control structures that are associated with tests and conditional and unconditional jumps are another example. Programming styles such as functional or logical programming make it possible to reduce this kind of bottleneck. This is the semantic gap (*cf.* § 3.1.5). Finally, the

17 Name of the university.

sequentiality that is inherent in the model makes it difficult to specify parallelism. This was not important in the early days, but today, this disadvantage weighs heavily on performance (*cf.* § V4-3.4).

Improvements have been introduced to speed up the communication flow rate between processor and memory. Memory, for example, has been segregated with the introduction of several levels of cache (*cf.* § 2.1). Its size was increased, and the subsystems were interleaved (*cf.* § 2.4.1 and 2.4.4 respectively in Darche (2012)).

3.4. Variations on a theme

The processor's main functional blocks are the execution unit, the control unit and the registers (Figure 3.2.1). Let us now look at these components in their environment. Since the processor communicates with the outside world, it has several internal buses of the same type, since this kind of interconnection enables communication between all of the microarchitecture's components. One or more data buses and an address bus carry information. These buses communicate with external buses via electronic buffers, that is, amplifiers that, when necessary, adjust voltage and current levels using logic-level translators (*cf.* § 3.8.2 in Darche (2004)). They play the role of logical isolator. They can also perform a storage function. They enable the use of buses by allowing for connection or disconnection to their three-state output (*cf.* § 3.4.1 of Darche (2004)). These roles are played by the MAR and MDR registers. Architectures can be classified according to their number of internal buses, from zero to three. Based on the number of buses and operands, both explicit and implicit, and their storage location (i.e. register, stack, random access memory), the number of fields and therefore the instruction size will vary proportionately (*cf.* § 3.5.1 and V4-1.1).

3.4.1. *Classification by bus*

An architecture with no buses uses the stack and is explained in § 3.5.1. The architecture in Figure 3.29 is a single internal bus architecture. This is an accumulator-based machine, with a register (Acc in the figure) always receiving an operand and the result of a computation for a dyadic operation, that is, one with two variables (*cf.* § V4-1.1). This architecture resembles the one used in the Z3 computer (development begun in 1938) described in Rojas and Hashagen (2000).

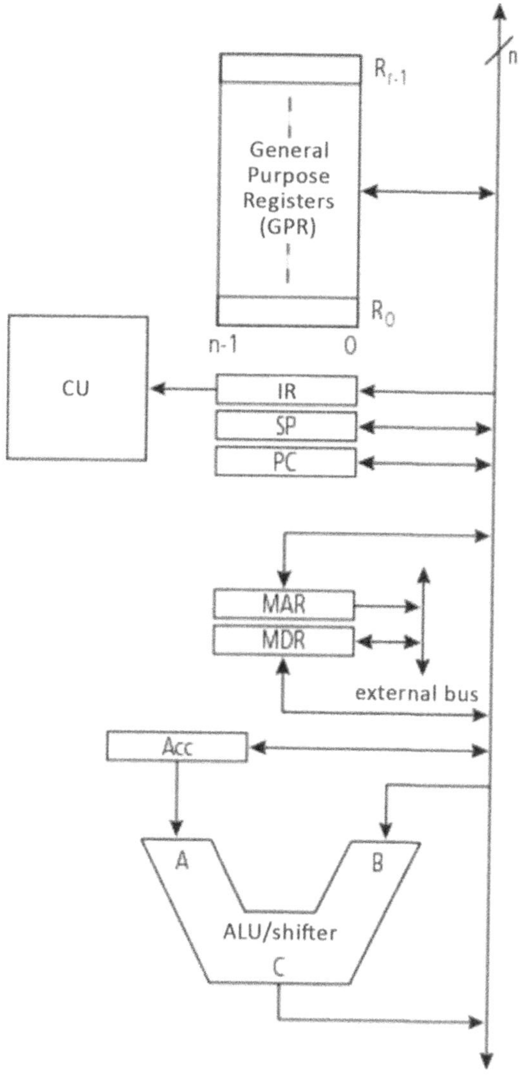

Figure 3.29. *Internal organization of a bus (control signals not shown)*

A commercial example of an MPU is Intel's 8080 microprocessor, which was based on the internal architecture of the 8008 (Figure 3.30). Another example is the Toshiba TLCS-12 (n = 12 bits).

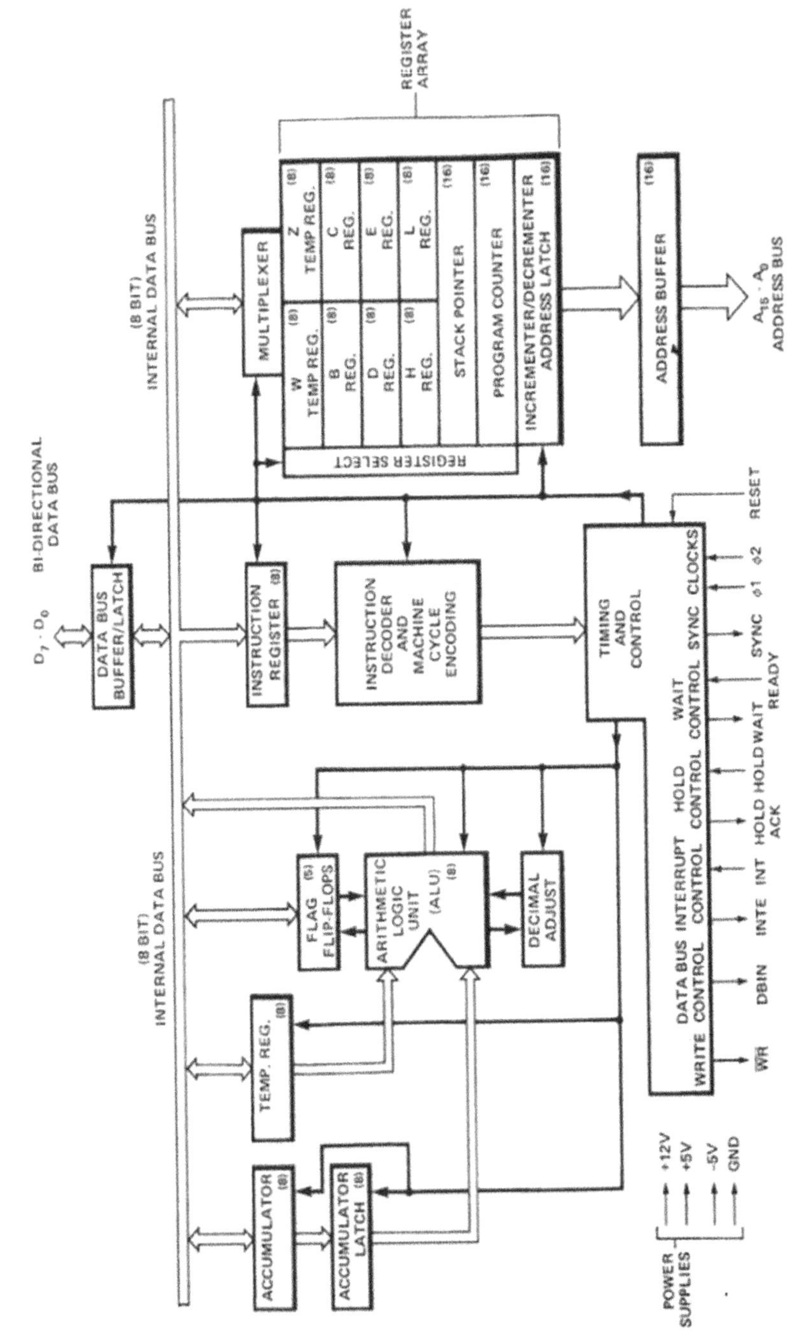

Figure 3.30. *Functional internal organization of Intel 8080A microprocessors with a single-bus internal data path (Intel 1975)*

Double internal bus architectures are the most common. The variations in Figure 3.31 are located at the accumulator, which can be connected to both buses (version b). It should be noted that some of the registers are bidirectional. In version a, a circuit enabling information passing between the internal buses can be implemented (bypass register).

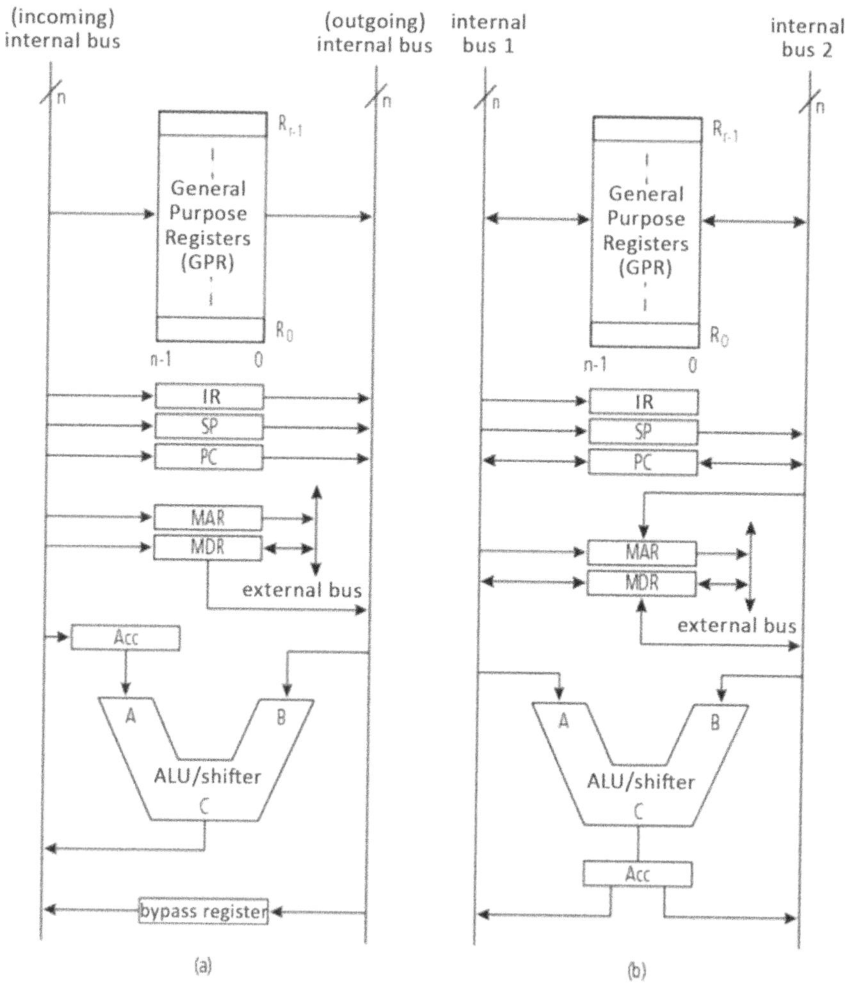

Figure 3.31. *Two variations of a double internal bus organization (CU and control signals not shown)*

A commercial example is the Motorola MC6800, which operated in 8-bit format (Figure 3.32). Its organization can be compared to the preceding single bus approach. Also note that, for performance reasons, the ports on each register are bidirectional, contrary to those in the preceding figure. The address bus was cut in two to make internal transfers independent (Bennett *et al.* 1977) but logically still only form one bus.

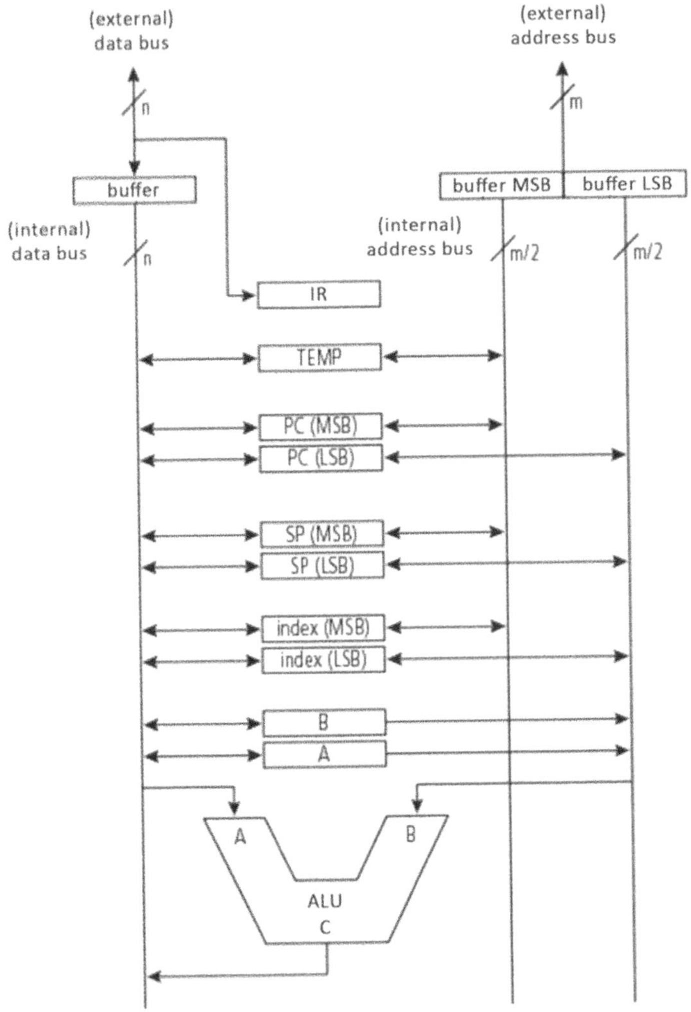

Figure 3.32. *Internal functional organization of the Motorola MC6800 microprocessor with double internal bus data path*

Another example is the PACE MPU from NS, whose structure is shown in Figure 3.33. Contrary to the preceding example, one of the internal buses is extended externally via a multiplexed address/data bus. Several 8-bit accumulators AC_i ($i \in [0, 3]$) make it possible to increase the locality of computations. Note the presence of a 10-word capacity stack whose full or empty status can be detected and indicated via interrupt (*cf.* Chapter V4-5).

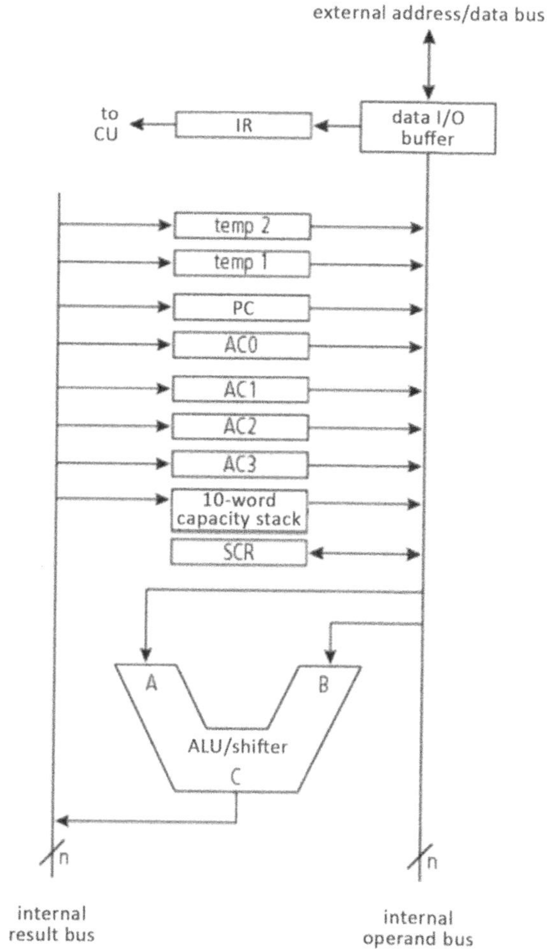

Figure 3.33. *Functional internal organization of the PACE microprocessor from NS with a double internal bus data path*

Figure 3.34 presents a three-bus architecture. Its value lies in its ability to transfer operands and the result of a dyadic operation in a single instruction cycle.

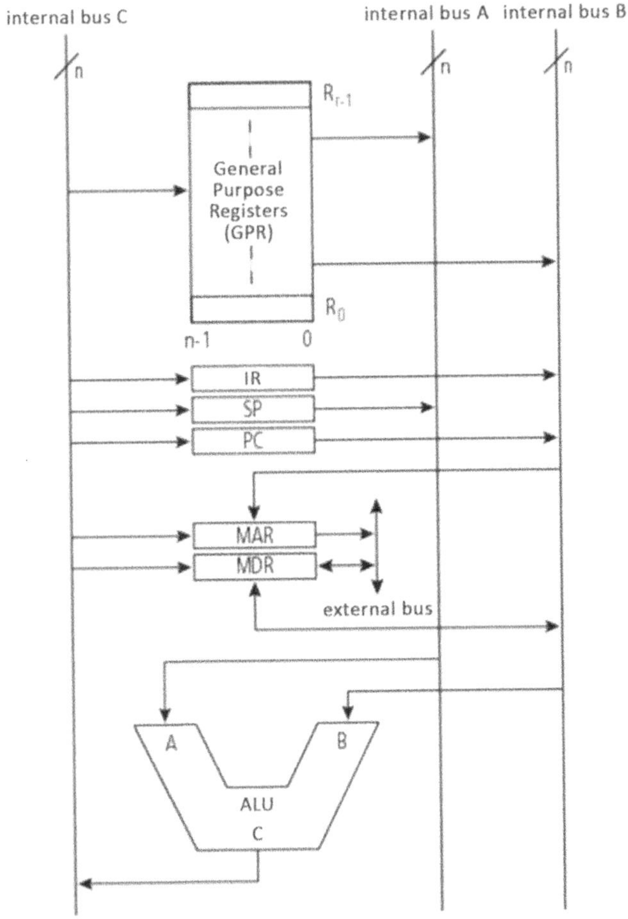

Figure 3.34. *Internal three-bus organization (CU and control signals not shown)*

The number of buses will have an effect on the ability to simultaneously address operands and the storage location of the result during execution of an instruction, and therefore its syntax and encoding (*cf.* Chapter V4-1). A study on these different kinds of buses can be found in Tseng and Siewiorek (1981, 1982). Section 3.5.1 shows the different types of addressing depending on the number of buses.

3.4.2. *Harvard architectures*

To avoid bottlenecks, the Harvard Mark I computer (1944) stored code and data in two distinct memories that operated independently (Figure 3.35). Each possesses its own communication path (i.e. bus). Access conflicts are thus avoided. Parallelism is intrinsic to this model. A consequence is that a given address will correspond to several storage locations, each belonging to separate address spaces. The name of the university was applied to this architecture. The Harvard architecture therefore predates the von Neumann architecture. Instruction memory is read-only, while data memory is read-write. The bus size, particularly in terms of addresses, cannot be equal.

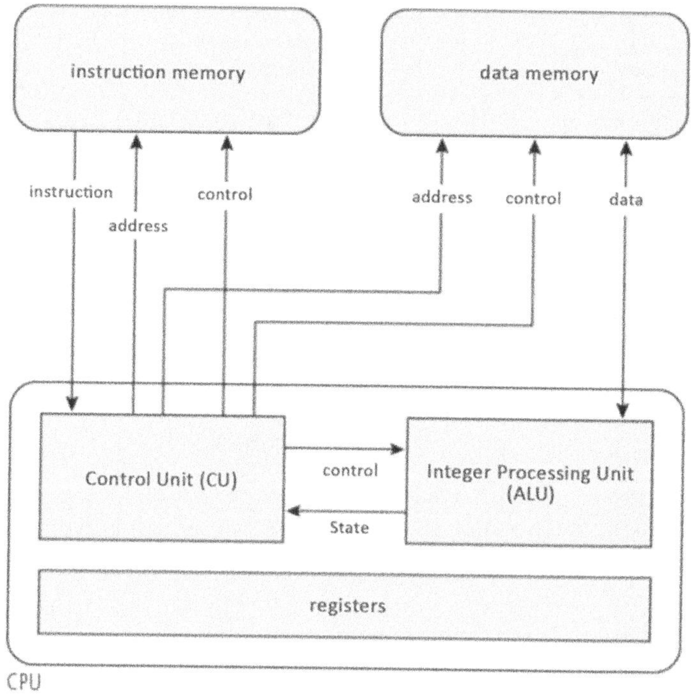

Figure 3.35. *Pure Harvard architecture*

Several versions were subsequently proposed. The modern variants gathered under the "modified Harvard architecture" umbrella are a mix of von Neumann and Harvard architectures. The x86 family is a commercial example. As shown in Figure 3.36, we see the former's unified memory, as well as specialized memory closer to the processor to improve flow rate with cache memory for specialized contents (split cache). In relation to the original model, address zero refers to a single memory cell in the unified memory containing instructions and data, but the communication buses are separated for the caches.

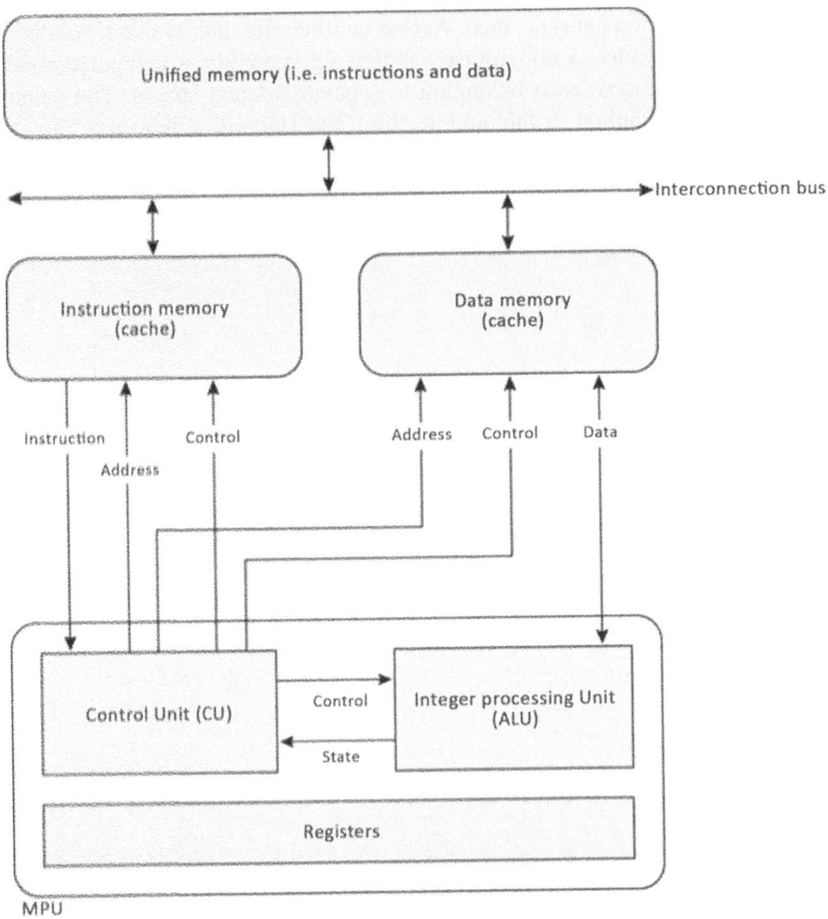

Figure 3.36. *Example of a modified Harvard architecture (x86 family)*

Microprocessors specialized for digital signal processing (DSP) and microcontrollers (MCU for MicroController Unit, *cf.* respectively § V3-1.1 and V3-5.3) have preferred to adopt this architecture because it is more efficient for these applications. There will be variations in implementation. An example concerns instruction memory accessible via programming (operation equivalent to a write, but more complex) to be able to store a program (this is the case for flash EEPROM (Electrically Erasable Programmable ROM) memory). We should also mention microcontrollers from the Maxim MAXQ® family, which can fetch an instruction in any type of memory. The Atmel AVR family, for example, can read or write constants in instruction memory thanks to specialized instructions such as `lpm` (Load Program Memory) or `spm` (Store Program Memory). Figure 3.37 shows the data path with, on the dotted line, an additional path that makes it possible to read data, which will be constants in the case of non-volatile memory (i.e. ROM) in instruction memory for the SHARC® architecture. This architecture integrates an instruction cache that is not shown. This variant is called the super-Harvard architecture, which uses (at least) two memory banks for data. This provides a first memory reserved for programs and the remainder for data. This makes it possible to parallelize signal processing instructions such as `MAC (multiply-and-accumulate)`, because two simultaneous accesses to operands for the computation are possible.

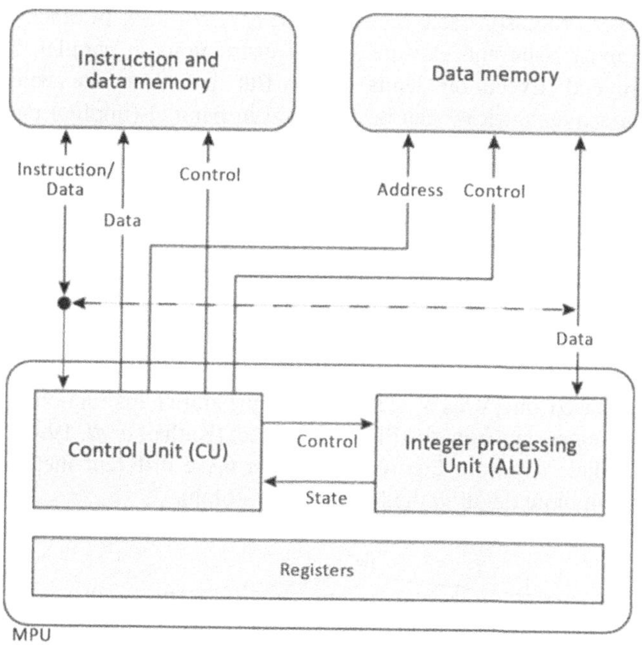

Figure 3.37. *Simplified architecture of a SPARC® family processor*

3.4.3. *Parallelism*

To speed up sequential computation in von Neumann machines, it was necessary to move to parallelization. There are several types of parallelism at the level of instructions or data. As a first look, we discuss parallelism at the instruction level, among activity threads or the cores. An example of data parallelism is vector-based architecture (*cf.* § V4-2.7.1).

NOTE.– This section is illustrated by the MPU examples in § V3-4.7.

3.4.3.1. *Instruction-level parallelism*

Instruction-Level Parallelism (ILP) brings together design techniques from other families of processors and compilers to overcome sequential execution. The first research along these lines dates to the end of the 1960s – beginning of the 1970s (Jouppi 1989). These techniques first appeared in microprocessors in the 1980s to speed up execution of instructions, particularly those related to transfers between the CPU and main memory (and vice versa) and to arithmetic computation with integer and floating-point numbers. Improving performance requires executing more than one Instruction Per Processor cycle (i.e. IPC > 1, *cf.* § V4-3.4). In other words, the microprocessor must issue and execute several instructions in parallel. There will therefore be several Execution Units (EU). But how can we detect which instructions in a sequential flow can be executed in parallel (implicit parallelism), and where should this detection take place? Looking over the development and execution chain, two candidates come to mind. They are the compiler and the microprocessor. In the former case, the compiler will detect a potential parallel between instructions. In the latter case, the microprocessor will do this dynamically. Two conflicting schools exist for controlling these execution units. They are distinguished by the type of control, dynamic or static, of these execution units. The former case involves a superscalar approach, and the latter uses (Very) Long Instruction Word ((V)LIW) and Transport Triggered Architecture (TTA, Corporaal 1995), which is based on (V)LIW. The Explicitly Parallel Instruction Computing (EPIC) approach, emerging from the PlayDoh project (Kathail *et al.* 1993, 2000) is a potential intermediate solution. Figure 3.38 shows these different methods, which will be described in more detail in the forthcoming Volume 2.

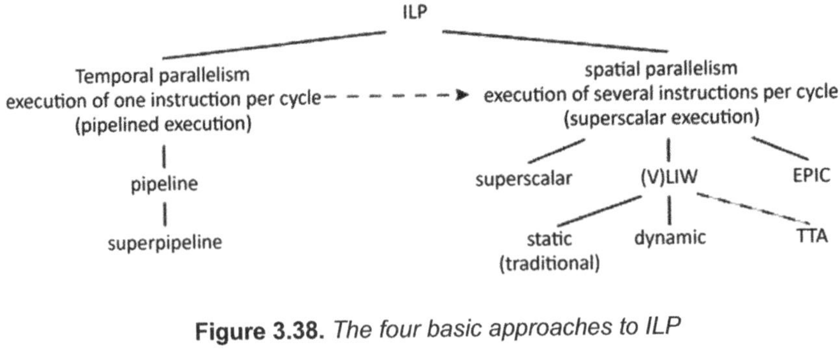

Figure 3.38. *The four basic approaches to ILP*

Architectures are classified based on a variety of criteria. The first was to consider the instruction set. Thus, there are CISC and RISC type architectures. CISC stands for Complex Instruction Set Computer. Two historical representatives are the System/360 (Amdahl *et al.* 1964) and VAX (Levy and Eckhouse 1989) architectures. RISC stands for Reduced Instruction-Set Computer (*cf.* V2, forthcoming). The convergence of the two forms has led to the modern version of processors, called CRISC for Complex-Reduced ISC. To speed up execution, the Very Long Instruction Word (VLIW) architecture and its descendant, the EPIC architecture, gathers together several instruction fields per instruction word. As an illustration, we can mention the ISA, with a minimal number of instructions, or MISC (Minimal ISC) with an instruction (OISC for One ISC, also referred to as SISC for Single ISC[18] (Azaria and Tabak 1983), or URISC for Ultimate RISC (Mavaddat and Parhami 1988)) and finally the ultimate solution with ZISC (Zero Instruction Set Computer, Lindblad *et al.* 1995), which is a neuronal co-processor from IBM. We will conclude by mentioning WISC (Writable ISC), a theoretical processor from Koopman (1987a, 187b) and NISC (No ISC) from Gajski (2003, 2005).

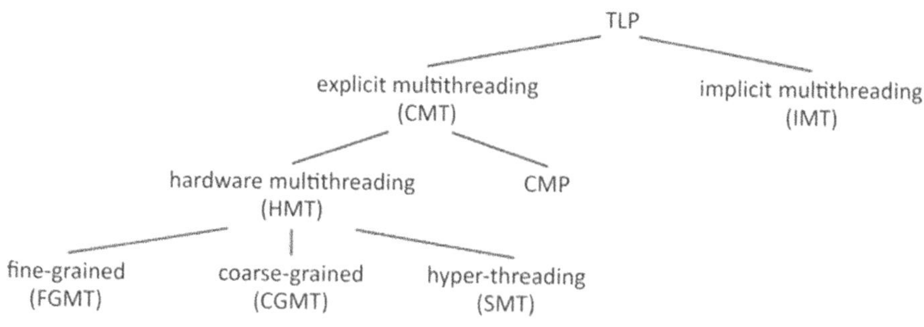

Figure 3.39. *Simplified classification of TLP architectures*

3.4.3.2. *Thread level*

After increasing the frequency of the processor's clock and having taken advantage of parallelism at the cycle level (ILP) with the pipeline and superscalar approaches such as VLIW or EPIC, Thread-Level Parallelism (TLP) was proposed, which is also referred to as multithreaded parallelism. It breaks down along the lines of two approaches, explicit or CMT (Chip MultiThreading) and implicit. The former is further divided into Hardware MultiThreading (HMT) and Chip MultiProcessing (CMP). Finally, hardware multithreading can be very Fine-Grained (FGMT) or

18 This should not be confused with Special ISC (*cf.* § V2-9.2), or, in the case of the illustration, Small ISC!

Coarse-Grained (CGMT), or in the form of hyperthreading. Originally called Simultaneous parallel MultiThreading (SMT) by its inventors (Tullsen *et al.* 1995, 1996), hyper-threading consists of transforming parallelism at the activity thread level into parallelism at the instruction level. With the Implicit MultiThreading (IMT) approach, threads are generated implicitly by the hardware or the compiler.

3.4.3.3. *Multicore architectures*

Figure 3.40 shows the evolution of the clock frequency over time (middle curve). It stopped increasing after 2005 because of power dissipation problems (second curve). This led to the stagnation of computation power (fourth curve). Knowing that the number of integrated transistors on a chip continues to increase (last curve), commercial producers began to increase the number of processors or cores (first curve).

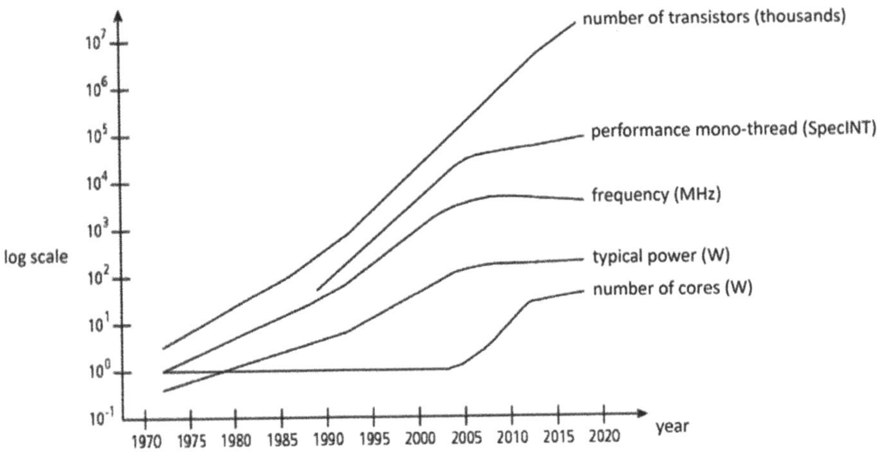

Figure 3.40. *Variation of characteristics over time (based on (Leavitt 2012))*

A multicore microprocessor or (S)CMP ((Single) Chip Multiprocessor) is made up of several independent cores gathered on the same chip (die). We speak of dual-core, quad-core, etc. The first multicore microprocessor was the IBM Power 4 (Tendler *et al.* 2002). When their number exceeds several hundred or even a thousand cores, we must speak of many-core and massively multi-core approaches (Borkar 2007).

Each core is a modern, pipelined, even superscalar microprocessor, with several levels of cache. All the cores, on the other hand, share the last level of cache and the external interface. Since 2010, chips have integrated a GPU (Graphics Processing Unit) and a memory controller. Figure 3.41 illustrates our point with an example of a component, here a second-generation Intel® Core™ i7 microprocessor manufactured in 32 nm engraving technology and clocked at 3.4 GHz.

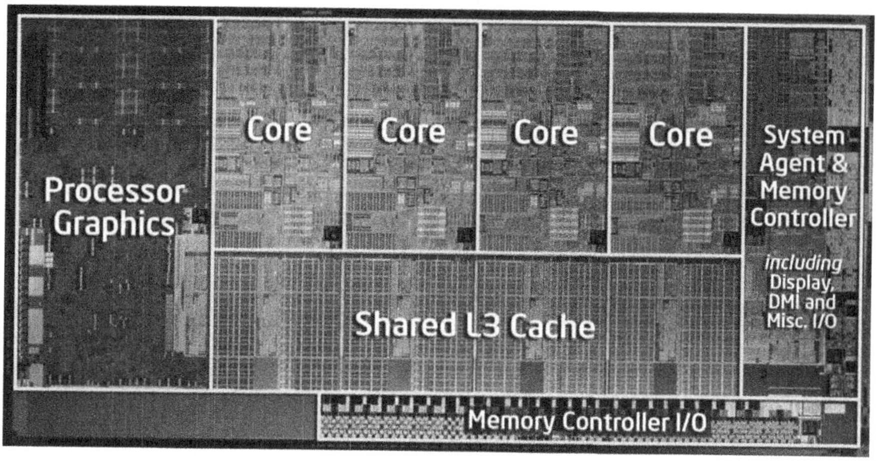

Figure 3.41. *Microphotograph of an Intel Sandy Bridge quad-core i7 (source: Intel 2011). For a color version of this figure, see www.iste.co.uk/darche/microprocessor1.zip*

A multi-core chip can be symmetric or asymmetric. SMP stands for Symmetric (shared memory) MultiProcessing. In the first category, the cores can be identical (homogeneous cores approach). For the second category, also called the heterogeneous cores approach, one or more of the cores is more powerful than the others.

3.5. Instruction set architecture

Abbreviated as ISA, this refers to the architecture of the processor seen by the programmer (in the sense of Figure 3.4(a)). It is the interface between software and hardware, providing only the hardware details necessary for programming and compilation. The architecture exposes a common, or at least ascending, set of instructions. Hence, commercial producers also call it the programmer model, since it primarily refers to the processor's instruction set. It is an abstract view of the hardware. The ISA was initially relevant to a family of machines of a given class, then to a single processor and, finally, to a family of processors. Two examples from the first category are, for mainframe computers, the IBM System/360 and System/370 lines and, for minicomputers, the PDP and VAX lines from Digital

Equipment Corporation (DEC), and in the case where a series of machines have upward software compatibility (*cf.* § V4-3.3.2 and 3.3.3). The first microprocessors had their own ISA[19]. Then, Intel successively created the evolution of the x86 architecture (Intel 1989), the IA-32 (Intel 2003) and the Intel 64 (Intel 2017). We should also mention the RISC-based Arm® instruction set architecture (Arm 2019), implemented in the MIPS32 (MIPS 2001a) and the MIPS64 (MIPS 2001b), the PowerPC (IBM 2017) and the SPARC (Weaver and Germond 1994).

The ISA primarily defines the Instruction Set (IS). This set will constitute the target language for a compiler. However, it also specifies the architecture of the processor by specifying the storage components, data format, (memory) model, processor execution modes and hardware and software interrupt model.

3.5.1. *Storage components*

The potential information storage components are the General-Purpose Register (GPR, *cf.* § V3-3.1), the main memory and the stack (based on registers or in main memory, *cf.* § V4-4.1). A way to classify ISAs is to use as criteria the locations for storing the operands (explicit) and the result. Thus, five classes can be defined (Figure 3.42), which are the stack, accumulator, register-memory, register-register or load-store architecture and memory-to-memory. Each class will have a number of internal buses.

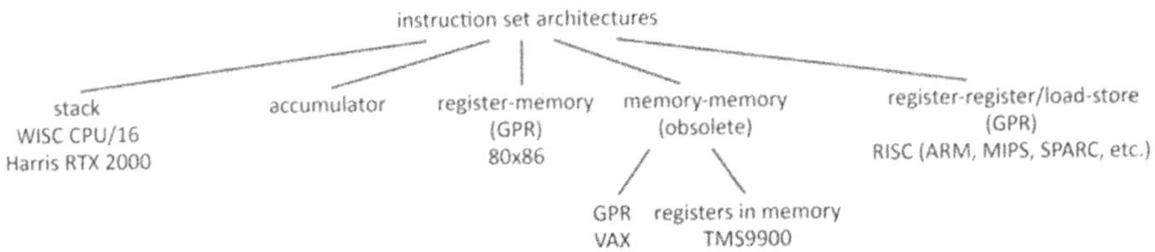

Figure 3.42. *Classes of instruction set architectures with examples*

From the programming point of view, each class corresponds to a pair (o, a) with maximum number of operands o and number of memory references a, as shown in Table 3.5. The number of internal buses will vary depending on the class.

19 With a few exceptions such as the Intel 8080 with the Zilog Z80 or the Motorola MC680X (X = 0, 2 or 9).

ISA classes	Maximum number of operands o	Number of memory addresses a	Examples	Types
Stack	0	0 (Implicit address)	Transputer	Stack
Accumulator	1	1	Intel 8080, Motorola MC680x	CISC
Register-memory	2	1	IBM System/360 and System/370, Intel 80x86, Motorola MC68000, TI TMS320C54x	CISC
Memory-memory	2	2	VAX	CISC
Load/store (register-register)	3	0	MIPS, SPARC, PowerPC, Arm®, Alpha, SuperH	RISC
Memory-memory	3	3	VAX-11®	CISC

Table 3.5. *Characteristics of architecture classes (according to Hennessy and Patterson (2007) modified)*

The stack or pushdown-store architecture works only with LIFO access memory (Last-In, First-Out, *cf.* § V4-4.1). The stack management primitives are the `push pop` instructions. We also speak of a 0-address or zero operand machine. The location of the operands is implied. They should always be at the top of the stack, as shown in Figure 3.43. The operation uses them by popping them off the stack, and the result is implicitly stored on the top of the stack. A sample program is given below. The M_i ($i \in [1, 3]$) are the locations in memory. The add statement only uses implicit operands[20] stored in the stack. Assuming that, with each access of the stack, a push or pop is carried out depending on the type of access, a series of instructions for an addition could be:

`push M1`; stack ← M1
`push M2`; stack ← M2
`add`; stack ← stack + stack

20 The semantics of the term "operand" of an operation is, in this case, Assembly Language (AL); in other words, the operand specified after the mnemonic (i.e. abridged instruction, *cf.* § V4-2.1). This references either a "traditional" operand (i.e. the value used for the computation (mathematical definition)) or a result.

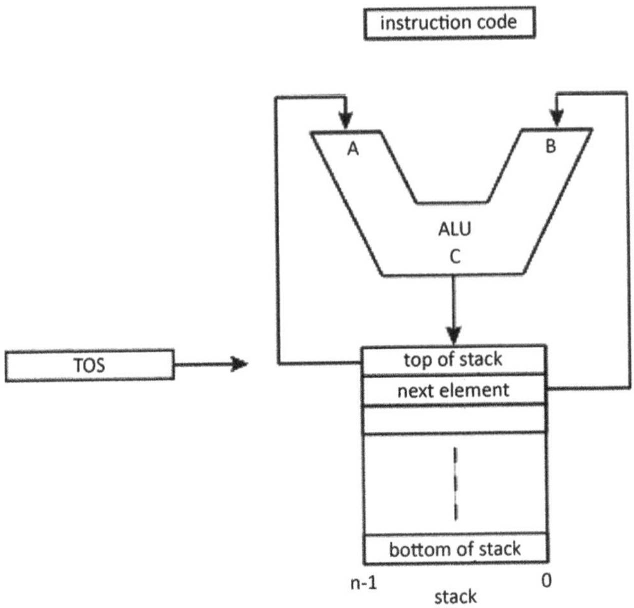

Figure 3.43. *Zero-address stack architecture (from Nurmi (2007), modified)*

Variants can use one operand with reference (one-operand instruction) and another on the stack or two operands with reference with the storage of the result on the stack (Koopman 1989). The code is thus more concise. In the following example, an address field is added to the operation, and the storage of the result on the top of the stack is implicit.

`push M1`; stack ← M1
`add M2`; stack ← stack + M2

We should mention two pioneering machines, the KDF9 from English Electric (Lavington 1980) and the Burroughs B5000. For pocket calculators, we can point to the HP35, which used the modified post-fixed notation also called Reverse Polish Notation (RPN), which was invented by the philosopher Jan Lukasiewicz. Koopman (1989) studied this architecture.

The accumulator architecture was presented earlier. In this architecture, an operand is implicitly stored in the accumulator. There is at most one access to main memory (Figure 3.44). For a dyadic function, the use of an implicit work register will imply the presence of a single address (case of the Whirlwind computer) in the coding of the instruction. A sample program is given below. It should be noted that access to the operand M1 is implicit for the addition instruction.

```
load M1; Acc ← M1
add M2; Acc ← Acc + M2
store M3; M3 ← Acc
```

The only purpose is to limit the instruction size. The IAS was one of the first machines with one address. Another example was the ICL 2900 central computer (Buckle 1978). An example of a machine (on paper) with one address was the MARIE (Machine Architecture that is Really Intuitive and Easy) from Null and Lobur (2003).

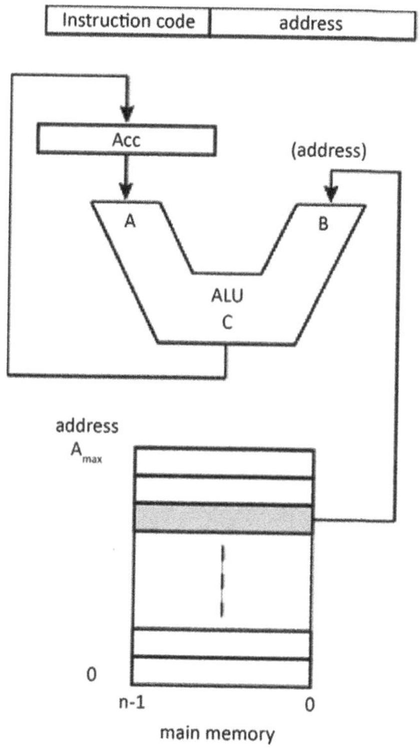

Figure 3.44. *One-address architecture, with accumulator (from (Nurmi 2007), modified)*

In a machine with two memory addresses, the instructions have two reference fields for the operands. Examples of implementation include the IBM System/360 and /370 families and the UNIVAC Solid State computer. We must mention the notion of the one-and-a-half address computer with, for the two-operand instructions, a memory reference and another for a register (hence the 0.5 by memory address space) or a constant. Two examples are the PDP-6 and PDP-10 minicomputers (Bell 1978). The x86 architecture also falls into this category. From a historical point of view, Reilly (2003) includes in this category the pioneering computers with cylindrical memory (drum-based computers), which specified address of the next instruction in the previous one.

In a GPR-type architecture, all or some of the operands are preferably stored in registers for general use to speed up the execution time. An example implementation is the VAX-11® from DEC. The variants are the load-store architecture, register-(to-)memory and memory-(to-)memory. With load-store, also called register-register, there are no instruction operand(s) in memory (Figure 3.45). RISC microprocessors like the Arm® family from the company of the same name are representatives of load-store architecture. In the register-memory variant, at least one operand is in a register.

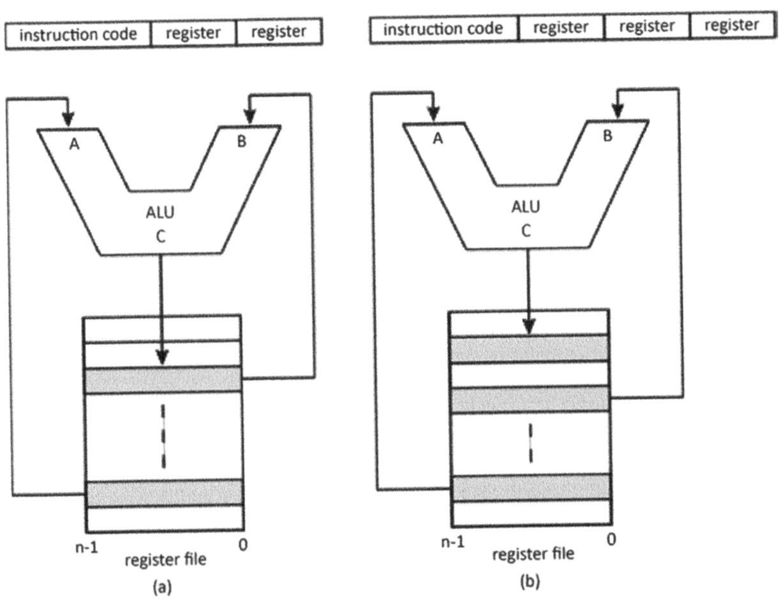

Figure 3.45. *Architecture with two (a) and three (b) register references (from Nurmi (2007), modified)*

In a register-register architecture, only the `load` and `store` instructions access the memory to (un)load the registers containing the operands and the result of computation. The other instructions only use the registers as memory to improve access time. Execution time is therefore very short and is the same for all instructions. The use of registers leads to simplified instruction encoding (*cf.* § V4-1.1). Their size is fixed and small. The counterpart is a longer program length. The RISC approach is an example of this architecture. A sample program is given below. It should be noted that the references to the operands and, here, to the result are explicit.

load R1, M1; R1 ← M1
load R2, M2; R2 ← M2
add R3, R1, R2; R3 ← R1 + R2
store M3, R3; M3 ← R3

One advantage of a register-memory architecture is not having to fetch an operand in memory (which would require an additional instruction). It generalizes the accumulator architecture. Block transfer is therefore not suitable without adapting the architecture (*cf.* § V4-2.8.1). In addition, for the sake of reducing the instruction size, the number of registers is generally low (ten is the order of magnitude) to have a wide address field. The execution time for an instruction also varies depending on the location of the operands. In the version in Figure 3.46(a), the operands are not equivalent in the case of a binary operation (i.e. with two operands). Indeed, the destination operand (the one on the left in the case of an MPU in the x86 family) is destroyed by the result of the computation, as this sequence of instructions shows:

move R1, M1; R1 ← M1
add R1, M2; R1 ← R1 + M2
move M3, R1; M3 ← R1

An example program in relation to Figure 3.46(b) is given below. It should be noted that the references to the operands and to the result are explicit.

load R1, M1; R1 ← M1
add R3, R1, M2; R3 ← R1 + M2
store M3, R3; M3 ← R3

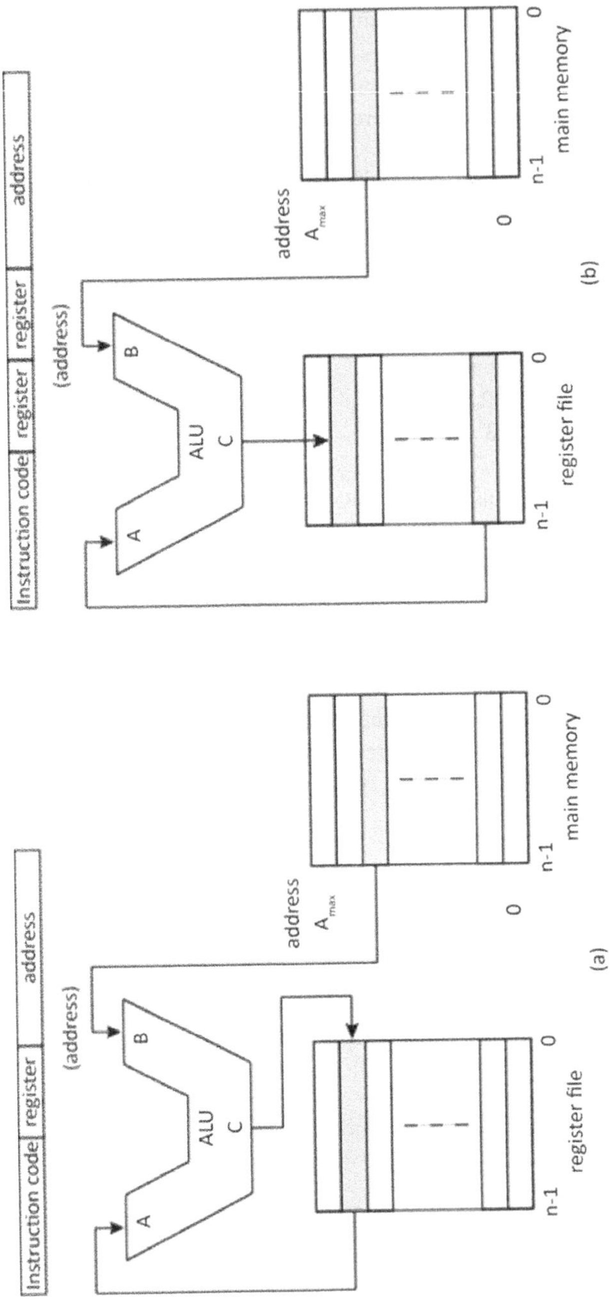

Figure 3.46. *Memory-register architectures (from Nurmi (2007), modified*

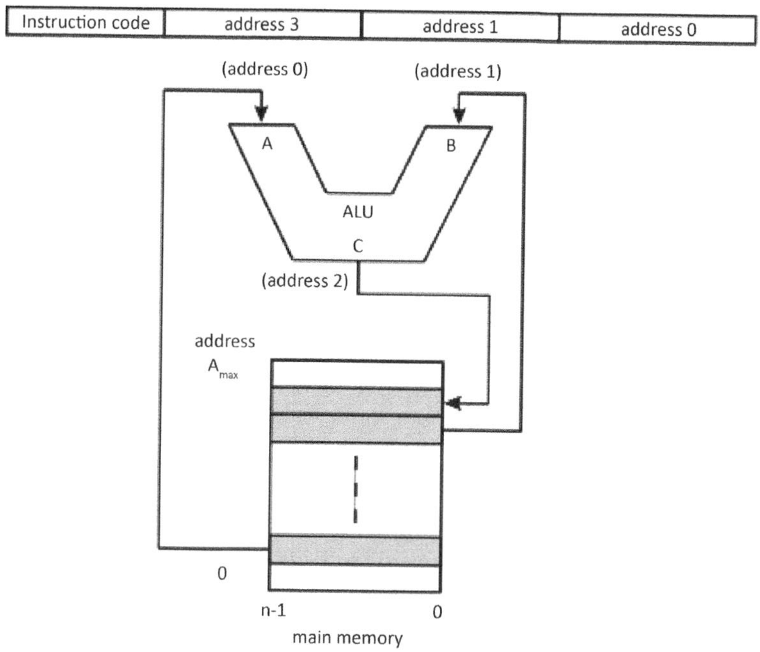

Figure 3.47. *Three-address architecture (from Nurmi (2007), modified*

In memory-memory architecture, all operands are in memory (Figure 3.47). An instruction references at most three operands in memory. The instruction size is therefore large and variable depending on the addressing mode. In a machine with three addresses, there are two buses for the source operands (source buses A and B) and one for the result. The advantage is that this decreases the number of internal cycles by increasing the parallelism linked to the transfer. An example of these machines is the CDC 6600/6700 family (i.e. CYBER 70 model 76). A code example for a hypothetical machine would be:

`add M3, M2, M1`; M3 ← M1 + M2

One notable exception is the IBM 650, where the second address pointed to the next instruction (IBM 1955; Knuth 1986). Three or four addresses with a pointer to the next instruction are the last two variants, an example being the SEAC (Standards Electronic Automatic Computer, Greenwald *et al.* 1953).

The distinctive TMS9900 microprocessor from Texas Instruments (TI 1976) is an example of a memory-memory architecture with user registers installed in main memory. A WP (Workspace Pointer) points to a bank of 16 register words serving as registers. The value lies in the speed of context change (*cf.* § V4-4.2.2) since one only needs to change the value of WP. The last three locations (registers 13:15) are used to save the three unique internal registers accessible to the programmer, which are SC for the return address, the status register (ST) and WP. Therefore, there is no need for a stack. It is no longer used for performance reasons, since main memory has a much higher latency than a register (by a factor of about 30). This architecture has an inherent bottleneck because everything happens in memory. It was therefore abandoned. In addition, access to memory compared to a register is time-consuming.

For reference, EDVAC (Gluck 1953) was a four-address machine.

3.5.2. *Data format and type*

ISA characterizes the type of data (natural or relative integers, floating-point numbers, numbers in BCD, alphanumeric data, character strings, etc.), the size and the associated vocabulary. A 64-bit processor will handle integers in 8 (byte), 16 (halfword), 32 (word) 64 (doubleword) and 128 (quadword) formats. If it has a computation unit for floating-point numbers, then it will manipulate basic scalar data or, for more modern components, vector data (*cf.* § V4-2.7.1).

3.5.3. *Instruction set*

Defining an instruction set consists of defining the operations, the format of the instructions, their coding (code operation) and their addressing modes (*cf.* § V4-1.2), and the number, type and size of the explicit operands. The instructions are classified in families (*cf.* § V4-2.1). Several instruction sets, generally inclusive, can exist for the same architecture. An IS is generally fixed, but it can be dynamic on demand (DISC for Dynamic Instruction Set Computer) by reprogramming, for example, an FPGA (Field-Programmable Gate Array, *cf.* § 4.3.2 in Darche (2004)) as proposed by Wirthlin and Hutchings (1995). The definition of the instructions takes place at the assembly language level, with the mnemonic (i.e. short name, *cf.* § V4-2.1), its semantics, the syntax of the instructions, the methods of addressing the operands and the result. The instruction size defines the total width (i.e. the number of bits) and the different fields of the instruction code. This size can be fixed or variable (*cf.* § V4-1.1). Historically, the IAS handled two instructions per address, and the IBM 701 only one, which has become the standard today except for special architectures such as Very Long Instruction Word (*cf.* V2). Chapter 5 presents all these aspects.

3.5.3.1. *Properties*

An instruction set has properties. Orthogonality expresses the independence of the instructions from the types of data. It is linked to the notions of completeness and consistency. Completeness is the fact that each type of data has a full set of operations. The consistency of an instruction set characterizes the degree of availability of an instruction set for the different types of data. Weak consistency would mean that the add statement is provided but subtraction is not for a given data type.

Another property is symmetry. An instruction set is said to be symmetric if any instruction can use any addressing mode and any register. This can also apply to data formats and types or to the updating of flags. Variations in the definition are acceptable. Vajda (1986) talks about independence between instructions, data types and addressing modes. A first example is the VAX, whose instructions were independent of the addressing modes. Another example is the fact that mathematical exceptions are thrown transparently without specialized instructions. This simplifies the hardware and, in particular, the life of the system programmer!

A final property is the simplicity of the instruction set. The architecture that best illustrates this is called RISC (*cf.* V2, forthcoming). The purpose of this architecture was to accelerate computation speed by choosing the most frequently used instructions and optimizing their execution.

All these concepts are detailed in § V4-3.1.3.

3.5.4. *Memory model*

The (memory) model specifies the order in which bits and bytes are stored in memory (i.e. little and big-endian orders, *cf.* § 2.6.2 in Darche (2012)). It also indicates the access unit. For example, Intel's x86 MPU architecture uses byte addressing. It specifies whether the information should be aligned to the word and the behavior in the event of unaligned memory access.

Unaligned access will generally cause an exception or slow execution (case of the x86 family). For the most powerful architectures, it describes virtual memory with address translation from logical memory to physical memory, memory protection, cache management and synchronization of access to memory shared by several PEs (Processing Element).

3.5.5. *Execution modes*

As the processor executes at least two processor execution modes (i.e. supervisor and user, *cf.* § V4-3.2.2), there will be two ISA specifications, the application level programmers' model and the system level programmers' model. Each will have its own instruction set or, more exactly, the supervisor (or system) mode will include the other set. A mode can also have, for reasons of upward compatibility (*cf.* § V4-3.3.3), sub-modes linked to the data format. We can point to, for example, the AArch64 and AArch32 modes of the Arm® family (Arm 2019). The consequences will also relate to the other elements of the ISA such as storage and the (memory) model.

3.5.6. *Miscellaneous*

The interrupt model specifies the types of interrupts. It details the request mechanism, where the interrupt vectors are located and how the contextual backup/restore process takes place. This mechanism is explained in detail in V4-5. More generally, ISA defines the data structures specific to an SE such as descriptor tables (examples from Intel include GDT for Global Descriptor Table, LDT for Local Descriptor Table and IDT for Interrupt Descriptor Table), page tables or process control blocks.

3.6. Basic definitions for this book

This section is dedicated to the basic definitions that apply to this book. A processor (hardware) is a programmable functional unit composed of at least one Control Unit (per instruction) and one Integer Processing Unit (IPU). The control unit is responsible for fetching the instructions and the associated operands of a program from main memory, for decoding them and for generating the control flow for the processing unit, which is responsible for execution (definition ISO/IEC 2382-1: 1993 extended). It has its own storage area, a basic one in the form of registers or an advanced one in the form of a cache for the most powerful processors. The integer processing unit or IU (Integer Unit) is a computation unit dedicated to processing integers (*cf.* § 2.5 in Darche (2000)), signed as the 2^n's complement or not as natural binary or BCD (Binary Coded Decimal). The GPRs (*cf.* § V3-3.1.1) enable storage of the operands. They can be grouped in the form of a bank (register file, bank of registers). This is referred to as multi-port memory. Registers dedicated to management (i.e. specialized registers, see § V3-3.1.1) maintain the state of the processor. In general, the processor is generally dedicated to computation. It can also be dedicated to a function or a domain such as I/O. We speak of I/O Processors (IOP). It will then have registers of the CSR type (Control and Status Register, *cf.* § 2.2.1 in Darche (2003) and § 3.8). Hardware accelerators such as a computation unit dedicated to the processing of real numbers in standardized fixed and floating-point representations (*cf.* §4 in Darche (2000)) or an FPU (Floating-Point Unit) or any other co-processor (CP for CoProcessor) can be added to it. The microprocessor, the microcontroller or the DSP are examples of processors as "discrete components". More generally, a computation element, that is, a processor, will be designated by PE (Processing Element) or, preferably, PU (Processing Unit). A (central) computing unit or (C)PU ((central) processing unit) or central processor is a functional unit that contains one (uniprocessor) or several processors (multiprocessor). The integrated version is the microprocessor, which is the central unit of the microcomputer. We also speak of a "MicroProcessing Unit" (MPU). The microprocessor is at the origin of the microcomputer[21] or C and its industry.

To facilitate the modeling of architectures, it may be useful to define generic entities. A processor consists of one or more computation elements or PE. A PE is the entity that performs computations. It consists of several functional units including the CU and the IPU. For microprocessors, a PE is equivalent to a core. Associated with this PE, there is the Memory Element (ME) and the Communication Element (CE). In a generic parallel architecture, a processing node is made up of several processors and, depending on the model, local memory.

3.7. Conclusion

In this chapter, we have defined the fundamental concepts, computational model and architecture of a computer. A computational model is a high-level abstraction that explains how computations are performed. We have more specifically described the control flow computation model, which uses a data by reference mechanism to access shared memory cells. The control mechanism is originally sequential with a single control thread passed from instruction to instruction. However, the mechanism can be parallelized (*cf.* Farrell *et al.* 1979; Hopkins *et al.* 1979). The dataflow computation model has a data by value mechanism and a parallel control mechanism. This means that the data is passed directly to the instructions and that, as before, the literals are stored with the instruction code. The runtime consumes the data tokens, which can no longer be reused.

Computer design can be broken down into three levels: the study of behavior – the functional aspect of computers; its organization – the structural aspect; and its implementation in a given technology. In modern vocabulary, these three levels are respectively called the architecture of the instruction set or ISA, the microarchitecture and implementation. ISA refers to the architecture of the processor

21 Computer whose central unit is made up of at least one microprocessor.

as seen by the programmer. Microarchitecture refers to the operational units and their interactions (i.e. relationship), which implement the architecture specifications.

We then illustrated the concepts of computational model and architecture with the so-called von Neumann approach. A computer following the latter has a sequential control flow. It executes a program, an ordered sequence of instructions, stored in main memory. Each of these instructions can be followed by one or more operands, which can be a literal datum, an address referencing it, or the reference to a register or a target (instruction) address during a disconnection (*cf.* § V4-2.4). The binary word representing the instruction has a variable or fixed format depending on the ISA.

Conclusion of Volume 1

The microprocessor is at the heart of current digital systems. This programmable logic component sequentially executes the instructions of a program stored in main memory. This first introductory volume to the field presented the basic concepts of how a computer works.

The introduction presented the different technologies that make up computers: mechanics, electromechanics and electronics. With regard to the latter, the different generations have been described according to their technologies. A classification of families of computers was then proposed. The analog approach has not been forgotten, and this chapter has ended with the integration of components in microelectronics and its limits.

A review of the function of storage and of former and current technologies was made in the second chapter. Associated concepts such as information storage order and alignment were then discussed. Finally, modeling and classification were proposed.

In the third chapter, the fundamental concepts, computational model and architecture of a computer have been defined. A computational model is a high-level abstraction that explains how computations are performed. We have more specifically described the computation model with control flow and data flow. The architectural aspect is then addressed. Computer design can be broken down into three levels: the study of behavior – the functional aspect of computers; its organization – the structural aspect; and its implementation in a given technology. In modern vocabulary, these three levels are known respectively as Instruction Set Architecture (ISA), microarchitecture and implementation. ISA refers to the architecture of the processor as seen by the programmer. Microarchitecture refers to the operational units and their interaction (i.e. relationship), which meets the specifications of the architecture. The notions of computational model and architecture were then illustrated with the so-called von Neumann approach. A computer following the latter has a sequential control flow. It executes a program, an ordered sequence of instructions, stored in main memory. Each of these instructions can be followed by one or more operands, which can be a literal datum, an address referencing it or the reference to a register or a target (instruction) address during a transfer of control, that is, during a break in the instruction flow.

The following volume is devoted to the communication features of digital systems.

Exercises

Here are some exercises that complement the concepts presented in this book. Their numbering refers to the chapter with which they are associated.

Chapter 1. Exercises

E1.1. The notion of a complement is used in machine arithmetic to implement subtraction. There are two types, which are the true and restricted complements denoted respectively ^ and ¯. They were studied in § 4.2 of Darche (2000). Show that it is possible to subtract by using addition.

Answer. For the limited complement, a good example is the Pascaline (Figure 1.4). The method is as follows:

$$S = A - B = (10^n - 1) - (10^n - 1 - A + B) = (10^n - 1) - S' = \bar{S'} \quad [1.3]$$

$$with\, S' = \bar{A} + B$$

Another approach is formula [1.4], more restrictive because it is necessary to increment the result at the end of addition.

$$A - B = A + (10^n - 1 - B) + 1 \qquad [1.4]$$

Take an example of size n = 3. Let S = A - B = 704 - 196 = 508. We have:

$$\bar{A} = 999 - 704 = 295$$

$$S' = \bar{A} + B = 295 + 196 = 491$$

$$S = \overline{S'} = 999 - 491 = 508$$

If we now consider the representation in addition to 2^n, we must use the following formula:

$$\hat{A}_B = B^n - A_B = (B^n - 1) - A_B + 1 = \bar{A}_B + 1 \quad [1.5]$$

Let us use the previous example. Let S = A - B = 704 - 196 = 508, we have:

$$\bar{B} = 999 - 196 = 803$$

$$S = A - B = A + (-B) = A + \hat{B} = 704 + 803 + 1$$
$$= 1508 \text{ (= 508 if the value is truncated in the n = 3 digit format)}$$

Chapter 3. Exercises

E3.1. What is the major difference between the von Neumann and Harvard architectures?

Answer. The von Neumann architecture (*cf.* § 3.2.2) has a unified memory. This means that the instructions and the data are stored in a single memory. The Harvard architecture (*cf.* § 3.4.2) stores them in two separate memories (memory with specialized content).

E3.2. To which internal operation is the comparison reduced (`comp` operator)?

Answer.

$$A \text{ comp B} \Leftrightarrow A - B \text{ comp } 0 \quad [3.2]$$

This relation means that the comparison operation (<,>, = and combinations of these) is reduced to a subtraction and a comparison with respect to zero. This justifies the presence of the binary indicators (flags) ZF, SF, CF and OF in the status register (*cf.* § V3-3.1.5).

Acronyms

This section includes all of the acronyms used in this volume. They will be introduced once per chapter.

General

A

A	Address
ABC	Atanasoff–Berry Computer
Ac or Acc	Accumulator register
AL	Assembly Language
ALGOL	ALGOrithmic Language
ALU	Arithmetic and Logic Unit
AR	Arithmetic Register
AS/400	Application System/400
ASCC	Automatic Sequence Controlled Calculator (IBM)
ASIC	Application-Specific Integrated Circuit
ASM	Application-Specific Memory
ASP	Application Service Provider

B

b	bit (cf. BIT)
B	Byte
BASIC	Beginner's All-purpose Symbolic Instruction Code
BBSRAM	Battery-Backed SRAM
BCD	Binary Coded Decimal
BE	Big Endian
BiCMOS	Bipolar CMOS
BiE	Bi-Endian
BINAC	BINary Automatic Computer
BIOS	Basic Input/Output System
BIT	BInary digiT or Binary digIT
BJT	Bipolar Junction Transistor

C

CA	Central Arithmetical part or Central Arithmetic logic unit
CAD	Computer-Assisted/Aided Design
CAD	Computer-Assisted/Aided Drawing
CAM	Content-Addressable Memory
CC	Central Control part or unit
CC	Condition Code
CC	Control Counter
CCU	Computer Control Unit
CD	Compact Disk
CD-ROM	CD Read-Only Memory
CE	Chip Enable (cf. CS)
CE	Communication Element
CF	Carry Flag

CFG	Control Flow Graph
CGMT	Coarse-Grained MultiThreading
CISC	Complex Instruction Set Computer
Clk	(input) Clock
CM	Central Memory
CMOS	Complementary MOS
CMP	Chip MultiProcessor
CMP	Chip MultiProcessing
CMT	Chip MultiThreading
CO	COntrol-driven
COBOL	COmmon Business Oriented Language
COTS	Commercial Off-The-Shelf
COW	Cluster of Workstations
CP	CoProcessor
CP	Control Path
CP/M	Control Program for Microcomputers (Digital Research)
CPSD	Cell-Phone-Sized Device
CPU	Central Processing Unit
CR	Control Register
CRISC	Complex-Reduced Instruction Set Computer
CS	Chip Select (cf. CE)
CSP	Communicating Sequential Processes
CSR	Control and Status Register
CU	(Central) Control Unit

D

D	Data
D	Device

DA	DAta-driven
DDF	Dynamic Dataflow
DE	DEmand-driven
DIL	Dual-In-Line
DIP	DIL Package
DISC	Dynamic Instruction Set Computer
DMA	Direct Memory Access
DP	Data Path
DPU	Data Processing Unit
DQ	Data input/output
DR	Data Register
DRAM	Dynamic RAM
DSP	Digital Signal Processor
DTL	Diode–Transistor Logic

E

EAROM	Electrically Alterable ROM, one of the two types of EEPROM
ECC	Error Checking and Correcting/Error-Correcting Code
ECF	Exceptional Control Flow
ECL	Emitter Coupled Logic
EDAC	Error Detection And Correction (cf. ECC)
EDSAC	Electronic Delay Storage Automatic Calculator
EDVAC	Electronic Discrete Variable Automatic Computer
EEPROM	Electrically EPROM
E2PROM	Electrically EPROM
ELSI	Extra LSI (Fujitsu)
ENIAC	Electronic Numerical Integrator And Computer
EPIC	Explicitly Parallel Instruction Computing

EPROM	Erasable PROM
EU	Execution Unit
EX	EXecute phase
EXOR	EXclusive OR (cf. XOR)

F

FD	Floppy Disk
FDD	FD Drive
FDE	Fetch-Decode-Execute cycle
FDX	Fetch-Decode-eXecute cycle
FEEPROM	Flash EEPROM (definition JEDEC – JESD88C)
FET	Field Effect Transistor
FF	Flip-Flop
4GL	4th Generation Languages
FGMT	Fine-Grained MultiThreading
FIFO	First In, First Out
FORTRAN	FORmula TRANslation
FPGA	Field-Programmable Gate Array
FPU	Floating-Point Unit
FR	Function table Register
FSM	Finite State Machine
FW	FirmWare

G

GDT	Global Descriptor Table (Intel)
GPR	General-Purpose Register
GPU	Graphics Processing Unit/Graphics Processor Unit
GSI	GigaScale Integration

H

HD	Hard Disk
HDD	HD Drive
HDL	Hardware Description Language
HLL	High-Level Language
HMI	Human–Machine Interface
HMOS	High-density MOS (Depletion-load NMOS)
HMT	Hardware MultiThreading
HPC	High-Performance Computing
HW	HardWare

I

I	Input
IaaS	Infrastructure-as-a-Service
IBR	Instruction Buffer Register
ICU	Instruction Control Unit
ID	Instruction Decode
I/D	Instructions/Data
IDT	Interrupt Descriptor Table (Intel)
IF	Instruction Fetch
ILP	Instruction-Level Parallelism
IMT	Implicit MultiThreading
I/O	Input/Output
IO	Input/Output (rarely used)
IOP	I/O Processor
IoT	Internet of Things
IP	Instruction Path
IP	Instruction Pointer (Intel x86) (cf. SC and PC)

IPU	Integer Processing Unit
IR	Instruction Register
IRAM	Intelligent RAM
IS	Instruction Set
ISA	Instruction Set Architecture
ISBN	International Standard Book Number
ISC	Instruction Set Computer
ISM	Infinite State Machine
ISP	Instruction Set Processor
IT	Information Technology

J

JFET	Junction FET
JPEG	Joint Photographic Experts Group

K

K	Kitchen

L

LAN	Local Area Network
LDT	Local Descriptor Table (Intel)
LE	Little Endian
LIFO	Last In, First Out
Lisp	LISt Processing
LIW	Long Instruction Word
LSI	Large-Scale Integration

M

M	Memory
MAC	Multiply-and-ACcumulate
MADC	Manchester Automatic Digital Computer
MADM	Manchester Automatic Digital Machine
MAN	Metropolitan Area Network
MAR	Memory Address Register
MARIE	Machine Architecture that is Really Intuitive and Easy
MCU	MicroController Unit (preferred)
MCU	MicroComputer Unit
MDR	Memory Data Register
ME	Memory Element
ME	passing MEssages
MEMS	MicroElectroMechanical System
MIPS	Microprocessor without Interlocked Pipeline Stages from MIPS Technologies (therefore called MIPS Computer Systems)
MISC	Minimal ISC
MLM	Multi-Level Memory
MoC	Model of Computation
MOS	Metal-Oxide Semiconductor
MOSFET	MOS FET
MPEG	Moving Picture Experts Group
MPP	Massively Parallel Processor/Processing
MPU	MicroProcessor Unit
MQ	Multiplier-Quotient Register
MROM	Mask ROM or Mask-programmed ROM (JEDEC)
MSD	Mass Storage Device

MSI	Medium Scale Integration
MSS	Mass Storage System

N

NAND	Not AND
NISC	No ISC
NMOS	Negative (channel) MOS
NOVRAM	Non-Volatile RAM (cf. NVRAM and NVSRAM)
NOW	Network of Workstations
NVM	Non-Volatile Memory
NVSRAM	Non-Volatile SRAM (cf. NOVRAM)

O

O	Output
ObS	On-board System
OEM	Original Equipment Manufacturer
OF	Operand Fetch
OF	Overflow Flag
OISC	One Instruction Set Computer (sometimes SISC)
OS	Operating System
OTPROM	One-Time EPROM

P

PA	PAttern-driven
PaaS	Platform-as-a-Service
PACE	Precision Analog Computing Element
PAD	Personal Audio Device
PALM	Put All Logic in Microcode

PA/VD	Personal Audio/Video Device
PC	Personal Computer
PC	Program Counter (cf. SC and IP)
PCB	Printed Circuit Board
PCU	Program Control Unit (Carter 1995) (cf. DSP from Motorola)
PDA	Personal Digital Assistant
PDP	Programmable Data Processor (DEC)
PE	Processing Element, Processor Element
PET	Personal Electronic Transactor (Commodore International)
PI/O	Peripheral (Input–Output)
PISO	Parallel In Serial Out
PMOS	Positive (channel) MOS
PMS	Processor, Memory, Switch descriptive system
PN	dataflow Process Networks
POWER	Performance Optimization With Enhanced RISC
PowerPC	POWER Performance Computing
PROLOG	*PROgrammation en LOGique* (programming in logic)
PROM	Programmable ROM
PS/2	Personal System/2
PSR	Processor Status Register
PSRAM	Pseudo-Static RAM
PU	Processing Unit
PVD	Personal Video Device

Q

Qubit	Quantum bit

R

RAM	Random Access Memory
RC	Read Cycle
RFC	Request For Comments
RISC	Reduced Instruction Set Computer
RMW	Read-Modify-Write
ROM	Read-Only Memory
RPN	Reverse Polish Notation
RT	Register Transfer (cf. RTL)
RTL	RT Language (preferred over RT Level)
RW or R/W	Read/Write

S

SaaS	Software-as-a-Service
SBC	Single-Board Computer
SC	Sequence Counter (cf. IP and PC)
(S)CMP	(Single-)Chip Multiprocessor
SDF	Synchronous Dataflow
SDRAM	Synchronous DRAM
SEAC	Standards Electronic Automatic Computer
SF	Sign Flag
SFF	Small Form Factor
SH	SHared data
SI	*Système International d'unités* (International System of Units)
SIPO	Serial In Parallel Out
SISC	Single Instruction Set Computer (sometimes OISC)
SISC	Special Instruction Set Computer

SL	linear resolution with Selection Function
SLD	Selective Linear Definite clause (cf. SL)
SLSI	Super LSI
SLT	Solid Logic Technology (IBM)
SMP	Symmetric (shared memory) MultiProcessing
SMP	Simultaneous Multi-threaded Parallelism
SMT	Simultaneous MultiThreading
SoC	System on (a) Chip, System-on-Chip
SP	Stack Pointer
SPARC	Scalable Processor ARChitecture
SPOOL	Simultaneous Peripheral Operations On-Line
SR	Selectron Register
SR	Shift Register
SRAM	Static RAM
SRP	Synchronous-Reactive Programming
SSD	Solid-State Disk
SSI	Small-Scale Integration
SSRAM	Synchronous SRAM
ST	Status Register (TMS9900)
SW	SoftWare

T

TLP	Thread-Level Parallelism
TT	Time-Triggered
TTA	Transport Triggered Architecture
TTL	Transistor–Transistor Logic

U

ULSI	Ultra LSI
UNIVAC	Universal Automatic Computer
URISC	Ultimate RISC
URL	Uniform Resource Locator
USB	Universal Serial Bus
UV	UltraViolet
UV-EPROM	UltraViolet EPROM

V

VAX	Virtual Addressed eXtended (DEC)
VLIW	Very LIW
VLSI	Very LSI
VM	Virtual Memory
VoIP	Voice over IP

W

W	Write
WAN	Wide Area Network
WB	Write Back
WC	Write Cycle
WE	Write Enable
WISC	Writable Instruction Set Computer
WP	Workspace Pointer (TMS9900)
WSN	Wireless Sensor Network

X

XOR	eXclusive OR (*cf.* EXOR)

Z

ZF	Zero Flag
ZISC	Zero Instruction Set Computer

Miscellaneous

µC	Microcontroller
µP	Microprocessor
2D or 2-D	Two-dimensional
3D or 3-D	Three-dimensional
3M	a megabyte of memory, a block of resolution of at least one Megapixel and with computation power of a million instructions per second (MIPS)
5M	Megabyte memory, Megapixel display, MIPS processor power, 10+ Megabyte disk drive and 10 Megabit/s network

Measurement units/prefixes

b/s or bps	bit(s) per second
bpspp	bps per pin
E	exa (= 10^{18})
Exbi	exabinary (prefix Ei)
FLOPS	Floating Point Operations Per Second
G	giga (= 10^{9})
Gb	gigabit
GB	gigabyte
GB/s or GBps	gigabyte(s) per second
Gib	gibibit
Gibi	gigabinary (prefix Gi)
GiB	gibibyte

Gops	gigaoperation(s) per second
IPC	Instructions Per Cycle
k	kilo (= 1000)
K	kilobinary (= 1024) – a deprecated prefix; the capital letter indicates the value of the prefix (which we have selected for this work)
kb	kilobit (= 1000 b)
Kb	kilobit (= 1024 b) – former multiple, to be avoided
KB	kilobyte (1024 bytes)
kBps	kilobyte(s) per second
Kib	kibibit
Kibi	kilobinary (prefix Ki)
KiB	kibibyte
M	mega (= 10^6)
Mebi	megabinary (prefix Mi)
MFLOPS	Million FLOating-point Operations Per Second
Mib	mebibit
MiB	mebibyte
MIPS	Million Instructions Per Second
P	peta (= 10^{15})
Pebi	pebibinary (prefix Pi)
PFLOPS	PetaFLOPS
SPECfpxx	System Performance Evaluation Corporation floating point, xx = year
T	tera (= 10^{12})
Tb	terabit
Tbps	terabit per second
TB	terabyte
TBps	terabyte per second
Tebi	tebibinary (prefix Ti)

Tib	tebibit
TiB	tebibyte
Y	yotta (= 10^{24})
Yobi	yobibinary (prefix Yi)
Z	zetta (= 10^{21})
Zebi	zebibinary (prefix Zi)

Temporal characteristics

t_a	access time
t_c	cycle time
t_{RC}	Read Cycle time
T_{ref}	Reference time (DRAM refresh)
t_{WC}	Write Cycle time

Companies and Organizations

ACM	Association for Computing Machinery
AFIPS	American Federation of Information Processing Societies
AFISI	*Association Française d'Ingénierie des Systèmes d'Information*
AIEE	American Institute of Electrical Engineers
AMD	Advanced Micro Devices, Inc.
ARM	Acorn RISC Machine; later Advanced RISC Machines
BBC	British Broadcasting Corporation
CDC	Control Data Corporation
DEC	Digital Equipment Corporation
EAI	Electronic Associates, Inc.
HP	Hewlett-Packard
IAS	Institute for Advanced Study
IBM	International Business Machines Corporation

ICL	International Computers Limited
IEC	International Electrotechnical Commission
IEDM	International Electron Devices Meeting
IEEE	Institute of Electrical and Electronics Engineers
IETF	Internet Engineering Task Force
Inria	*Institut national de recherche en informatique et en automatique*
ISO	International Organization for Standardization
ISSCC	IEEE International Solid-State Circuits Conference
ITRS	International Technology Roadmap for Semiconductors
JEDEC	Joint Electron Device Engineering Council (Solid-State Technology Association)
MIT	Massachusetts Institute of Technology
MITS	Micro Instrumentation Telemetry Systems
NS	National Semiconductor
PARC	Xerox Palo Alto Research Center
RCA	Radio Corporation of America
SGI	Silicon Graphics, Inc.
TI	Texas Instruments
TRS	Tandy RadioShack

Trademark (™)

Microflame	NS

Registered Trademarks (®)

AMD	AMD
Ethernet	Xerox Corporation
Intel	Intel
Pentium	Intel

PS/2	International Business Machines Corporation
UNIX	AT&T
Windows	Microsoft Corporation

References

Preface

Darche, P. (2000). *Architecture des ordinateurs – Représentation des nombres et codes – Cours avec exercices corrigés*. Collection Support IUT. Éditions Gaëtan Morin. November.

Darche, P. (2002). *Architecture des ordinateurs – Fonctions booléennes, logiques combinatoire et séquentielle – Cours avec exercices et exemples en VHDL*. Éditions Vuibert. March.

Darche, P. (2003). *Architecture des ordinateurs - Interfaces et périphériques - Cours avec exercices corrigés*. Editions Vuibert. June.

Darche, P. (2004). *Architecture des ordinateurs - Logique booléenne: implémentations et technologies*. Editions Vuibert. November.

Darche, P. (2012). *Mémoires à semi-conducteurs: principe de fonctionnement et organisation interne des mémoires vives - Volume 1*. Editions Vuibert. January. Un des quatre ouvrages sélectionnés pour le prix AFISI (Association Française d'Ingénierie des Systèmes d'Information) du meilleur livre informatique.

Chapter 1

Anderson, T.E., Culler, D.E., and Patterson, D.A. (1995). A case for NOW (Networks of Workstations). *IEEE Micro*, 15(1), 54–64. February.

Andrews, E.G. (1963). Telephone switching and the early bell laboratories. *The Bell System Technical Journal (BSTJ)*, 341–353. March. Also in (La Porte and Stibitz 1982, 13–19).

Andrews, E.G. and Bode, H.W. (1950). Use of the relay digital computer. *Electrical Engineering*, 69(2), 158–163. February. Also in (La Porte and Stibitz 1982, p. 5–13).

Architecture Technology Corporation (1991). Minisupercomputers. Architecture Technology Corporation Report. September.

Arnold, B. (2009). Shrinking possibilities. *IEEE Spectrum*, 46(4), 26–28 and 50–56. April.

Ascher, M. (1983). The logical-numerical system of Inca quipus. *IEEE Annals of the History of Computing*, 5(3), 268–278. July.

Aspray, W. (ed.) (1990). *Computing Before Computers*. Iowa State University Press.

Bardeen, J. and Brattain, W.H. (1948). The transistor, a semi-conductor triode. *Physical Review*, 74(2), 230–231. July 1948. Republished in *Proceedings of the IEEE*, 86(1), 29–30. January.

Bardeen, J. and Brattain, W.H. (1950). Three-Electrode Circuit Element Utilizing Semiconductive Materials. American patent no. 2524035. Application number: US3346648A. Application date: June 17, 1948. Publication date: October 3.

Belak, J. (1993). Harnessing the killer micros: Applications from LLNL's massively parallel computing initiative. *Theoretica Chimica Acta*, 84(4), 315–323. January.

Bell, C.G. (1986). Toward a history of (Personal) workstations. *ACM Conference on the History of Personal Workstations*. Conference date: January 9–10. Also in (Goldberg 1988, 1–50).

Bell, C.G. (2008a). Bell's law for the birth and death of computer classes. *Communications of the ACM (CACM)*, 51(1) *50th Anniversary Issue: 1958–2008*, 86–94. January.

Bell, C.G. (2008b). Bell's law for the birth and death of computer classes: A theory of the computer's evolution. *IEEE Solid-State Circuits Society (ISSCS) Newsletter*, 13(4), 8–19. Fall.

Bell, G. (2014). STARS: Rise and fall of minicomputers (Scanning Our Past). *Proceedings of the IEEE*, 102(4), 629–638. April.

Besk, G.R., Yen, D.W.L, and Anderson, T.L. (1993). The cydra 5 minisupercomputer: Architecture and implementation. *The Journal of Supercomputing*, 7(1/2) *Special Issue on Instruction-Level Parallelism*, 143–180. May.

Brinkman, W.F. (1997). A history of the invention of the transistor and where it will lead us. *IEEE Journal of Solid-State Circuits (JSSC)*, SC-32(12), 1858–1865. December.

Bromley, A.G. (1982). Charles babbage's analytical engine, 1838. *IEEE Annals of the History of Computing*, 4(3), 196–217. July.

Bromley, A.G. (1987). Charles babbage's tabulations using the 1832 model of difference engine no. 1. Technical Report 304. Basser Department of Computer Science, The University of Sydney, Australia. April.

Brooks III, E.D. (1989). Attack of the killer micros. Teraflop computing panel. *Supercomputing'89*. Conference date: November 13–17. Conference location: Reno, Nevada, USA.

Burger, R.M., Cavin III, R.K., Holton, W.C., and Sumney, L.W. (1984). The impact of ICs on computer technology. *IEEE Computer*, 17(10), 88–95. October.

Burley, R.M. (1987). An overview of the 4 systems in the VAX 8800 family. *Digital Technical Journal*, 1(4), 10–19. February.

Bush, V. (1931). The differential analyzer: A new machine for solving differential equations. *Journal of The Franklin Institute*, 212(4), 447–488. October.

Bush, V. and Caldwell, S.H. (1945). A new type of differential analyzer. *Journal of The Franklin Institute*, 240(4), 255–326. October.

Campbell-Kelly, M. (1987). Charles babbage's table of logarithms (1827). Research Report 106 (RR106). Department of Computer Science, University of Warwick. September.

Campbell-Kelly, M. (1988). Charles babbage's table of logarithms (1827). *IEEE Annals of the History of Computing*, 10(3), 159–169. July/September.

Carson, J.H. (ed.) (1979). Tutorial: Design of microprocessor systems. Initially presented at *Tutorial Week 79*, December 10–14, 1979, San Diego, California, USA. Institute of Electrical and Electronics Engineers (IEEE).

Cass, S. (2005). Genius on the block: The foundations of the computing age go up for auction. *IEEE Spectrum*, 42(7), 40–45. July.

Ceruzzi, P.E. (2003). Zuse computers. *Encyclopedia of Computer Science*, 4th edition, 1876–1877. John Wiley and Sons Ltd.

Ceruzzi, P.E. (2013). Inventing the computer (Scanning Our Past). *Proceedings of the IEEE*, 101(6), 1503–1508. June.

Computer World (1976). Cray-1 has power of five 370/195s. *Computer World*, 21, August 23.

Darche, P. (2000). *Architecture des ordinateurs - Représentation des nombres et codes - Cours avec exercices corrigés*. Collection Support IUT. Edition Gaëtan Morin. November.

Darche, P. (2002). *Architecture des ordinateurs - Fonctions booléennes, logiques combinatoire et séquentielle - Cours avec exercices et exemples en VHDL*. Edition Vuibert. March.

Darche, P. (2003). *Architecture des ordinateurs - Interfaces et périphériques - Cours avec exercices corrigés*. Editions Vuibert. June.

Darche, P. (2004). *Architecture des ordinateurs - Logique booléenne: implémentations et technologies*. Editions Vuibert. November.

Darche, P. (2012). *Mémoires à semi-conducteurs: principe de fonctionnement et organisation interne des mémoires vives - Volume 1*. Editions Vuibert. January. Un des quatre ouvrages sélectionnés pour le prix AFISI (Association Française d'Ingénierie des Systèmes d'Information) du meilleur livre informatique.

Davis, E.M., Harding, W.E., Schwartz, R.S., and Corning, J.J. (1964). Solid logic technology: Versatile, high-performance microelectronics. *IBM Journal of Research and Development*, 8(2), 102–114. April.

DEC (1975 1976). LSI-11, PDP-11/03 User's Manual. 1st Edition, September 1975. 2nd Printing (Rev). November 1975. 3rd edition (Rev), May. Digital Equipment Corporation.

Denning, P.J. (1971). Third generation computer systems. *ACM Computing Surveys (CSUR)*, 3, 176–210. December.

Doerr, J. (1978). Low-cost microcomputing: The personal computer and single-board computer revolutions. *Proceedings of the IEEE*, 66(2), 117–130. February. Also in (Carson 1979, 110–123).

Electronic Associates Inc. (1964). EAI 231R-V Analog Computer Information Manual. Electronic Associates Inc.

Ellsworth, M.J., Campbell, L.A., Simons, R.E., Iyengar, M.K., Schmidt, R.R., and Chu, R.C. (2008). The evolution of water cooling for IBM large server systems: Back to the future. *11th Intersociety Conference on Thermal and Thermomechanical Phenomena in Electronic Systems (ITHERM 2008)*. Conference date: May 28–31.

Essinger, J. (2004). *Jacquard's Web: How a Hand-Loom Led to the Birth of the Information Age*. Oxford University Press.

Etiemble, D. (2016). Introduction aux systèmes embarqués, enfouis et mobiles. Article Réf. H8000 V2. Techniques de l'Ingénieur. August 10.

Feng, W. (2003). Making a case for efficient supercomputing. *Queue - Power Management Queue*, 1(7), 54–64. October.

Foster, I. and Kesselman, C. (eds) (2003). *The Grid 2, Blueprint for a New Computing Infrastructure*. The Elsevier Series in Grid Computing, 2nd edition. Morgan Kaufmann.

Foster, I., Kesselman, C., and Tuecke, S. (2001). The anatomy of the grid: Enabling scalable virtual organizations. *International Journal of Supercomputer Applications*, 15(3), 200–222. Fall.

Gaspard Clair Francois Marie Riche (Baron de) Prony (De Prony 1825). Recueil de cinq tables, pour faciliter et abréger les calculs des formules relatives au mouvement des eaux dans les canaux découverts et les tuyaux de conduite. Imprimerie royale. September.

Gernelle, F. (1974). Ordinateur, en particulier pour des applications en temps réel. Brevet d'invention no. 73.03553. Institut National de la propriété Industrielle. Filing date: 1 February 1973. Decision date: August 19.

Godderz, J.E. (1976). The most significant bits. *ACM SIGMINI (Special Interest Group on Minicomputers newsletter) Newsletter*, 2(4-5), 5. September.

Goldberg, A. (ed.) (1988). *A History of Personal Workstations*. ACM Press (Addison-Wesley Publishing Company).

Goldstein, C. (1999). La naissance du nombre en Mésopotamie. *La Recherche*, special edition no. 2, L'Univers des Nombres, 10–12. August.

van de Goor, A.J. (1989). *Computer Architecture and Design*. Addison-Wesley Publishing Company, Inc.

Grattan-Guinness, I. (1990). Work for the hairdressers: The production of de Prony's logarithmic and trigonometric tables. *IEEE Annals of the History of Computing*, 12(3), 177–185. July/September.

Haghighi, S. (2001). Server computer architecture. In (Oklobdzij 2001, section 5.1, section II Computer Systems and Architecture, Chapter 5 - Computer Architecture and Design).

Hartree, D.R. (1948). A historical survey of digital computing machines. In (Hartree *et al.* 1948, 265–271). December.

Hartree, D.R., Newman, M.H.A., Wilkes, M.V., Williams, F.C., Wilkinson, J.H., and Booth, A.D. (1948). A discussion on computing machines. *Proceedings of the Royal Society of London, Series A, Mathematical and Physical Sciences*, 195(104), 265–287. December 22.

Helmers, C. (1976). Trends in pplications. *Byte*, 1(9), 4, 6, 90, 92, 94 and 96. May.

Hewlett-Packard (1968). Powerful computing genie: $4900. Ready, willing and able. Hewlett-Packard. Advertisement for the HP 9100. *Science*, 162(3849), 6. October 4.

Hewlett-Packard (1998). *Proceedings of the IEEE*, 86(1) *Special Issue: 50th Anniversary of the Transistor*. January.

Hill, M.D., Jouppi, N.P., and Sohi, G.S. (2000). *Readings in Computer Architecture*. Morgan Kaufmann Publishers Inc.

Hohn, F. (1955). Some mathematical aspects of switching. *The American Mathematical Monthly*, 62(2), 75–90. February.

Hollerith, H. (1884a). Art of Compiling Statistics. United States Patent 0395782. Application number: US143805XA. Filing date: September 23.

Hollerith, H. (1884b). Apparatus for Compiling Statistics. United States Patent 0395783. Application number: US28493988DA. Filing date: 09/23/1884.

Hollerith, H. (1887). Art of Compiling Statistics. United States Patent 0395781. Application number: US24062987DA. Filing date: June 8.

Ifrah, G. (1994). *Histoire universelle des chiffres*. Editions Robert Laffont, Paris.

ITRS Emerging Research Devices Technology Working Group (2001). International Technology Roadmap For Semiconductors-Executive Summary. ITRS Emerging Research Devices Technology Working Group.

Kaeslin, H. (2008). *Digital Integrated Circuit Design: From VLSI Architectures to CMOS Fabrication*. Cambridge University Press.

Keller, A.C. (1962). Relays and switches. *Proceedings of the Institute of Radio Engineers (IRE)*, 50(5), 932–934. May.

Kim, E.E. and Toole, B.A. (1999). Ada and the first computer. *Scientific American*, 280(5), 76–81. May.

La Porte, D. and Stibitz, G.R. (1982). Eloge: E. G. Andrews, 18981980. *IEEE Annals of the History of Computing*, 4(1), 4–19. January.

Libes, S. (1978). *Small Computer Systems Handbook*. Hayden Book Company, Inc.

Lilen, H. (1979). *Circuits Intégrés JFET-MOS-CMOS: Principes et Applications*, 3rd edition. Editions Radio.

Marguin, J. (1994). *Histoire des instruments et machines à calculer, Trois siècles de mécanique pensante*, 1642–1942. Editions Hermann.

Matzke, D. (1997). Will physical scalability sabotage performance gains? *IEEE Computer*, 30(9), 37–39. September.

Meindl, J.D. (1984). Ultra-large scale integration. *IEEE Transactions on Electron Devices*, 31(11), 1555–1561. November.

Meindl, J.D. (1995). Low power microelectronics: Retrospect and prospect. *Proceedings of the IEEE*, 83(4), 619–635. April.

Metropolis, N. and Worlton, J. (1980). A trilogy on errors in the history of computing. *IEEE Annals of the History of Computing*, 2(1), 49–59. January.

Moore, G.E. (1965). Cramming more components onto integrated circuits. *Electronics*, 38(8), 114–117. April 19. Republished in (Hill *et al.* 2000, 56–59).

Moore, G.E. (1975). Progress in digital integrated electronics. *International Electron Devices Meeting (IEDM)*, 11–13. Republished in (Moore 2006).

Moore, G.E. (2006). Progress in digital integrated electronics. Technical Literature. *IEEE Solid-State Circuits Society (SSCS) Newsletter*, 20(3), 36–37. September.

Moto-Oka, T. (1982). 5th Generation Computer Systems. *International Conference on 5th Generation Computer Systems*, Moto-Oka, T. (ed.). October 19–22, 1981, Tokyo, Japan. Elsevier.

Nabielsky, J. and Skelton, A.P. (1981). A virtual terminal management model. Request For Comments (RFC) 782. The MITRE Corporation. Internet Engineering Task Force (IETF). January.

Nelson, D.L. and Bell, C.G. (1986). The evolution of workstations. *IEEE Circuits and Devices Magazine*, 2(4), 12–16. July 1986.

Oklobdzija, V.G. (ed.) (2001). *The Computer Engineering Handbook*. CRC Press.

Osborne, A. (1980). *An Introduction to Microcomputers: Volume 1 - Basic Concepts*, 2nd edition. Osborne/McGraw-Hill.

Patterson, D.A. (1995). Microprocessors in 2020. *Scientific American*, 273(3), 62–67. September.

Pfister, G. (1998). *In Search of Clusters*, 2nd edition. Prentice Hall.

Pugh, E.W. (2013). Stars: IBM system/360. *Proceedings of the IEEE*, 101(11), 2450–2457. November.

Rau, B.R., Yen, D.W.L., Wei, Y., and Towle, R.A. (1989). The Cydra 5 departmental supercomputer. Design philosophies, decisions, and trade-offs. *IEEE Computer*, 22(1), 12–35. January.

Roberts, E.W. and Yates, W. (1975a). ALTAIR 8800: The most powerful minicomputer project ever presented – can be built for under $400. ALTAIR 8800 Minicomputer, Part I. *Popular Electronics*, 7(1), 33–38. January.

Roberts, E.W. and Yates, W. (1975b). Build the ALTAIR minicomputer. ALTAIR 8800 minicomputer, Part II. *Popular Electronics*, 7(2), 56–58. February.

Rochain, S. (2016). *De la mécanographie à l'informatique. 50 ans d'évolution*. ISTE Editions, London.

Rojas, R. (1997). Konrad Zuse's legacy: The architecture of the Z1 and Z3. *IEEE Annals of the History of Computing*, 19(2), 5–16. April/June.

Scientific American (1997). The solid-state century: The past, present and future of the transistor. *Scientific American*, Special Issue, 8(1). January 22.

Schultz, G.W., Holt, R.M., and McFarland, H.L. (1973). A guide to using LSI microprocessors. *IEEE Computer*, 6(6), 13–20. June.

Seraphim, D.P. and Feinberg, I. (1981). Electronic packaging evolution in IBM. *IBM Journal of Research and Development*, 25(5), 617–629. September.

Shannon, C.E. (1938). A symbolic analysis of relay and switching circuits. *Transactions of the American Institute of Electrical Engineers (AIEE)*, 57, 713–723. Also in (Shannon 1993).

Shannon, C.E. (1953). Realization of all 16 switching functions of two variables requires 18 contacts. Bell Laboratories Memorandum. November 17.

Shannon, C.E. (1993). In *Claude Elwood Shannon, Collected Papers*. Sloane, N.J.A. and Wyner, A.D. (eds). IEEE Press.

Shapiro, F.R. (2000). Origin of the term "personal computer": Evidence from the JSTOR electronic journal archive. Comments, Queries, and Debates. Werner Buchholz. *IEEE Annals of the History of Computing*, 22(4), 70–71. October–December.

Shiva, S.G. (2006). *Advanced Computer Architectures*. CRC Press.

Siewiorek, D.P., Bell, C.G., and Newell, A. (1982). *Computer Structures: Principles and Examples*. McGraw-Hill Book Company.

Small, J.S. (2001). *The Analogue Alternative. The Electronic Analogue Computer in Britain and the USA, 1930–1975*. Routledge.

Smith, J.E. and Nair, R. (2005). *Virtual Machines. Versatile Platforms for Systems and Processes*. Morgan Kaufmann Publishers. Elsevier Inc.

Speiser, A.P. (1980). The relay calculator Z4. *IEEE Annals of the History of Computing*, 2(3), 242–245. July.

Sterling, T., Becker, D.J., Savarese, D., Dorband, J.E., Ranawake, U.A., and Packer, C.V. (1995). Beowulf: A parallel workstation for scientific computation. *1995 International Conference on Parallel Processing (ICPP)*, I (Architecture), I-11–I-14. CRC Press. August 14–18, University of Illinois at Urbana-Champain, Illinois, USA.

Stiefel, M.L. (1978). Single board computers. *Mini-Micro Systems*. September. Republished in (Carson 1979, 124–133).

Succi, S., Ayati, B.P., and Hosoi, A.E. (1996). A six lecture primer on parallel computing. Technical Report CS-96-11. University of Chicago. Chicago, IL, USA.

Sullivan, P., Callander, M.A. (Sr.), Lundberg, J.R., Stamm, R.L., and Bowhill, W.J. (1990). The VAX 6000 model 400 scalar processing module. *Digital Technical Journal*, 2(2), 27–35. Spring.

Suri, P.K. and Mittal, S. (2012). A comparative study of various computing processing environments: A review. *International Journal of Computer Science and Information Technologies (IJCSIT)*, 3(5), 5215–5218. October.

Swade, D.D. (1993). Redeeming charles babbage's mechanical computer. *Scientific American*, 268(2), 86–91. February.

Swade, D.D. (2001). *The Difference Engine: Charles Babbage and the Quest to Build the First Computer*. Viking Press.

Swade, D.D. (2005). The construction of charles babbage's difference engine No. 2. *IEEE Annals of the History of Computing*, 27(3), 70–88. July/September.

Tanenbaum, A. (2005). *Architecture de l'ordinateur*, 5th edition. Pearson Education.

Treleaven, P.C. (1981). 5th generation computer architecture analysis. *International Conference on 5th Generation Computer Systems*, 265–275. October 19–22, 1981,Tokyo, Japan. In (Moto-Oka *et al.* 1982).

Treleaven, P.C. and Lima, I.G. (1982). Japan's 5th generation computer systems. *IEEE Computer*, 15(8), 79–88. August.

Truitt, T.D. and Rogers, A.E. (1964). *Introduction au Calcul Analogique: Principes et Applications*. Dunod.

Weiss, E. (1996). Konrad zuse obituary. *IEEE Annals of the History of Computing*, 18(2), 3–5. Summer.

Weste, N.H.E. and Harris, D. (2010). *CMOS VLSI Design: A Circuits and Systems Perspective*, 4th edition. Addison-Wesley Longman, Inc.

Wickes, W.E. (1968). *Logic Design with Integrated Circuits*. John Wiley & Sons Inc.

Xanthopoulos, T. (2009). *Clocking in Modern VLSI Systems*. Series on Integrated Circuits and Systems. Thucydides Xanthopoulos Editor.

Zuse, K. (1993). *The Computer - My Life*. Springer-Verlag.

Chapter 2

Amdahl, G.M., Blaauw, G.A., and Brooks, F.P. (1964). Architecture of the IBM system/360. *IBM Journal of Research and Development*, 8(2), 87–101. April.

Belady, L.A., Parmelee, R.P., and Scalzi, C.A. (1981). The IBM history of memory management technology. *IBM Journal of Research and Development*, 25(5), 491–504. September.

Bell, C.G., Mudge, J.C., and McNamara, J.E. (eds) (1978). *Computer Engineering: A DEC View of Hardware Systems Design*. Digital Press.

Buchholz, W. (1956). Memory word length. Stretch Memo no. 40. 3. July 31.

Buchholz, W. (ed.) (1962). *Planning a Computer System - Project Stretch*. McGraw-Hill Book Company, Inc.

Buchholz, W. (1977). The word "Byte" comes of age. *Byte*, 2(2), 144. February.

Chen, P.M. and Patterson, D.A. (1993). Storage performance-metrics and benchmarks. *Proceedings of the IEEE*, 8(9), 1151–1165. September.

Chisvin, L. and Duckworth, R.J. (1989). Content-addressable and associative memory: Alternatives to the ubiquitous RAM. *IEEE Computer*, 22(7), 51–64. July.

Ciminiera, L. and Valenzano, A. (1987). *Advanced Microprocessor Architectures*. Electronic Systems Engineering Series. AddisonWesley Publishing Co.

Cohen, D. (1981). On holy wars and a plea for peace. *IEEE Computer*, 14(10), 48–54. October. Original: IEN (Internet Engineering Note) 137. USC/ISI (University of Southern California /Information Sciences Institute). April 1.

Darche, P. (2002). *Architecture des ordinateurs - Fonctions booléennes, logiques combinatoire et séquentielle - Cours avec exercices et exemples en VHDL*. Edition Vuibert. March.

Darche, P. (2003). *Architecture des ordinateurs - Interfaces et périphériques - Cours avec exercices corrigés*. Editions Vuibert. June.

Darche, P. (2012). *Mémoires à semi-conducteurs: principe de fonctionnement et organisation interne des mémoires vives - Volume 1*. Editions Vuibert. January. Un des quatre ouvrages sélectionnés pour le prix AFISI (Association Française d'Ingénierie des Systèmes d'Information) du meilleur livre informatique.

Digital Equipment Corporation (1983). PDP-11 Architecture Handbook. Order Code: EB-23657-18. Digital Equipment Corporation (DEC).

Gifford, D. and Spector, A. (1987). Case study: IBM's system/360–370 architecture. *Communications of the ACM (CACM)*, 30(4), 291–307. April.

Gray, J. and Shenay, P. (1999). Rules of thumb in data engineering. December 1. *16th International Conference on Data Engineering (ICDE'00)*, 3. February 28–March 3.

Handy, J. (1998). *The Cache Memory Book*, 2nd edition (First Edition in 1993). Academic Press.

IEEE (1996). IEEE Standard for High-Bandwidth Memory Interface Based on Scalable Coherent Interface (SCI) Signaling Technology (RamLink). IEEE Std 1596.4-1996. Approved March 19.

IEEE (2002a). Draft Standard for Prefixes for Binary Multiples. IEEE Std P1541/D5. The Institute of Electrical and Electronics Engineers. New York, USA. April 18.

IEEE (2002b). IEEE Std 1541-2002: IEEE Standard for Prefixes for Binary Multiples.

International Electrotechnical Commission (2000). Letter symbols to be used in electrical technology-Part 2: Telecommunications and electronics-Symboles littéraux à utiliser en électrotechnique - Partie 2: Télécommunications et électronique. International Electrotechnical Commission. IEC 60027-2 - Edition 2.0 Bilingual. 22 November.

Meinadier, J.-P. (1971 1988). *Structure et Fonctionnement des Ordinateurs*. Librairie Larousse, Paris.

Nakagomi, T., Holzbach, M., Van Meter, R., III, and Ranade, S. (1993). Re-defining the storage hierarchy: An ultra-fast magneto-optical disk drive. *12th IEEE Symposium on Mass Storage Systems: "Putting all that Data to Work"*, 267–274. April 26–29.

Patterson, D. (2004). Latency lags bandwith. *Communications of the ACM (CACM)*, 47(10), 71–75. October.

Patterson, D. (2005). Latency lags bandwidth. *2005 IEEE International Conference on Computer Design: VLSI in Computers and Processors (ICCD 2005)*, 3–6. October 2–5.

Self, K. (1999). Memory in megabytes and/or mebibytes. *IEEE Spectrum*, 36(8), 18. August.

Chapter 3

Ackerman, W.B. (1982). Data flow languages. *IEEE Computer*, 15(2), 15–24. February.

Agha, G.A. (1985). Actors: A model of concurrent computation in distributed systems. Technical report 844. Massachusetts Institute of Technology (MIT) Artificial Intelligence Laboratory. Cambridge, MA, USA. June.

Agha, G.A. (1986). *Actors: A Model of Concurrent Computation in Distributed Systems*. MIT Press, Cambridge, MA, USA.

Amdahl, G.A., Blaauw, G.A., and Brooks, F.P., Jr. (1964). Architecture of the IBM system/360. *IBM Journal of Research and Development*, 8(2), 87–101. April.

ARM (2019). ARM Architecture Reference Manual. ARMv8, for ARMv8-A Architecture Profile. Arm® DDI 0487D.b (ID042519). Arm® Limited.

Azaria, H. and Tabak, D. (1983). Design considerations of a single instruction microcomputer – A case study. *Microprocessing and Microprogramming*, 11(3–4), 187–194. March–April.

Backus, J. (1978). Can programming be liberated from the von Neumann Style? A functional style and its algebra of programs. *Communications of the ACM (CACM)*, 21(8), 613–641. August.

Baer, J.-L. (1984). Computer architecture. *IEEE Computer*, 17(10), 77–87. October.

Bell, J.R. (1973). Threaded code. *Communications of the ACM (CACM)*, 16(6), 370–372. June.

Bell, C.G. and Newell, A.C. (1970). The PMS and ISP descriptive systems for computer structures. *1970 Spring Joint Computer Conference (Spring AFIPS'70)*, 351–374. Conference date: May 5–7.

Bell, C.G. and Newell, A. (1971). *Computer Structures: Readings and Examples*. McGraw-Hill Computer Science Series. McGraw-Hill Book Company.

Bell, C.G., Kotok, A., Hastings, T.N., and Hill, R. (1978). The evolution of the DEC system 10. *Communications of the ACM (CACM)*, 21(1), 44–63. January.

Bennett, T.H., Kouvoussis,A.E., and Wiles, M.F. (1977). Microprocessor chip register bus structure. American patent no. 4004281. Assignee: Motorola, Inc. Application number: 05/519133. Filing date: October 30, 1974. Publication date: January 18.

Blaauw, G.A. and Brooks, F.P. Jr. (1996). *Computer Architecture: Concepts and Evolution*. Addison-Wesley Professional.

Borkar, S. (2007). Thousand core chips: A technology perspective. *44th Annual Design Automation Conference (DAC'07)*, 746–749. June 4–8. San Diego, CA, USA.

Brooks, F.P. Jr. (1975 1995). *The Mythical Man-Month: Essays on Software Engineering*. 20th Anniversary Edition. Other Editions in 1975 and 1982. Addison-Wesley.

Bryant, R.E. and O'Hallaron, D.R. (2016). *Computer Systems: A Programmer's Perspective*, 3rd edition. Addison Wesley.

Buchholz, W. (1953). The systems design of the IBM type 701 Computer. *Proceedings of the IRE*, 41(10), 1262–1275. October.

Buchholz, W. (ed.) (1962). *Planning a Computer System – Project Stretch*. McGraw-Hill Book Company, Inc.

Buck, J.T. (1993). Scheduling dynamic dataflow graphs with bounded memory using the token flow model. Doctor of Philosophy in Engineering-Electrical Engineering and Computer Sciences Dissertation, University of California at Berkeley.

Buck, J.T. and Lee, E.A. (1993). Scheduling dynamic dataflow graphs with bounded memory using the token fow model. *1993 IEEE International Conference on Acoustics, Speech, and Signal Processing (ICASSP-93)*, 1, 429–432. April 27–30. Minneapolis, MN, USA.

Buckle, J.K. (1978). *The ICL 2900 Series*. MacMillan Press Ltd.

Burks, A.W., Goldstine. H.H., and von Neumann, J. (1946–1947). Preliminary discussion of the logical design of an electronic computing instrument. Part I, 1. Report prepared for U.S. Army Ordnance Department. 28 June 1946-2 September. In CD-ROM by (Shriver and Smith 1998) and in (Taub 1963, 34–79).

Carter, J.W. (1995). *Microprocessor Architecture and Microprogramming: A State-Machine Approach*. Prentice Hall International Limited, London.

Ceruzzi, P. (2000). "Nothing new since von Neumann": A historian looks at computer architecture, 1945–1995. In (Rojas and Hashagen 2000, 195–217).

Corporaal, H. (1995). Transport triggered architectures: Design and evaluation. PhD Dissertation, Delft University of Technology (TU Delft). September 13.

Dahl, O.J. and Nygaard, K. (1966). SIMULA – An ALGOL-based simulation language. *Communications of the ACM (CACM)*, 9(9), 671–678. September.

Dally, W.J. and Wills, D.S. (1989). Universal mechanism for concurrency. *Proceedings of PARLE. Lecture Notes in Computer Science (LNCS)*, 365, 19–33. Springer Verlag, Berlin.

Darche, P. (2000). *Architecture des ordinateurs – Représentation des nombres et codes – Cours avec exercices corrigés*. Collection Support IUT. Éditions Gaëtan Morin. November.

Darche, P. (2002). *Architecture des ordinateurs – Fonctions booléennes, logiques combinatoire et séquentielle – Cours avec exercices et exemples en VHDL*. Éditions Vuibert. March.

Darche, P. (2003). *Architecture des ordinateurs - Interfaces et périphériques - Cours avec exercices corrigés*. Editions Vuibert. June.

Darche, P. (2004). *Architecture des ordinateurs - Logique booléenne: implémentations et technologies*. Editions Vuibert. November.

Darche, P. (2012). *Mémoires à semi-conducteurs: principe de fonctionnement et organisation interne des mémoires vives - Volume 1*. Editions Vuibert. January. One of four books selected for the AFISI (Association Française d'Ingénierie des Systèmes d'Information) prize for the best book on computing.

Dasgupta, S. (1990). A hierarchical taxonomic system for computer architectures. *IEEE Computer*, 23(3), 64–74. March 1990. See also (Schmidt and Dasgupta 1990).

Dennis, J.B. (1980). Data flow supercomputers. *IEEE Computer*, 13(11), 48–56. November.

Edwards, S.A. (1997). The Specification and Execution of Heterogeneous Synchronous Reactive Systems. PhD Thesis. Technical Report No. UCB/ERL M97/31. Electrical Engineering and Computer Sciences (EECS) Department, University of California, Berkeley.

Estrin, G. (1952). A description of the electronic computer at the institute for advanced studies. *1952 ACM National Meeting (ACM'52)*, 95–109. Toronto, Canada.

Estrin, G. (1953). The electronic computer at the institute for advanced study. *Mathematical Tables and Other Aids to Computation*, 7(42), 108–114. April.

Farrell, E.P, Ghani, N., and Treleaven, P.C. (1979). Concurrent computer architecture and a ring based implementation. *6th Annual International Symposium on Computer Architecture (ISCA'79)*, 1–11.

Frizzell, C.E. (1953). Engineering description of the IBM type 701 computer. *Proceedings of the IRE*, 41(10), 1275–1287. October.

Gajski, D. (2003). NISC: The ultimate reconfigurable component. Technical Report TR 03-28. Center for embedded computer systems, University of California. October.

Gajski, D. (2005). No-instruction-Set-Computer Processor. United States Patent Application 20050097306. Application number: 10/ 944365. Filing date: 09/17/2004. Publication date: 05/05/2005.

Gajski, D.D. and Kuhn, R.H. (1983). Guest editors' introduction: New VLSI tools. *IEEE Computer*, 16(12), 11–14. December.

Gluck, S.E (1953). The electronic discrete variable computer. *Electrical Engineering*, 72(2), 159–162. February.

Godfrey, M.D. and Hendry, D.F. (1993). The computer as von Neumann planned it. *IEEE Annals of the History of Computing*, 15(1), 11–21. January. In CD-ROM by (Shriver and Smith 1998).

Goldstine, H.H. (1993). *The Computer from Pascal to von Neumann*. Princeton University Press.

Goldstine, H.H. and von Neumann, J. (1947–1948). Planning and coding of problems for an electronic computing instrument. Part II, Vols. 1 to 3. Three reports prepared for U.S. Army Ordnance Department. Republished in (Taub 1963, 80–235).

van de Goor, A.J. (1989). *Computer Architecture and Design*. Addison-Wesley Publishing Company, Inc.

Greenwald, S., Haueter, R.C., and Alexander, S.N. (1953). SEAC. *Proceedings of the IRE*, 41(10), 1300–1313. October.

Hartree, D.R., Newman, M.H.A., Wilkes, M.V., Williams, F.C., Wilkinson, J.H., and Booth, A.D. (1948). A discussion on computing machines. *Proceedings of the Royal Society of London, Series A, Mathematical and Physical Sciences*, 195(104), 265–287. December 22.

Hennessy, J.L. and Patterson, D.A. (2007). *Computer Architecture. A Quantitative Approach.* 4th edition. Morgan Kaufmann Publishers, Inc.

Hewitt, C. (1977). Viewing control structures as patterns of passing messages. *Artificial Intelligence*, 8(3), 323–364. June.

Hewitt, H., Bishop, P., and Steiger, R. (1973). A universal modular actor formalism for artificial intelligence. *3rd International Joint Conference on Artificial Intelligence (IJCAI)*, 235–245. August 20–23. Stanford University, Stanford California, USA.

Hoare, C.A.R. (1978). Communicating sequential processes. *Communications of the ACM (CACM)*, 21(8), 666–677. August. Republished in (Kuhn and Padua 1981).

Hopkin, R.P., Rautenback, P.W., and Treleavan, P.C. (1979). A computer supporting data flow, control flow and updateable memory. Technical Report 144, Computing Laboratory, University of Newcastle upon Tyne. September.

IBM (1955). IBM Presents The 650 Magnetic Drum Data Processing Machine. Reference Document: 32-6770. International Business Machines Corporation (IBM).

IBM (2017). Power ISA™. Version 3.0 B. IBM. March 29.

Intel (1975). Intel 8080 Microcomputer Systems User's Manual. Intel Corporation. September.

Intel (1981). Introduction to the iAPX 432 Architecture. Manual Order Number: 171821-001. Intel. August.

Intel (1989). 8086/8088 User's Manual, Programmer's and Hardware Reference. Intel.

Intel (2003). IA-32 Intel® Architectures Software Developer's Manual, Volume 1: Basic Architecture. Order Number 245470-012. Intel Corporation.

Intel (2017). Intel® 64 and IA-32 Architectures Software Developer's Manual. Order Number: 325462-062US. Intel Corporation. March.

Johnson, M. (1990). *Superscalar Microprocessor Design*. Prentice Hall Series in Innovative Technology. Prentice Hall.

Jouppi, N.P. (1989). The nonuniform distribution of instruction-level and machine parallelism and its effect on performance. *IEEE Transactions on Computers*, 38(12), 1645–1658. December.

Kahn, G. (1974). The semantics of a simple language for parallel programming. *IFIP Congress*, 471–475. August 5–10. Stockholm, Sweden.

Kathail, V., Schlansker, M.S., and Rau, B.R. (1993). HPL PlayDoh architecture specification: Version 1.0. HPL Technical Report HPL-93-80. HP Laboratories Palo Alto.

Kathail, V., Schlansker, M.S., and Rau, B.R. (2000). HPL-PD architecture specification: Version 1.1. HPL Technical Report HPL-93-80(R.1). HP Laboratories Palo Alto. February (Revised).

Kilburn, T. (1948). A storage system for use with binary digital computing machines. PhD Thesis, University of Manchester. 13 December.

Knuth, D.E. (1986). The IBM 650: An appreciation from the field. *IEEE Annals of the History of Computing*, 8(1), 50–55. January–March.

Koopman, P. Jr. (1987a). Writable instruction set, stack oriented computers: The WISC concept. *1987 Rochester Forth Conference*. June 9–13. University of Rochester. *The Journal of Forth Application and Research*, 5(1).

Koopman, P. (1987b). The WISC concept. *Byte*, 12(4), 187–193. April.

Koopman, P.J. Jr. (1989). *Stack Computers: The New Wave*. Mountain View Press.

Kopetz, H. (1998). The time-triggered model of computation. *19th IEEE Real-Time Systems Symposium (RTSS'98)*, 168–177. December 2–4. Madrid, Spain.

Kowalski, R. (1979). Algorithm = Logic + Control. *Communications of the ACM (CACM)*, 22(7), 424–436. July.

Kuhn, R.H. and Padua, D.A. (eds) (1981). *Tutorial on Parallel Processing*. IEEE Press.

Lavington, S.H. (1980). *Early British Computers*. Manchester University Press.

Leavitt, N. (2012). Will power problems curtail processor progress? *IEEE Computer*, 45(5), 15–17. May.

Lee, E.A. and Messerschmitt, D.G. (1987a). Static scheduling of synchronous data flow programs for digital signal processing. *IEEE Transactions on Computers*, C-36(1), 24–35. January.

Lee, E.A. and Messerschmitt, D.G. (1987b). Synchronous data flow. *Proceedings of the IEEE*, 75(9), 1235–1245. September.

Levy, H.M. and Eckhouse, R.H. Jr. (1989). *Computer Programming and Architecture: The VAX*, 2nd edition. Digital Equipment Corporation (DEC).

Lindblad, T., Lindsey, C.S., Minerskjöld, M., Sekhniaidze, G., Székely, G., and Eide, A. (1995). Implementing the new zero instruction set computer (ZISC036) from IBM for a Higgs Search. *Letter to the Editor. Nuclear Instruments and Methods in Physics Research*, Section A, 357(1), 192–194. April.

Marlet, R. (2012). *Program Specialization*. ISTE, London and John Wiley & Sons, New York.

Masini, G., Napoli, A., Colnet, D., Léonard, D., and Tombre, K. (1990). *Les langages à objets*. Inter Editions.

Mavaddat, F. and Parhami, B. (1988). URISC: The ultimate reduced instruction set computer. *International Journal of Electrical Engineering & Education*. 25(4), 327–334. October.

McCulloch, W.S. and Pitts, W. (1943). A logical calculus of the ideas immanent in nervous activity. *Bulletin of Mathematical Biophysics*, 5(4), 115–133. December.

Metropolis, N. and Worlton, J. (1980). A trilogy on errors in the history of computing. *IEEE Annals of the History of Computing*, 2(1), 49–59. January.

Minsky, M.L. (1967). *Computation: Finite and Infinite Machines*. Prentice-Hall, Inc.

MIPS Technologies, Inc. (2001a). MIPS32™ Architecture For Programmers. Volume I: Introduction to the MIPS32™ Architecture. Document Number: MD00082, Revision 0.95. MIPS Technologies, Inc.. March 12.

MIPS Technologies, Inc. (2001b). MIPS64™ Architecture For Programmers. Volume I: Introduction to the MIPS64™ Architecture. Document Number: MD00083, Revision 0.95. MIPS Technologies, Inc.. March 12.

Moore, B.L. (1949). The Mark III Calculator. *Second Symposium on Large-Scale Digital Calculating Machinery*, XXVI, 11–19. 13–16 September. The Annals of the Computation Laboratory of Harvard University. Harvard University Press. Cambridge, MA, 1951.

Moto-Oka, T. (ed.) (1982). Fifth generation computer systems. *International Conference on Fifth Generation Computer Systems*. October 19–22, 1981. Tokyo, Japan. Elsevier.

Nature (1948). Calculating machines. *Nature*, 161(4097), 712–713. May 8.

von Neumann, J. (1945). First draft of a report on the EDVAC. contract no. W-670-ORD-4926 Moore School of Electrical Engineering, University of Pennsylvania. June 30. See also (Godfrey and Hendry 1993). In CD-ROM of (Shriver and Smith 1998).

Nguyen, V. and Hailpern, B. (1986). A generalized object model. *1986 SIGPLAN Workshop on Object-Oriented Programming (OOPWORK'86)*. June 9–13, 1986. Yorktown Heights, New York, USA. *ACM SIGPLAN (Special Interest Group on Programming Languages) Notices*, 21(10), 78–87. October.

Null, L. and Lobur, J. (2003). MarieSim: The MARIE computer simulator. *ACM Journal of Educational Resources in Computing (JERIC)*, 3(2), Article no. 1. June.

Nurmi, J. (ed.) (2007). *Processor Design. System-on-Chip Computing for ASICs and FPGAs*. Springer.

Patterson, D., Anderson, T., Cardwell, N., Fromm, R., Keeton, K., Kozyrakis, C., Thomas, R., and Yelick, K. (1997a). A case for intelligent RAM. *IEEE Micro*, 17(2), 34–44. March/April.

Patterson, D., Anderson, T., Cardwell, N., Fromm, R., Keeton, K., Kozyrakis, C., Thomas, R., and Yelick, K. (1997b). Intelligent RAM (IRAM): Chips that remember and compute. *1997 IEEE International Solid-State Circuits Conference (ISSCC'97)*. 6–8 February. San Francisco, USA.

Patterson, D., Kozyrakis, C.E., Perissakis, S., Anderson, T., Asanovic, K., Cardwell, N., Fromm, R., Colbus, J., Gribstad, B., Keeton, K., Thomas, R., Treuhaft, N., and Yelick, K. (1997c). Scalable processors in the billion transistor Era: IRAM. *IEEE Computer*, 30(9), 75–78. September.

Patterson, D., Asanovic, K., Brown, A., Fromm, R., Colbus, J., Gribstad, B., Keeton, K., Kozyrakis, C.E., Martin, D., Perissakis, S., Thomas, R., Treuhaft, N., and Yelick, K. (1997d). Intelligent RAM (IRAM): The industrial setting, applications, and architectures. *IEEE International Conference on Computer Design (ICCD'97)*, 2–7. October.

Profit, A. (1970). *Structure et technologie des ordinateurs*. Armand Colin.

Randell, B. and Treleaven, P.C. (1983). *VLSI Architecture*. Prentice-Hall.

Reddi, S.S. and Feustel, E.A. (1976). A conceptual framework for computer architecture. *Computing Surveys*, 8(2), 277–300. June.

Reilly, E.D. (2003). *Milestones in Computer Science and Information Technology*. Greenwood Press.

Rojas, R. and Hashagen, U. (eds) (2000). *The First Computers: History and Architectures*. MIT Press.

Ross, H.D. (1953). The arithmetic element of the IBM type 701 computer. *Proceedings of the IRE*, 41(10), 1287–1294. October.

Schmidt, U. and Dasgupta, S. (1990). Comments, with reply on "A Hierarchical Taxonomic System for Computer Architectures". *IEEE Computer*, 23(6), 6. June.

Shiva, S.G. (2006). *Advanced Computer Architectures*. CRC Press.

Shriver, B. and Smith, B. (1998). *The Anatomy of a High-Performance Microprocessor: A Systems Perspective*. IEEE Press.

Sima, D., Fountain, T., and Kacsuk, P. (1997). *Advanced Computer Architectures: A Design Space Approach*. Addison-Wesley Longman Limited.

Stern, N. (1980). John von Neumann's influence on electronic digital computing, 1944–1946. *IEEE Annals of the History of Computing*, 2(4), 349–362. October.

Swartzlander, E.E. Jr. (1976). *Computer Design Development: Principal Papers*. Hayden Book Company, Inc.

Taub, A.H. General (ed.) (1963). *John von Neumann: Collected Works. Vol.: Design of Computers, Theory of Automata and Numerical Analysis*. Pergamon Press.

Tendler, J.M., Dodson, J.S., Fields, J.S. Jr. (Steve), Le, H., and Sinharoy, B. (2002). Power4 system microarchitecture. *IBM Journal of Research and Development*, 46(1), 5–27. January.

Texas Instruments Incorporated (1976). TMS9900 Microprocessor Data Manual. Texas Instruments Incorporated. December.

Treleaven, P.C. (1981). 5th generation computer architecture analysis. *International Conference on 5th Generation Computer Systems*, 265275. October 19–22. Tokyo, Japan. In (Moto-Oka *et al.* 1982).

Treleaven, P.C. (1983). Decentralised computer architectures for VLSI. In (Randell and Treleaven, 348–380).

Treleaven, P.C. (1990). *Parallel Computers*. Wiley, New York.

Treleaven, P.C. and Hopkins, R.P. (1981). Decentralized computation. *8th Annual Symposium on Computer Architecture*, 279–290. May, Paris, France.

Treleaven, P.C. and Lima, I.G. (1984). Future computers: logic, data flow, ..., Control Flow? *IEEE Computer*, 17(3), 47–58. March.

Treleaven, P.C. and Vanneschi, M. (eds) (1987). *Future Parallel Computers, An Advanced Course*. Pisa, Italy, June 9–20. *Lecture Notes in Computer Science (LNCS)*, 272. Springer-Verlag.

Treleaven, P.C., Brownbridge, D.R., and Hopkins, R.P. (1982). Data-driven and demand-driven computer architectures. *ACM Computing Surveys (CSUR)*, 14(1), 93–143. March.

Treleaven, P.C., Refenes, A.N., Lees, K.J., and McCabe, S.C. (1987). Computer architectures for artificial intelligence. In (Treleaven and Vanneschi, 416–492).

Tseng, C.-J. and Siewiorek, D.P. (1981). The modeling and synthesis of bus systems. *18th Design Automation Conference (DAC'81)*, 471–478. June 29–July 1. Nashville, Tennessee, USA.

Tseng, C.-J. and Siewiorek, D.P. (1982). *The Modeling and Synthesis of Bus Systems*. DRC-18-42-82. Paper 65. Department of Electrical and Computer Engineering. Carnegie Institute of Technology. April.

Tullsen, D.M., Eggers, S.J., and Levy, H.M. (1995). Simultaneous multithreading: Maximizing on-chip parallelism. *22nd Annual International Symposium on Computer Architecture (ISCA)*, 392–403. June 22–24. Santa Margherita Ligure, Italy.

Tullsen, D.M., Eggers, S.J., Emery, J.S., Levy, H.M., Lo, J.L., and Stammy, R.L. (1996). Exploiting choice: Instruction fetch and issue on an implementable simultaneous multithreading processor. *23nd Annual International Symposium on Computer Architecture (ISCA)*, 191–202. May 22–24. Philadelphia, PA, USA.

Turing, A.M. (1937a). On computable numbers, with an application to the entscheidungsproblem. *Proceedings of the London Mathematical Society*. Series 2, 42, Part 1, 230–265.

Turing, A.M. (1937b). On computable numbers, with an application to the entscheidungsproblem. A correction. *Proceedings of the London Mathematical Society*, Series 2, 43, Part 1, 544–546.

Turing, A.M. and Girard, J.-Y. (1995). *La machine de Turing*. Le Seuil, Paris.

Vajda, F. (1986). Super micros – objectives and approaches. *Microprocessing and Microprogramming*, 17(1), 1–17. January.

Weaver, D.L. and Germond, T. (eds) (1994). The SPARC architecture manual. Version 9. SPARC International, Inc. PTR Prentice Hall.

Wilkes, M.V. (1951). The best way to design an automatic computing machine. *Report of the Manchester University Computer Inaugural Conference*, 16–18. Electrical Engineering Department of Manchester University. Manchester, England. July. Republished in (Swartzlander 1976; Williams and Campbell-Kelly 1989). Also in *IEEE Annals of the History of Computing*, 8(2), 118–121. April 1986.

Williams, M.R. and Campbell-Kelly, M. (1989). *The Early British Computer Conferences*. MIT Press, Cambridge, MA, USA

Williams, F.C. and Kilburn, T. (1948). *Electronic Digital Computers*. Letters to Editor. *Nature*, 162(4117), 487. September 25.

Williams, F.C. and Kilburn, T. (1949). A storage system for use with binary digital computing machines. *Proceedings of the IEE - Part II: Power Engineering*, 96(50), 183–200. April.

Wirthlin, M.J. and Hutchings, B.L. (1995). A dynamic instruction set computer. *1995 IEEE Symposium on FPGAs for Custom Computing Machines*, 99–107. April 19–21. Napa Valley, CA, USA.

Index

This index covers all 5 volumes in this series of books.

B

C

D

E

F

G

H

I

J

L

M

N

O

S

T

U

V

W

Other titles from

iSTE

in

Computer Engineering

2020

LAFFLY Dominique
TORUS 1 – Toward an Open Resource Using Services: Cloud Computing for Environmental Data
TORUS 2 - Toward an Open Resource Using Services: Cloud Computing for Environmental Data
TORUS 3 - Toward an Open Resource Using Services: Cloud Computing for Environmental Data

LAURENT Anne, LAURENT Dominique, MADERA Cédrine
Data Lakes
(Databases and Big Data Set – Volume 2)

OULHADJ Hamouche, DAACHI Boubaker, MENASRI Riad
Metaheuristics for Robotics
(Optimization Heuristics Set – Volume 2)

SADIQUI Ali
Computer Network Security

2019

BESBES Walid, DHOUIB Diala, WASSAN Niaz, MARREKCHI Emna
Solving Transport Problems: Towards Green Logistics

CLERC Maurice
Iterative Optimizers: Difficulty Measures and Benchmarks

GHLALA Riadh
Analytic SQL in SQL Server 2014/2016

TOUNSI Wiem
Cyber-Vigilance and Digital Trust: Cyber Security in the Era of Cloud Computing and IoT

2018

ANDRO Mathieu
Digital Libraries and Crowdsourcing
(Digital Tools and Uses Set – Volume 5)

ARNALDI Bruno, GUITTON Pascal, MOREAU Guillaume
Virtual Reality and Augmented Reality: Myths and Realities

BERTHIER Thierry, TEBOUL Bruno
From Digital Traces to Algorithmic Projections

CARDON Alain
Beyond Artificial Intelligence: From Human Consciousness to Artificial Consciousness

HOMAYOUNI S. Mahdi, FONTES Dalila B.M.M.
Metaheuristics for Maritime Operations
(Optimization Heuristics Set – Volume 1)

JEANSOULIN Robert
JavaScript and Open Data

PIVERT Olivier
NoSQL Data Models: Trends and Challenges
(Databases and Big Data Set – Volume 1)

SEDKAOUI Soraya
Data Analytics and Big Data

SALEH Imad, AMMI Mehdi, SZONIECKY Samuel
Challenges of the Internet of Things: Technology, Use, Ethics
(Digital Tools and Uses Set – Volume 7)

SZONIECKY Samuel
Ecosystems Knowledge: Modeling and Analysis Method for Information and Communication
(Digital Tools and Uses Set – Volume 6)

2017

BENMAMMAR Badr
Concurrent, Real-Time and Distributed Programming in Java

HÉLIODORE Frédéric, NAKIB Amir, ISMAIL Boussaad, OUCHRAA Salma, SCHMITT Laurent
Metaheuristics for Intelligent Electrical Networks
(Metaheuristics Set – Volume 10)

MA Haiping, SIMON Dan
Evolutionary Computation with Biogeography-based Optimization
(Metaheuristics Set – Volume 8)

PÉTROWSKI Alain, BEN-HAMIDA Sana
Evolutionary Algorithms
(Metaheuristics Set – Volume 9)

PAI G A Vijayalakshmi
Metaheuristics for Portfolio Optimization
(Metaheuristics Set – Volume 11)

2016

BLUM Christian, FESTA Paola
Metaheuristics for String Problems in Bio-informatics
(Metaheuristics Set – Volume 6)

DEROUSSI Laurent
Metaheuristics for Logistics
(Metaheuristics Set – Volume 4)

DHAENENS Clarisse and JOURDAN Laetitia
Metaheuristics for Big Data
(Metaheuristics Set – Volume 5)

LABADIE Nacima, PRINS Christian, PRODHON Caroline
Metaheuristics for Vehicle Routing Problems
(Metaheuristics Set – Volume 3)

LEROY Laure
Eyestrain Reduction in Stereoscopy

LUTTON Evelyne, PERROT Nathalie, TONDA Albert
Evolutionary Algorithms for Food Science and Technology
(Metaheuristics Set – Volume 7)

MAGOULÈS Frédéric, ZHAO Hai-Xiang
Data Mining and Machine Learning in Building Energy Analysis

RIGO Michel
Advanced Graph Theory and Combinatorics

2015

BARBIER Franck, RECOUSSINE Jean-Luc
COBOL Software Modernization: From Principles to Implementation with the BLU AGE® Method

CHEN Ken
Performance Evaluation by Simulation and Analysis with Applications to Computer Networks

CLERC Maurice
Guided Randomness in Optimization
(Metaheuristics Set – Volume 1)

DURAND Nicolas, GIANAZZA David, GOTTELAND Jean-Baptiste, ALLIOT Jean-Marc
Metaheuristics for Air Traffic Management
(Metaheuristics Set – Volume 2)

MAGOULÈS Frédéric, ROUX François-Xavier, HOUZEAUX Guillaume
Parallel Scientific Computing

MUNEESAWANG Paisarn, YAMMEN Suchart
Visual Inspection Technology in the Hard Disk Drive Industry

2014

BOULANGER Jean-Louis
Formal Methods Applied to Industrial Complex Systems

BOULANGER Jean-Louis
Formal Methods Applied to Complex Systems:Implementation of the B Method

GARDI Frédéric, BENOIST Thierry, DARLAY Julien, ESTELLON Bertrand, MEGEL Romain
Mathematical Programming Solver based on Local Search

KRICHEN Saoussen, CHAOUACHI Jouhaina
Graph-related Optimization and Decision Support Systems

LARRIEU Nicolas, VARET Antoine
Rapid Prototyping of Software for Avionics Systems: Model-oriented Approaches for Complex Systems Certification

OUSSALAH Mourad Chabane
Software Architecture 1
Software Architecture 2

PASCHOS Vangelis Th
Combinatorial Optimization – 3-volume series, 2nd Edition
Concepts of Combinatorial Optimization – Volume 1, 2nd Edition
Problems and New Approaches – Volume 2, 2nd Edition
Applications of Combinatorial Optimization – Volume 3, 2nd Edition

QUESNEL Flavien
Scheduling of Large-scale Virtualized Infrastructures: Toward Cooperative Management

RIGO Michel
Formal Languages, Automata and Numeration Systems 1: Introduction to Combinatorics on Words
Formal Languages, Automata and Numeration Systems 2: Applications to Recognizability and Decidability

SAINT-DIZIER Patrick
Musical Rhetoric: Foundations and Annotation Schemes

TOUATI Sid, DE DINECHIN Benoit
Advanced Backend Optimization

2013

ANDRÉ Etienne, SOULAT Romain
The Inverse Method: Parametric Verification of Real-time Embedded Systems

BOULANGER Jean-Louis
Safety Management for Software-based Equipment

DELAHAYE Daniel, PUECHMOREL Stéphane
Modeling and Optimization of Air Traffic

FRANCOPOULO Gil
LMF — Lexical Markup Framework

GHÉDIRA Khaled
Constraint Satisfaction Problems

ROCHANGE Christine, UHRIG Sascha, SAINRAT Pascal
Time-Predictable Architectures

WAHBI Mohamed
Algorithms and Ordering Heuristics for Distributed Constraint Satisfaction Problems

ZELM Martin *et al.*
Enterprise Interoperability

2012

ARBOLEDA Hugo, ROYER Jean-Claude
Model-Driven and Software Product Line Engineering

BLANCHET Gérard, DUPOUY Bertrand
Computer Architecture

BOULANGER Jean-Louis
Industrial Use of Formal Methods: Formal Verification

BOULANGER Jean-Louis
Formal Method: Industrial Use from Model to the Code

CALVARY Gaëlle, DELOT Thierry, SÈDES Florence, TIGLI Jean-Yves
Computer Science and Ambient Intelligence

MAHOUT Vincent
Assembly Language Programming: ARM Cortex-M3 2.0: Organization, Innovation and Territory

MARLET Renaud
Program Specialization

SOTO Maria, SEVAUX Marc, ROSSI André, LAURENT Johann
Memory Allocation Problems in Embedded Systems: Optimization Methods

2011

BICHOT Charles-Edmond, SIARRY Patrick
Graph Partitioning

BOULANGER Jean-Louis
Static Analysis of Software: The Abstract Interpretation

CAFERRA Ricardo
Logic for Computer Science and Artificial Intelligence

HOMES Bernard
Fundamentals of Software Testing

KORDON Fabrice, HADDAD Serge, PAUTET Laurent, PETRUCCI Laure
Distributed Systems: Design and Algorithms

KORDON Fabrice, HADDAD Serge, PAUTET Laurent, PETRUCCI Laure
Models and Analysis in Distributed Systems

LORCA Xavier
Tree-based Graph Partitioning Constraint

TRUCHET Charlotte, ASSAYAG Gerard
Constraint Programming in Music

VICAT-BLANC PRIMET Pascale *et al.*
Computing Networks: From Cluster to Cloud Computing

2010

AUDIBERT Pierre
Mathematics for Informatics and Computer Science

BABAU Jean-Philippe *et al.*
Model Driven Engineering for Distributed Real-Time Embedded Systems

BOULANGER Jean-Louis
Safety of Computer Architectures

MONMARCHE Nicolas *et al.*
Artificial Ants

PANETTO Hervé, BOUDJLIDA Nacer
Interoperability for Enterprise Software and Applications 2010

SIGAUD Olivier *et al.*
Markov Decision Processes in Artificial Intelligence

SOLNON Christine
Ant Colony Optimization and Constraint Programming

AUBRUN Christophe, SIMON Daniel, SONG Ye-Qiong *et al.*
Co-design Approaches for Dependable Networked Control Systems

2009

FOURNIER Jean-Claude
Graph Theory and Applications

GUEDON Jeanpierre
The Mojette Transform / Theory and Applications

JARD Claude, ROUX Olivier
Communicating Embedded Systems / Software and Design

LECOUTRE Christophe
Constraint Networks / Targeting Simplicity for Techniques and Algorithms

2008

BANÂTRE Michel, MARRÓN Pedro José, OLLERO Hannibal, WOLITZ Adam
Cooperating Embedded Systems and Wireless Sensor Networks

MERZ Stephan, NAVET Nicolas
Modeling and Verification of Real-time Systems

PASCHOS Vangelis Th
Combinatorial Optimization and Theoretical Computer Science: Interfaces and Perspectives

WALDNER Jean-Baptiste
Nanocomputers and Swarm Intelligence

2007

BENHAMOU Frédéric, JUSSIEN Narendra, O'SULLIVAN Barry
Trends in Constraint Programming

JUSSIEN Narendra
A TO Z OF SUDOKU

2006

BABAU Jean-Philippe *et al.*
From MDD Concepts to Experiments and Illustrations – DRES 2006

HABRIAS Henri, FRAPPIER Marc
Software Specification Methods

MURAT Cecile, PASCHOS Vangelis Th
Probabilistic Combinatorial Optimization on Graphs

PANETTO Hervé, BOUDJLIDA Nacer
Interoperability for Enterprise Software and Applications 2006 / IFAC-IFIP I-ESA'2006

2005

GÉRARD Sébastien *et al.*
Model Driven Engineering for Distributed Real Time Embedded Systems

PANETTO Hervé
Interoperability of Enterprise Software and Applications 2005